A blue-sky day at the Swiss Paragliding Open in Fiesch, Switzerland. Photo: Martin Scheel / azoom.ch

Thermal Flying

A GUIDE FOR PARAGLIDER AND HANG GLIDER PILOTS

by
Burkhard Martens

About this book

Thermal Flying was first published in German in 2005. It was an instant hit, and was quickly reprinted and translated into many different languages, including Russian, French, Italian, Spanish, Japanese, Chinese, Polish, Czech and Portuguese. The English edition was first published in 2006 and was updated some years later by Mads Syndergaard for its second edition in 2013. This third edition has also again been updated, taking into account the development in technology and equipment. The art of thermal flying however, and the natural phenomena described within these pages, remain timeless and unchanging. The techniques pilots use to find and use thermals are the same today as they were 20 years ago or more. Burki has published several books since Thermal Flying, but Thermal Flying was and will remain a true classic. When we at Cross Country heard Burki was looking for a partner to help him reprint the English-language edition, we jumped at the chance. We have done our best to retain Burki's unique, accessible style which has made him such a favourite with pilots worldwide. We hope we have done him justice! The Cross Country team

About Cross Country magazine

Cross Country was established in 1988 by Sherry Thevenot, an artist who married into the hang gliding scene and wanted to reflect the spirit of free flight through magazines. The magazine somehow just slotted right in, and it has grown ever since – it is now read by pilots around the world in both digital and print. It has always been edited and owned by pilots, and always will be. Find us online at *xcmag.com* and join us on social media *@xcmag*

Publisher's info

Cross Country International
Tollgate, Beddingham
Lewes
BN8 6JZ, UK
www.xcmag.com

Third edition published: August 2021 / Re-printed February 2023
Photographs and text copyright Cross Country International Ltd. All rights reserved. No part of this book may be reproduced in any form or by any means without permission in writing from the publisher. This is not a teach-yourself manual – please learn with a qualified instructor at an approved school. Free flight is an evolving discipline, theories adapt, equipment is superseded and advice changes: please send feedback to editor@xcmag.com.

Author: Burkhard Martens
Original team: Nina Brümmer, Volker Schwaniz, David Welsh and Mads Syndergaard
Cross Country team: Bastienne Wentzel, Charlie King, Marcus King and Ed Ewing
Photographs: By the author unless credited otherwise
Front cover photo: Martin Scheel / azoom.ch
Contact the author: *thermikwolke.com*
Contact the publisher: *xcmag.com*
ISBN: 978-1-8380173-6-1

> "If you want to fly,
> you have to give up the things
> that weigh you down"
>
> *Toni Morrison, writer and Nobel Prize winner*

Patent registration no. 10-2020-0045494 (South Korea), EP20208575.9 (Europe)

WHEN NATURE MEETS ENGINEERING

The "Wave Leading Edge" is inspired by the tubercles of the humpback whale and has been realised through the "GIN LAB", a wind tunnel project run in collaboration with Ulsan National Institute of Science and Technology in South Korea.

The Wave Leading Edge delays the airfoil separation point, which increases lift for all angles of attack and decreases drag at low angles of attack. The result is a wing that has more performance, yet is easier to fly.

LAB

www.gingliders.com

ADVANCE

PIONEERING SPIRIT AND SWISS PRECISION.
advance.swiss

SINCE 1988

In the beginning was curiosity. It still shapes us today. Meeting the needs of pilots is our benchmark: We offer them the highest quality and absolute reliability, both in the air and in customer service. That's how we went from pioneer to perfectionist.

Picture Adi Geisegger - Stockhorn, Switzerland

Reliable Paragliding Equipment
advance.swiss

Welcome to the world of thermal flying

When the first version of Thermal Flying was published back in May 2005 I really had no idea what to expect. Since then the enthusiasm that has followed me in our small flying community has all but overwhelmed me, and even pro pilots seem to have found useful parts in my book. Since then the book has been translated into many languages, and has evolved and developed alongside our sport.

In 2006 my old Paragliding World Cup friend Mads Syndergaard agreed to translate the German original into English, and also added many useful revisions. Bruce Goldsmith even wrote an entire chapter for that first English translation, which I feel enriched the book immensely.

Another one who deserves my profound gratitude is my wife Nina-Renate Brümmer. She has been patient beyond the call of duty, and she has been a valuable co-worker both as a photographer and as a motivator during the countless hours I have spent in front of the computer.

In 2021 the English edition has been revised and updated yet again, this time by the team at Cross Country Magazine. They have done a great job. It amazes me to think that what started as a personal project more than 15 years ago is still as valuable to pilots today as it was back then.

I was hooked on paragliding from the first flight, many years ago. Right from the first little hop into the air I knew that this was "it" for me. In the following years I flew as much as I possibly could as a full-time employed engineer – which was far too little for my taste. My idols were the club colleagues who had already been flying for two long years – I felt like they were untouchable in their skills.

To improve as quickly as possible I read everything I could lay my hands on, every book and every magazine. Manfred Kreipl's Thermalling Handbook, although hard to read, became my most trusted friend. The book had no pictures and only a few drawings, and I had to read many passages over and over to understand everything.

I also read all the theoretical material that we were issued for our exams. Most of this was fortunately much easier to read. My favourite texts concerned the

0.1 Panoramic flying in the heart of the Dolomites, South Tyrol, Italy. Photo: Nina Brümmer

0.2 Hang gliding over Lake Tegernsee, Germany

practicalities of flying; thermals, weather, trigger points, centring technique, valley winds – I devoured it all. Things like aviation law, navigation, aerodynamics and equipment knowledge also had to be learned for the test, but my heart was with the other subjects.

I wrote this book for all the pilots out there who feel just like I felt back then. It is about all the things that I, and many of my fellow students, found so intriguing when we first entered this wonderful world of free flying.

If something like this book had been available back then I truly think I could have sold a copy to each and every student in the class. But there are so many little hints and tricks in it that even old thermal hogs should be able to find some nuggets here and there.

What really caught me about flying is the playing in and with nature. We have all learned through our flying education how warm air will eventually rise as a thermal, but to actually find this rising air and use it to go right up to cloudbase is simply addictive.

To combine more thermals in one flight, to fly to the next expected trigger point and actually find lift, then use this lift to go further still; this is in my mind truly awe-inspiring. Whenever this happens, when my theories prove themselves in real life I feel particularly alive and fortunate.

So gliding towards a specific point on a hill and actually finding lift there is exhilarating every time. What it does for me is to prove that my understanding of nature is continually improving.

The other aspect of this game is the natural impressions gathered through a flight. Sometimes we're thermalling with raptors, sometimes flying over a flock of browsing geese.

And almost all the time we're enjoying spectacular views from a perspective that most people can only dream of. When flying over the Dolomites in the Italian Alps I can see the majestic main Alpine divide, an almost uninterrupted snow-covered ridge from horizon to horizon. Does anything really compare to this?

This book does not replace good instruction from experienced professionals. The first thermal experience should be gathered under supervision of a flight school, as strong thermals are not to be trifled with.

The book is written from a paraglider pilot's perspective, but all but a very few minor details may be directly applied to hang gliding as well. Descriptions of landscape-defined particularities like valley winds or the development of the average thermal strength during the day all refer to the Alpine region, from France to Slovenia, but may be applied to all mountainous regions. Whenever I'm referring to flatland regions this is always clearly stated.

Once you have mastered thermal flying the jump to cross country flying is relatively easy. I wish all fellow pilots all over the world lots of beautiful and exciting flights. May your own thermal flights be benign, and may Thermal Flying help you to get more out of them!

Stay high, fly far

Burki Martens

Burkhard Martens

Contents

Equipment 16

Your interaction with the equipment 16
Equipment for thermal flying 16
GPS 20

1 How thermals develop 22

How thermals develop 24
Thermal bubbles 25
Thermal-generated wind systems 26
Lift versus distance from a ridge 28
The ideal slope inclination 29
House thermals 30
Thermal duration 33
Visualising thermals 40
The vortex structure of thermals 42
Thermal influences 48
Rotating thermals 53
Thermal lifespan 55
Wind influence on thermals 58

2 Thermal generators and triggers 60

Albedo value 63
Factors to consider 63
Thermal triggers 66
Flatland thermal triggers 70
Cloud shadow 72
Different route choices in a valley 74

3 Flying in and around thermals 78

Turbulence 80
Using water to visualise rotor formation 85
Windward and leeward thermals 88
Blue thermals and clear-air thermals 92
Magic air and reverse thermals 94
Convergence 96
Inversions 104

0.3 Clouds mark the lift in Andalucia, Spain. Photo: Adi Geisegger

0.4 Taking the second climb on a flight from Gourdon in the south of France. Photo: Marcus King

Thermal lunch break	109
Dust devils	112
Smoke and dust as thermal markers	113
Systematic thermal hunting	114

4 Clouds — 120

Forming, dissipating	122
Locating the area of best climb	123
Cloud associated dangers	126
Gust fronts	128
Escaping from clouds	133
Cloud domes	134
Dolphin-flying under cloud streets	138
What else can the clouds reveal?	140

5 Clouds and weather — 150

Cloud formations and what they tell us	152
The 10 most important cloud types	153
What can we learn about the weather from observing the wind?	162
The Coriolis Effect	163
Central European weather scenarios	164
Dangerous weather	165

6 Thermal-centring techniques — 168

How to find the best lift	171
Upwind and downwind sides of the thermal	172
Total Energy Compensation (TEC)	172
Important thermalling insights	174
What to do when you keep falling out of the side of a thermal?	175
Flatland Thermalling	176
Cores of different strengths next to each other	178
Reversing the turn direction	179
Wind shear	180
Rules for sharing thermals	182
Flying without a vario	186

7 Valley winds — 188

Glacier wind	192
Soarable ridges and valley-wind lee sides	196
The Venturi effect	198
Crossing a large valley	202
The sea breeze	204

13

8 Soaring 208

How to soar 210
Collison avoidance when soaring 212
Vector analysis of soaring winds 216
Finding and using embedded thermals when soaring 218
XC soaring 222
Soaring sand dunes 224
Cloud soaring 226

9 The temperature gradient 228

Radiosonde - Weather balloon 231
Roughly estimating the temperature gradient 231
Rules of thumb for applied use of the temperature gradient 232
Determining cloudbase and height 234
Identifying a subsidence inversion from a temperature-gradient diagram 235
Gliding forecast 239
World weather forecasting 240

10 Need-to-know 242

The polar curve 244
How to glide the furthest? 245
Active piloting 247
Training programme 249
Top-landing and slope-landing 254
Cross-country planning for beginners 256

11 Hints and tricks by Bruce Goldsmith 258

Thermalling on a hang glider - by Peter Achmüller 278

Conversion table

1 inch	=	2.54cm
1 foot	=	30.45cm
1 knot	=	1.852km/h
1 mph	=	1.61km/h
approx 200ft/min	=	1m/s

0.5 The launch in Rio de Janeiro. This unique take-off sees hang gliders launch from a ramp directly above the paraglider mat

Equipment

Your interaction with the equipment

To fly well the pilot needs to be in tune with the wing. In other words flying it must be *fun*. The passive safety should also correspond to the pilot's experience level, and finally the performance should be adequate.

The minimum descent rate for all recent wings is very close, so that if thermalling in normal lift is the only comparison parameter generally the best pilot, and not the best wing, will sit on top of the stack. The performance differences only become visible when gliding, and then only really when gliding at speed. Extreme differences may be seen when gliding at top speed into a headwind, whereas gliding with the wind doesn't tell us much about a wing's performance.

A pilot flying apprehensively under a high-performance wing will get less net performance out of it than they would if flying assertively with a Sports Class wing. This is due to the fact that a larger proportion of the pilot's mental capacity is then available for flying tactics and calculations rather than being tied up with worrying about the wing.

Current EN-A and EN-B wings have excellent performance. The first 120km FAI triangle was flown on a DHV 1-2 wing (low EN B) way back in 1998! Today, pilots regularly fly 200km and even 300km on intermediate gliders. It is the pilot beneath the wing that makes the difference.

Nobody should be fooled into believing that just switching to a hotter wing will automatically get them further, or even higher. Flying cross country is about finding and using lift, about having learned to trust your skills to consciously go to the most likely thermal sources and not just be stumbling around the skies and accidentally happening upon a thermal once in a while. Only when you have reached that level are you truly an XC pilot.

Equipment for thermal flying

Actually you don't really need much. Many pilots fly their first thermals with no vario, no flying boots and no gloves. No problem with that. People do fly thermals and go cross country without a vario, it is just a lot harder. And once we get used to the great little beeper most of us cannot really go anywhere without it.

So the most important investment, after the glider/harness combo, is the vario. The instrument of choice should have an integrated altimeter, both because in some countries flying XC is only allowed with one and because it helps you to develop a feeling for altitude. How many vertical metres does a specific transition burn? How high must I be at A to reach B, high

0.7 A condor joined me in a thermal while flying in the Sierra de Cordoba, Argentina

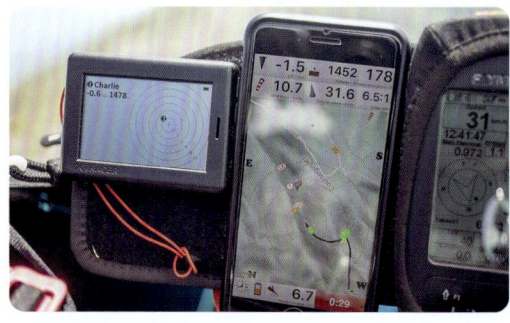

0.8 High-end varios and smartphone apps are generally overkill for the beginner., but techies may want them anyway!

*0.9 Well kitted-out Mexican pilot Patricia Garcia de Letona launches during a World Championship task
Photo: Marcus King*

0.10 A helmet vario is sufficient for thermalling. What's more, they are often solar-powered so never run out

0.11 Spot and Garmin inReach satellite trackers are used commonly by cross-country pilots. Regular position reports are sent by satellite, even where there is no mobile phone network available.

enough to connect with the next thermal? Many flights are also undertaken in regions where vertical airspace ceilings apply, so to avoid breaking the law, we must know how high we are. Whether you mount the vario on your flight deck, stick it to your helmet or tie it to your karabiner is a simply question of preference.

Sunglasses or goggles protect the eyes, also from the apparent wind, and sunscreen is indispensable at almost any altitude. A balaclava is important for cold days. Protective clothing like a flying suit or outdoor jacket and trousers is also a sensible investment.

Pilots spend a lot of time holding their hands in the air at great altitudes, and particularly in the springtime where the

> **HINT** If your only objective is local thermalling a helmet vario is totally adequate. I have one as a reserve on my helmet; if the main one fails I can always continue with the backup. I also use it for travelling and for tandem flying. The available helmet varios are small and reliable, and come in both battery- and solar-powered versions.

0.13 Pod harnesses keep you warm and improve glide angle performance by about 1 to 1.5 points when compared with an upright harness position. That's quite a lot – especially during accelerated flight. Disadvantages include increased twist potential, and they can be more complex to use. Occasional pilots should avoid them and stick with a sit-harness.

Tests in the Daimler wind tunnel made by Skywalk over the years have indicated that long tail fairings do not bring any real-world additional performance. The position of the cocoon, as shown here, provides a gain of 0.5 glide-angle points. The top surface of the cocoon should be almost parallel to the airflow, while the lower surface should be angled. Many pilots fly with the lower surface of the cocoon parallel to the airflow – this produces more resistance!

0.12 Normal seating position, not too reclined, not too upright. This allows for perfect weightshifting. And one foot on the accelerator!

air is still cold and the thermals go high, good gloves are important. The best are always a compromise because they must allow the pilot to feel the lines yet be warm enough to fend off the worst cold. The best hint is probably to stick heaters into your gloves. Large mitts can also be attached to a paraglider's brake lines or hang glider base-bar for extra warmth.

The harness must remain comfortable even during long flights and it should be easy to wriggle in after launch. I like my chest harness to be set around 43cm (17in) between the karabiners, and to fly in a semi-reclined position where I feel I have the optimal compromise between parasitic drag and the risk of getting twisted in the event of a mishap. Very laid-back flying positions increase the risk of riser twists.

The speed bar should not only be attached, it must also be adjusted correctly. When the legs are fully stretched the glider should be going at

0.14 A standard speed bar with an angled first step to ease the stepping into. The wire loop is used with one foot to get in, then both feet move to the actual bar and slowly accelerate to the desired speed

top speed. For most wings this means that the two pulleys on the risers touch. Short-legged pilots or pilots flying wings with long speedbar travel will often need a speedbar ladder to reach full speed, but these ladders are also useful for flying at half-speed with the legs stretched out – this is less tiring for the legs.

The brake-line length has to be perfect.

> **HINT** The higher the parasitic drag of the pilot gets, for example when sitting, or even standing up in the airflow, the higher the sink rate gets. Most people think that the speed decreases proportionally, but in fact the opposite is the case – the speed increases slightly!

> **HINT** I have my speed bar set up in a position that my legs are always resting on the first step of the ladder. This way all I need to do is stretch my legs to accelerate. Having to fiddle around to find it first is inefficient.

*0.15 **Left** Pulley-to-pulley at top speed. In this picture approximately one more centimetre may be pushed.*
***Right** A little trick to keep the speed bar out of the way when launching. A drawstring stopper holds it up until it is applied the first time in the air. Place the stopper beneath the Brummel hook of the speed system.*

0.16 My equipment for a long cross-country flight includes a vario/GPS, spare GPS, spare vario, Spot, radio, camera, mobile phone (switched on and stowed so I can reach it), something to eat and drink, spare batteries, a first-aid kit, maps, something to read, spare lines, a knife, my multifunctional tool and a repair kit

> **Exiting deep stalls**
> High sink values combined with little or no apparent wind may indicate that the wing has deep stalled. The quickest way to get it flying again is to either push both A-risers forward or to step on the speed bar.

Brakes that are set too long may pose a safety risk because they don't allow the pilot to control the wing to the max. Brake lines that are too short diminish the glide performance and may also be dangerous, as wings that are slowed down unnaturally may not pick up speed again after collapses.

The brakes should be adjusted in a position so that when they are let loose, absolutely no tension is applied to the trailing edge of the wing. Check the brake-line setting in flight by observing the trailing edge and verifying that there's no tension on any of the lines; the lines should bow out in a slight arc.

GPS

You don't need to have a GPS to thermal properly, in fact it's probably best not to have a GPS for your first few attempts. I do however, find a GPS very useful for flying and also when thermalling. For example, depending on how your instrument displays information, then you can observe things like the size of your turn radius, and the wind drift over several turns. If you fly a large circle near the ground, then you can easily guess the wind speed and direction by looking at the GPS track.

Aside from this useful in-flight information, being able to report your exact coordinates to a retrieve driver or if you have to emergency-land somewhere is a real safety bonus.

> **HINT** If you have a GPS which is unable to display airspace, then you can still enter control-zone corner positions as turnpoints. This can help you visualise the airspace and remind you of the height you should be at when close-by.

0.17 My two main instruments a few years ago. The reliable GPS 60 CS from Garmin and the top model from Bräuniger. I liked the IQ Compeo for its large, high-resolution display. The picture shows the complicated airspace you have to fly through to cross into the Zillertal from the Achensee. I change to the map view on the Compeo by pressing a button. I am in the glider wave airspace of the Innsbruck control zone in region 1, maximum allowed altitude 3,350m. I am flying east. In region 2 is the SRA 5 Innsbruck east airspace, maximum altitude approximately 2,950m. Region 3 shows the SRA2 Innsbruck airspace, maximum altitude 2,650m. I must descend to this altitude before I cross the line into this airspace and over to the Zillertal.

0.18 Flatland flying is generally associated with far more controlled airspace than when flying over mountain regions. Having a GPS with airspace display is important.
Photo: Skywalk / wolfgang-ehn.de

Don't Hesitate
To Levitate

1 How thermals develop

Climbing out together in a thermal, Westendorf, Austria Photo: Daniel Gassner

Chapter 1

The first steps:
How thermals develop

We use the word 'thermal' to describe the general phenomenon of warmer air rising through cooler air.

The principle is simple: the sun's rays heat some part of the ground more than the ground around it and this warm earth transfers its heat to the overlying air. Warm air is lighter than cold air, and once the temperature difference is high enough the parcel of warm air begins to rise.

The warmer air does not rise right away due to a certain inertia caused by gravitational forces and simple drag, but once a temperature difference of approximately 2°C has been reached it will generally release as a thermal. The higher the temperature difference becomes the stronger the thermal will be – this is also the reason why leeside thermals are often stronger, because hidden in the lee an air mass may have time to develop a larger temperature difference than on the windward side where all the air masses are continually stirred and mixed.

The thermal is now born. Its continuation depends on the surrounding air; the higher the temperature gradient (ie the steeper the temperature drops with altitude) the faster the thermal rises. The total height gain of the rising air mass also depends on the temperature gradient.

When the temperature gradient is high, and the decrease with altitude therefore large, we call the atmosphere unstable. When the temperature gradient is low, and the difference between ground level and higher levels is low, we call the atmospheric situation stable.

In stable air masses the thermal soon loses its energy and stops, but in unstable

1.1 Thermalling under a nice cloud in the Soča Valley in Slovenia. Cumulus clouds always mark the top of thermals

1.2 Blue thermals on the hill in Manilla, Australia, with active cumulus clouds in the distance. Photo: Nina Brümmer

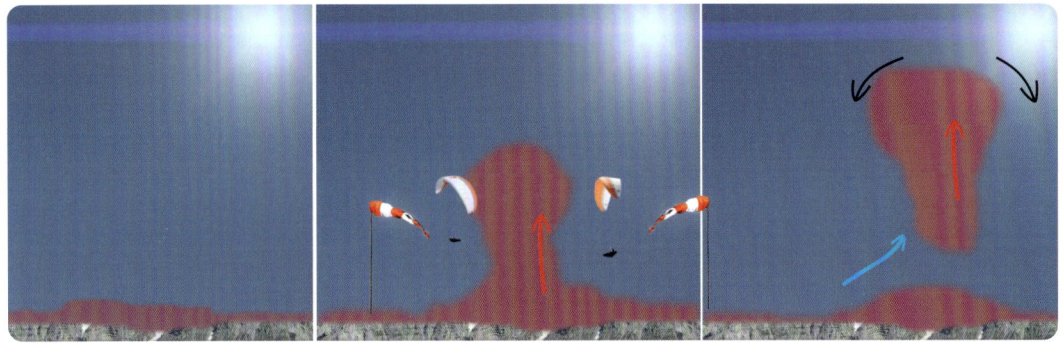

1.3 The formation of a thermal. The ground is heated up by the sun and transfers some of the heat to the air above. At some stage the temperature difference becomes so great that the heated air is no longer bound to the ground. The thermal lifts off. Both pilots in the centre photo are flying with a tailwind!

air it may rise very high. If the air is also humid, and there's no inversion below the dew point, cumulus clouds will develop and mark where the thermals are.

When the air is dry, or when the thermals are not rising very high, the thermals may remain 'blue' which means that no cumulus clouds are formed. We normally simply call these 'blue days'.

Thermal bubbles, pulsating thermals and thermal columns

When an individual air mass has reached the critical temperature and has started to rise, and the sun is not strong enough to heat the same area sufficiently to keep the thermal fed from below, we call it a thermal bubble. If another bubble forms in the same place shortly after it may be considered a pulsating thermal, see picture 1.3.

It is sometimes possible to actually see the warm air lying on the ground before it releases, just think of the shimmering of hot air over a road on a hot summer day.

If on the other hand we have a ground section that is receiving a strong influx of the sun's energy, and this is enough to keep feeding the thermal from below, we speak of thermal columns.

Because of the topography and the nature of the soil, thermal columns are more common in mountain regions, where a particular rocky mountain flank may be facing directly into the sun for extended periods. The thermals will often flow upwards following the terrain, and only release once they meet a distinct trigger point, sometimes only at the peak.

At the trigger point the thermal column loses its connection with the topography. Such a trigger point is normally fed from several good thermal generators below, which makes it easier to understand why it doesn't run out of warm air to propel upwards. Good trigger points near Alpine

1.4 A thermal column in the mountains. This cloud will remain where it is for several hours, sometimes smaller, sometimes growing bigger. House thermals are often this type of thermal

launches in mountain regions are often called 'house thermals' – fly there and you go up. This is then only valid for a specific period of the day, when the sun is reaching the thermal sources feeding the trigger point in question.

Thermal-generated wind systems in mountains

We have learnt that thermals aren't caused by the sun heating the air but rather by the sun heating the ground, which then heats the air. On slopes facing the sun the heated air may begin to flow upwards following the topography at a lower temperature difference than needed to release a real thermal bubble.

We call the winds that result 'anabatic winds'. You may have noticed that a particular launch site facing into the sun will often also face into wind regardless of the meteorological winds on any given day, thanks to this anabatic wind flow. This is however also a reason to be particularly alert with regard to windward and leeward sides, as it makes the situation less self-evident than one could sometimes wish.

Once the sun has changed its position in the sky and is no longer heating a particular mountain flank the soil begins to cool down. This immediately cools down the air directly above, and as cold air is heavier than warm air, the cool air begins to flow down the mountain.

This cool downward flow is called 'katabatic wind' which appears as soon as the slope is in shade. On launch sites facing east this may be observed in the middle of the afternoon, where a backwind will often set in regardless of the macro-meteorological wind direction.

When there's still snow on the upper reaches of the slopes the thermals coming from below will release at the snow line instead of near the crest. The cold air overlying the snow fields flows down the slope and meets the warm air rising from below, and the thermal is triggered.

The thermal even sucks in some of the surrounding air (see picture 1.3) and thus aggravates the situation, especially if the launch site is situated above the snow line; there'll be tailwind even if the meteorological wind is predicted to be straight on!

Generally it will still be possible to launch though, in one of the following brief phases:

- When the thermal releasing in front and below launch takes a short break

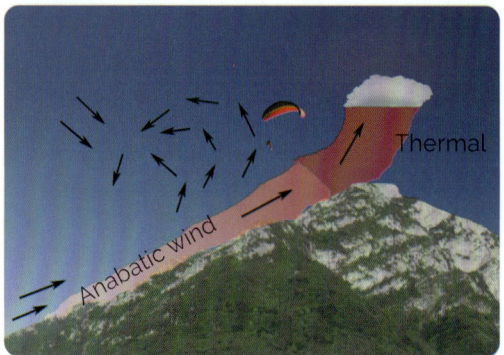

1.5 Anabatic winds caused by the sun heating a slope. Once the flow reaches the crest it releases and becomes a thermal. To replace the air that is disappearing upwards the surrounding air must flow into the area from all around.

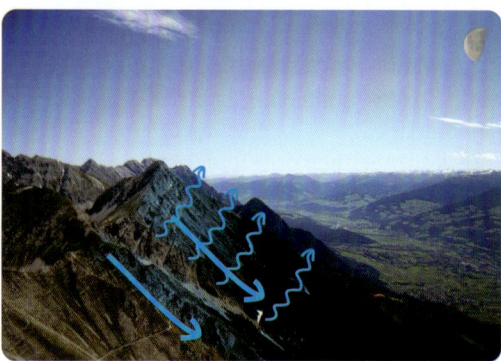

1.6 Katabatic winds flowing down the mountain. The flow begins almost as soon as the slope is in shade. The wavy arrows symbolise the long-wave radiation of heat to space from earth.

- When a gust of meteorological wind reaches the launch
- Or when just briefly we have no wind

The best launches for such conditions begin rather flat and then become steeper. A no-wind launch uses up a lot of runway!

1.7 *The pilot is leaning well forward to put enough energy into his launch procedure in no wind. Don't launch in a tailwind! Photo: Skywalk*

HINT Interesting things are present in the spring at many mountain launches. The valley is snow-free but the upper slopes, including the launch, are still covered. Over the snowy sections the cold air flows down katabatically and causes a tailwind on launch in spite of the meteorological wind being straight on!

*Garmisch, Germany
Photo: Skywalk*

Lift vs distance from a ridge

Researchers in the Inn valley in Austria set out to discover the correlation between the anabatic lift on a sunny ridge and the distance from the ridge. The results are in the table below.

The research shows that the best lift is not to be found right next to the ridge but 20-30m away (marked in yellow). The reason for this is the drag effect of the topography on the flow.

In the instance investigated, where the flow is 9km/h away from the ridge, it increases to 15km/h near the ridge and the lift is up to 1.5m/s 25 metres from the ridge. The 1.5m/s are the resultant of 10km/h=2.8m/s minus the paraglider sink value, which we set at 1.5m/s in this example (see the conversion table at the front).

The lift decreases as we distance ourselves more than 25 to 30m from the ridge until, 100m away, the ridge's influence on the apparent wind is no longer discernible.

HINT Soaring uncomfortably close is normally not beneficial. Besides, keeping a bit more distance will be good for the nerves!

Sink vs distance from a ridge

Once the slopes are in the shade the system reverses and the katabatic winds set in. They are not quite as strong as the anabatic winds but the distances

Table 1.1 Lift vs distance from a ridge

Distance (m)	5	10	15	20	25	30	35	45	90	100
Wind speed (km/h)	9	11	13	13	15	15	13	13	9	9
Vertical wind speed (km/h) (lifting component)	5.8	7.6	9.0	9.7	10	9.7	9.4	9.0	6.5	5.8

Picture 1.8 On the right-hand slope we can expect lift, on the left one we're pretty sure to encounter increased sinking. The sinking air will be felt as much as 100 metres away from the ridge.

are similar or a little shorter. For the pilot this means keeping at least 100m distance from shadowy slopes, see picture 1.6.

These rules apply to thermally generated anabatic/katabatic winds and not to macro-meteorological winds. In chapter 8, Soaring, we delve into the possibilities that these winds offer the passing pilot. Note that regions of dynamic lift caused by wind meeting an obstacle behave in a slightly different manner; these are frequently usable much further away from the ridge.

1.9 Soaring at such distances from the terrain is only possible in dynamic lift. Had it been anabatic lift the pilots would be much closer to the slope. Meduno, Italy

1.10 The moderately inclined launch at Fiesch, Switzerland. In the summer this slope delivers reliable thermals from around 10.30am to 11am.

1.11 The renowned Flimser Rock in Switzerland. It faces directly into the evening sun and is steep enough for the sun's rays to have their full effect. Due to wildlife preservation it is not allowed to approach this ridge low down.

The ideal slope inclination for generating and triggering thermals

"A slope facing directly into the sun at right angles warms up better than one that is either steeper or shallower."

This general rule is extremely useful. From it you can deduce the rules on the right for finding lift.

They hold true for the northern hemisphere – in the southern hemisphere exchange south with north and the same rules apply.

Rules for finding lift
1. In the morning the best lift is to be found coming off steep southeast facing slopes
2. Around noon the best slopes are the ones facing south and with a slightly flatter cross-section
3. In the afternoon we look for southwest facing slopes, and now again the steeper ones are good
4. In the evening we want steep west-facing slopes

Cloudbase

If the thermal has a cumulus cloud forming over it we call the base of the cloud the 'cloudbase'. The very young cumulus cloud needs a little time to properly define the base – in fact morning cumuli often dissolve before cloudbase is even properly defined.

1.12 Cumulus cloud with a well-defined base on the left. We can see that it is the result of four thermal pulsations, with the right one being active. Notice the indentation in the base of the right-hand cloud section; this is the clue to the active part.

House thermals and wandering thermals

Thermals that originate from a very defined, static source are often referred to as 'house thermals'. They are very common in the mountains, see picture 1.4.

In the flatlands, particularly on even ground, we may sometimes encounter 'wandering thermals'. These originate in one place but are pushed by the wind and continually fed from the warm air encountered by the thermal as it wanders along.

1.13 Pulsating thermal. The wind comes from the right, which is also where the thermal is generated. The cu's dissolve downwind. If crossing to this cloud we must aim for the little cloud on the right.

1.14 Pulsating thermal.

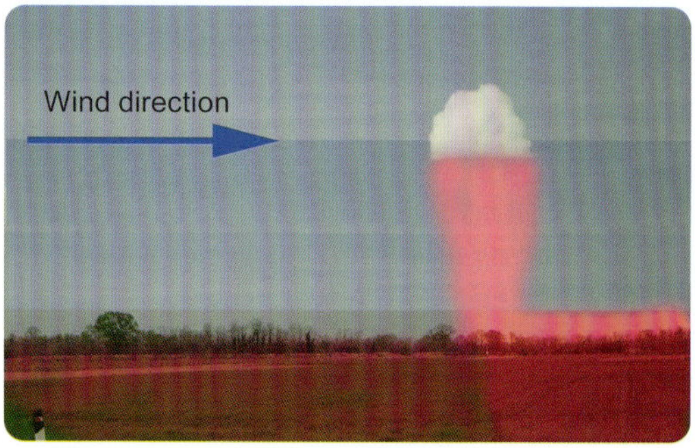

1.15 Wandering thermal. The wind pushes the entire thermal along so that it continues to receive warm air influx from the ground downwind. After the thermal has passed it takes a while before the ground can feed another thermal.

Sharing a thermal and reaching cloudbase in the south of France Photo: Marcus King

Thermals with several sources

In mountain regions we often find thermals feeding from several heat sources on the ground. This is something to have in mind during thermal-hunting so that we can optimise our glide path accordingly.

It is also to keep in mind when you are low down and fighting in weak lift. Keep scratching! As soon as the climb takes you up above the crestline the thermal will be joined by others and life will get easier.

HINT The right pilot is climbing better than the left one in picture 1.17. The pilot in the left, weaker core must decide if moving over to their colleague is worthwhile. Generally this is not the case as the loss of time/altitude in the process is high and we can never know how close we are to the joining of the thermals, where the weaker one will also get better.

HINT When a pulsating thermal is being pushed by the wind we find the next pulsation on the windward side of the previous one. In picture 1.13 the left cloud is dissolving and the right one is just forming – the best climb rates are to be found under the new cloud on the right!

EXPERIENCE The south face of the Laber near Garmisch in Germany is very thermally active but always in the lee and very turbulent due to the north wind caused by the local Alpine low pressure. The last time I flew to the Laber I aimed for a small crest just south of the main peak instead of battling it out in the lee. My little crest also produced a thermal, which even joined the Laber thermal once I got above the main peak, exactly as depicted in picture 1.17.

1.16 In this picture it is clear to see how the large cloud is being fed from several sources below.

1.17 Two thermal cores joining. Above the junction the thermal generally gets stronger and, at least for the pilot on the left, much wider and easier to centre. In this particular case it is probably not necessary for the left pilot to switch to the right core, see hint top left.

Thermal duration

How long a thermal remains active depends on several factors. In Europe we get the best conditions following a fresh influx of cold, unstable air masses, i.e. after a cold front has passed through. In these conditions the thermals may begin as early as 10am in the summer. In the evening we expect the thermal activity to shut down one or two hours before sunset.

Once the summer high-pressure has settled in it is common to see a 1-2 hour shortening of the usable time range during the day. This happens less in the spring

1.18 Ground-level inversion in the autumn. The ground fog must evaporate before usable thermals form. The cu's on the right stem from thermals forming on the mountain slopes above the inversion and indicate good flying conditions as long as we stay high.

1.19 In mountain regions the thermal activity begins earlier in the day than in the flatlands, and lasts longer into the evening. On east-facing rocky slopes thermals may begin very early whilst steep west-facing rocks may produce gentle lift surprisingly late. Dolomites, Italy. Photo: Nina Brümmer.

HINT Many flight instruments show the actual vario value, the average of 10 sec and also the average of 10 minutes. This is important to judge the quality of the thermals during the day.

33

1.20 On sunny high-pressure summer days the thermal development in the flatlands is often insufficient, whereas it may still be very good in the mountains. Notice the thick inversion over the flats. The location is the Isar Valley foothills in Germany

forming at valley bottom level until the sun has dissolved it. Sunny slopes above the inversion may produce usable thermals early in the day; see picture 1.18, but the good climbs only form once the inversion is gone. Older high-pressure situations may see the ground-level inversion last well into the day. There is more about this in chapter 3, Inversions, from page 106.

Thermal-strength development during the flying day

Glider pilots have set up a range of definitions for thermal strength. They apply to the large diameter circles flown by thermalling gliders, much larger than what we are able to do with our nimble aircraft. We can often stay in small, stronger cores and the given definitions are thus somewhat less useful for us.

The following times apply to the high summer in mountains in temperate regions. Assuming a recent influx of fresh cold air masses the thermals may begin to form as early as 8 or 8.30am, discernible by the little clouds forming over slopes facing east. To remain airborne we do however need something a little more substantial,

due to the more frequent influx of cold, unstable air giving the thermals a boost.

If the opposite situation, where the upper levels receive an influx of warm, stable air should happen the thermals will shut down earlier and generally need a higher excess temperature to rise.

In mountain valleys an inversion forms overnight due to the cooling of the ground-level air (in the winter this can often be seen as ground fog). This inversion prevents any thermals from

1.21 This is the Monte Avena launch above Feltre, Italy. Such extreme inversions effectively shut down all usable thermal activity. On this day we could barely remain airborne beneath the inversion but no thermals had the strength to punch through it. The thermal strength was comparable with picture 1.42. We later learned that the day had been really good in the high mountains, with thermal strength comparable to picture 1.40.

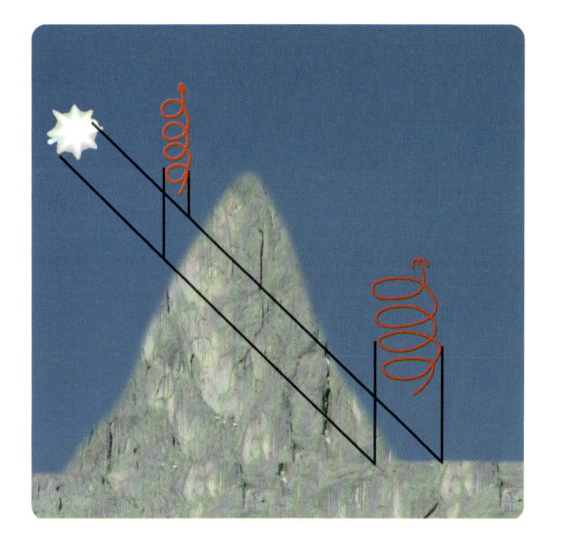

1.22 Thermals are usually stronger in the mountains than in the flatlands. Ground areas perpendicular to the sun absorb more energy than those lying at flatter angles, and heat the air better. Nevertheless flatlands thermals can be very strong. When thermaling the general rule is as follows: The stronger the thermal the bigger and flatter your circle can be

and this begins to become available around 10 to 11am. Anyone wishing to fly records should be on their way no later than 11am, and beginners wishing to learn thermalling are also advised to launch now. From noon the thermal development is at the most reliable and the strongest time, between 1pm and 3pm, is when the XC pilot can really make some distance – this is then also the time when the conditions are most demanding. From 4pm we begin to notice a weakening, making the air suitable for beginners once again, and from 6pm the thermals become weak enough that only exerienced pilots will usually remain flying. They will sometimes be able to keep going until 8pm.

The following values are meant as a suggestion only.

Weak: climb rates up to 1m/s
Medium: climb rates between 1 and 3m/s (200 - 600ft/min)
Strong: between 3 and 5m/s
Very strong: between 5 and 8m/s
Extreme conditions: above 8m/s

1.23 South launch, Speikboden, South Tyrol. The first gentle wisps are beginning to appear, and the Italian XC experts still have 15-30 minutes to get prepared. That is also the ideal time for beginners to learn about thermal flight

A classic and exciting spring day on the Aravis, France. Photo: Jérôme Maupoint

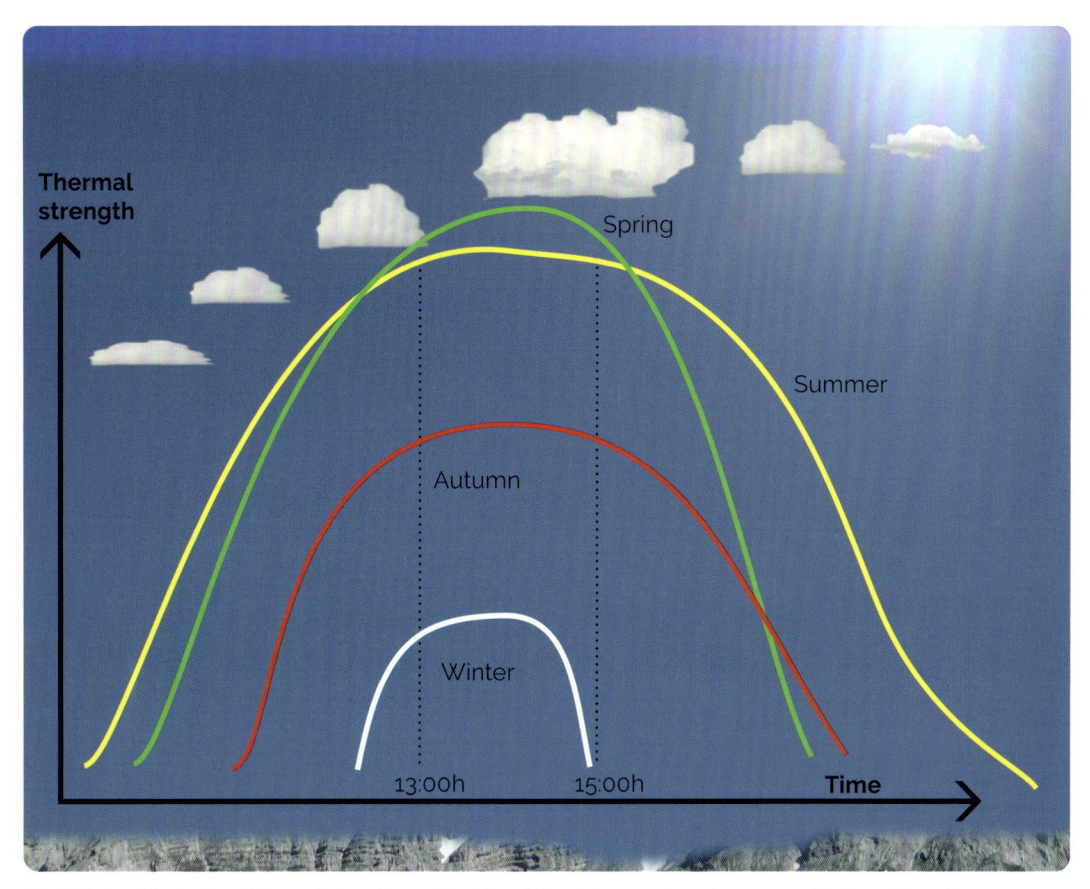

1.24 *This is an illustration of thermal strength as a function of time in temperate regions, across the four different seasons. Peak activity is between 13:00-15:00hrs. The Cu's above apply to the yellow summer curve.*

Values of up to 15m/s have been recorded! Note: 1 m/s is about 200 ft/min

These values apply to the peak vario readings, often only seen for brief moments during thermalling. A thermal averaging 3m/s over several minutes will surely have shown several peaks of 6-8m/s on the vario.

Large thermals are generally calmer and easier to core than small ones, where even experienced pilots often find themselves falling out the side now and again.

EXPERIENCE My own strongest climb ever was up to 12m/s and in total I have had no more than 10 thermals showing more than 10m/s on my vario in 22 years and more than 4,000 flights.

HINT Strong thermals are generally also more turbulent. This is the reason why it is not recommended that beginners fly during the strongest time of the day. The best time to gain your first thermalling experience is in the mornings and late afternoons.

EXPERIENCE Most pilots talk about peak values – these are usually just little jolts. Climb rates of 4-5m/s sustained over a 10-second average are a lot. Some instruments also calculate a 10-minute average – if this ever shows more than 3m/s then you have an extremely thermally-active day. In most cases this value is less than 2m/s.

37

Thermal strength through the different seasons

In springtime in temperate zones the air is generally unstable and the thermal activity begins earlier in the day, almost as early as in summer. Due to the lower angle of the sun it does however shut down one or two hours earlier – April in the Alps sees the last thermal activity around 6pm. In the autumn the thermals begin 1-2 hours later than in summer, and end as early as one or two hours before sunset. If any thermals form during the Alpine winter it will normally only be at the height of the day, i.e. around 12.30 to 2pm.

Winter thermals are almost always very weak, whereas spring thermals are renowned for their intensity. This is due to the generally cold air mass present, where even modest amounts of sun can cause a huge temperature difference, see picture 1.26. This in turn makes the springtime the most virulent and demanding season to fly, not to mention the extreme cold generally experienced at altitude at this time of year.

On April 20th the days are about as long as on August 20th. An analysis of the XC flights undertaken throughout the year shows that the longest flights in Europe are also flown during this time span. From April until June the thermals are strong and turbulent, from June this turbulence decreases and in August the thermals are generally relatively weak again. This does not however fully apply to central mountain regions like the inner Alps, where the strength and turbulence only decreases in September, or in places like the Dolomites where it may continue into October. In late autumn the thermal activity is low everywhere.

1.26 Spring thermalling. Much more common and always a cold experience. Cloudbase is high, and the thermals are strong and rough. This is Gréolières in southeast France Photo: Marcus King

1.25 Winter thermalling: Sadly a rare occurrence, and a weak one too. Generally encountered over snow-free south-facing slopes. In extremely cold and unstable air winter thermals may however form even over snow-clad forest slopes Photo: Wolfgang Kronwitter

1.27 *Autumn thermalling at Mittenwald-Karwendel, Germany, at the border with Austria. Often gentler, weaker, but strongest in central mountain regions. In the flatlands generally too weak to use. The picture shows a pilot climbing over steep south-facing mountains.*

Increasing stability as the year passes

By Volker Schwaniz

Experienced pilots know it well; the best thermals are to be found during springtime in spite of the fact that the summer has far higher temperatures and also more sunlight. So how can this be? The key to understanding this is insight into the development of the temperature at altitude during the year – because a difference in temperature between ground level and higher levels is a prerequisite for thermal development.

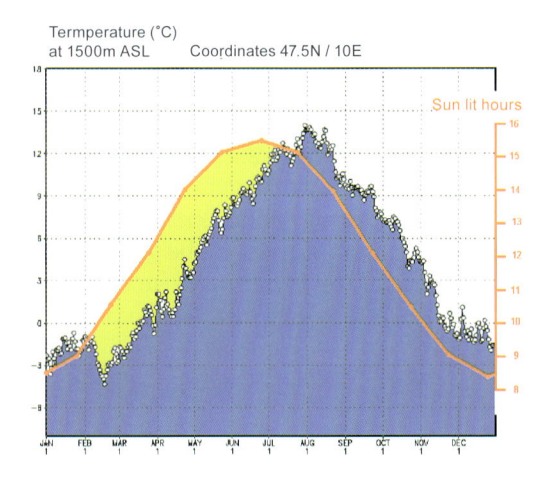

The orange graph shows the number of possible sunlight hours (indicating the possible ground heating effect) during the course of the year. In the northern hemisphere the maximum is reached on June 21st, and the minimum on December 21st. The black graph, and the blue area beneath it, show the average temperature at 1500m true altitude in the Alpine region. The horizontal parallel offset of the two graphs makes it beautifully clear that the yearly heating of the entire air mass is lagging behind the maximum available sunlight, and the excess energy thus available is greatest in the spring (the yellow area). This equals stronger thermals!

1.28 *Temperature development at 1,500m ASL and sunlight hours as a function of time around Arlberg, Austria. The temperature (blue area) lags behind the sunlight in the spring (yellow area) but is ahead in the autumn, which causes the increasing stability that we observe during the course of the year.*
Illustration: Volker Schwaniz

39

At the height of summer the intensity of the sunlight begins to weaken but the temperature at altitude still rises for quite some time, and this is exactly what causes the increasing stability. When the intensity of the sunlight decreases but the increase of temperature at altitude continues we have two factors, both contributing to the weakening of the thermal activity, both active at once. And although our senses tell us that we are right in the middle of the warm season, the point in time where the graphs meet is already behind us and the premises for the development of high and strong thermals have already deteriorated significantly within a very short time span.

If a high-pressure situation sets in we get an additional stable air mass with little temperature difference from ground level and up, which only adds to the negative equation. And finally the warm summer air can contain much more humidity, which increases the risk of thunderstorms developing.

1.29 Spring thermalling in Greifenburg, Austria. On the horizon are the eastern Alps

Why is cold air more unstable than warm air?

The stability of a given air mass does not depend primarily on the temperature, but on the temperature gradient. The temperature gradient indicates the decrease in temperature as a function of altitude, see also chapter 9. However, the temperature itself also plays a role:

Warm air can contain more humidity than cold air. When heating the air, the water vapour contained in it must also be heated, and this process requires more energy. The energy thus spent is not available for heating the air, which means that humid air heats slower than dry air. This is one of the reasons why spring thermals are better and stronger – the air that forms them contains less humidity and can be heated quicker.

But according to Volker Schwaniz the main reason why warm air impedes thermal development is the fact that the temperature gradient is less pronounced. A layer of warm, humid air lies on top of the ground layer and effectively stops the thermals before they get going.

Visualising thermals

Too bad that air is invisible, no matter if cold or warm. So to get the most of the conditions we need to be able to build a mental picture of the thermal we're circling in, to visualise it in our minds, see picture 1.4.

Some thermals are very large and may even be kilometres long, for example under long cloud streets. Others are small, narrow, or made up of several cores each showing significantly different climb rates. In the next pages we'll be showing a number of different thermal structures, to help you in your own visualisation process.

Thermalling with the last rays of the sun on steep west-facing flanks near the Furka Pass in Switzerland Photo: Advance

1.30 Four cumulus clouds forming. The ring shape indicates the presence of a vortex structure. Watching cumulus clouds form, bloom and fade is time well spent for pilots and can be done anywhere, including the landing field or café terrace

The vortex structure of thermals

Smoke rings blown by cigarette aficionados give a good visual clue as to the structure of thermal vortices.

We know from experience that the thermal is several times stronger in its core than closer to the edges. Why is that so? To explain it, the vortex-structure theory was developed. The accuracy of the theory can be affirmed often enough through observations: When the thermal rises the friction against the surrounding air slows it down along the edges. This sets off a rotating movement from the inside out, like when we turn out a sock. These vortices may be observed both in thermal bubbles and in thermal columns.

EXPERIENCE I had the most amazing experience surfing a vortex ring in a strong thermal once. I was going up at 9m/s on a no-wind day, and suddenly realised by looking at my GPS that my forward speed had gone to zero! At the time I was thinking hard about where that very strong headwind had suddenly come from, but today I realise that I was simply at the apex of the vortex ring, pointing right into the outflowing air (see illustration 1.31, pilot B). I eventually gained 1,500m vertically in very little time, flying straight practically on the spot! Impressive!

possible to sense the acceleration when moving over the core and into the tailwind, and the pilot should turn immediately to stay in the core and maximise her climb. The core of the vortex ring is rather turbulent and the pilot must continuously respond to the pitching of her wing and carry out adjustments to remain in the strongest lift.

Pilot C is still above the thermal. Only when he has descended down to the level, or it has climbed up to meet him, may he commence thermalling and gaining altitude.

Pilot D has fallen out of the side of the thermal and is heading away. Provided she's carrying a GPS she may notice her groundspeed picking up whilst her descent rate is also increasing.

Pilot E is approaching the thermal low down. He has a tailwind and already should see reduced descent – he's practically being sucked into the thermal. If he's not quick however he may miss the climb and find only sink below the thermal. His friends will climb out above him, leaving him searching fruitlessly for the climb. This is one of the most frustrating positions to be in for a pilot and is one of the reasons it is worth always topping up your height and staying high.

The example shows how important it is for each of us to always try to build up a mental picture of the thermal we're in; to visualise it. In this way we understand what is going on all the time in relation to which part of the thermal we're in, and make the most of it. This also allows us to re-enter the core quicker in case we lose it.

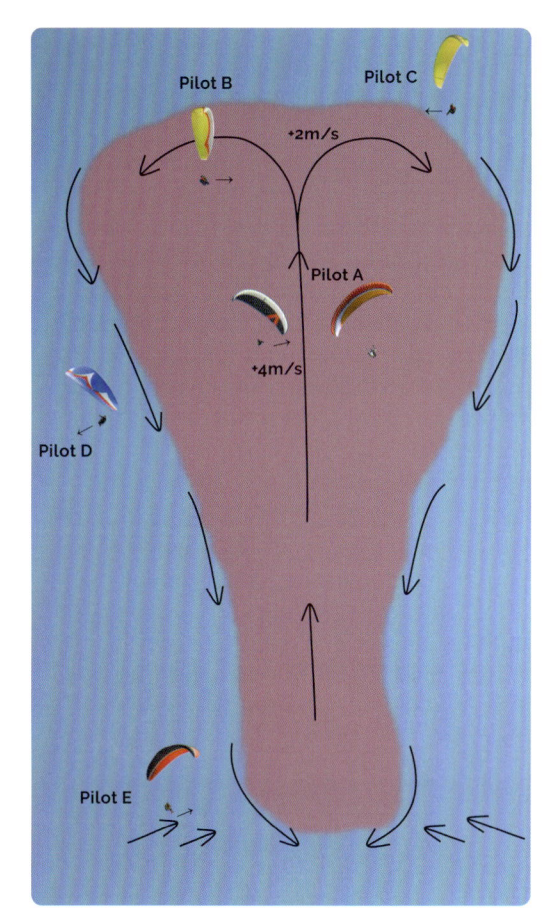

1.31 The vortex structure of thermals. This is an example of how an idealised thermal could look if we could see it. The net climb rate of the thermal may be 2m/s but in the core where Pilot A is we may experience 4m/s whereas the edges get only 1m/s. The horizontal component at B can be surprisingly strong – up to 30km/h in my experience.

Let's look at the significance of this vortex-ring structure for pilots A to E:
Pilot A is in the core of the thermal and is climbing twice as fast as pilot B, who is at the apex of the climb. Once pilot A catches up with B they will continue with identical climb rates.

Pilot B is flying against the headwind caused by the vortex ring. If she's carrying a GPS she may notice that her groundspeed is lower than it was shortly before. If she flies over the centre of the core she'll suddenly have a tailwind combined with lower climb rates. It is

> **HINT** If I'm flying straight and suddenly feel an increased drift towards one side, maybe even combined with reduced sinking, I always follow the drift immediately. Chances are I'll fly right into a thermal, just like Pilot E is about to do.

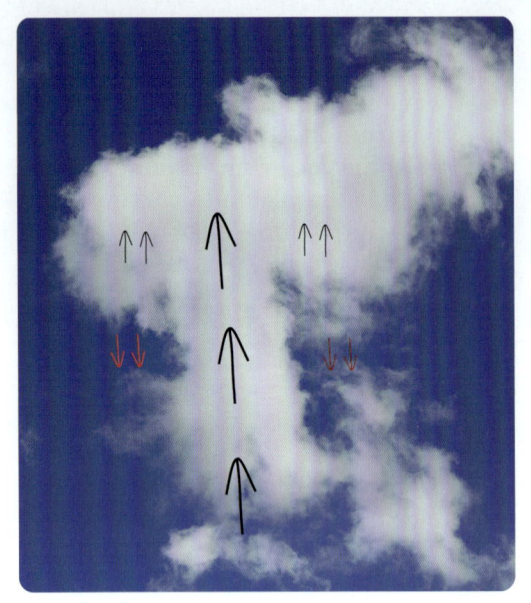

1.32 This is what we imagine a thermal looks like even though we can't see it. At the base a column which widens out like a mushroom at the top. Next to the column at the top you will generally find strong sink. Tactically it's best to fly blue thermals right to the top before leaving, with clouds you have to leave before getting sucked in.

The tail end of an isolated vortex-ring rising

Let's imagine two pilots trying to exploit the lower end of a thermal bubble rising as a vortex structure; one is 50m lower and soon gets left behind by the bubble, which due to his sinking through the surrounding air mass is always rising faster than him. But the other pilot who is 50m higher makes it into the centre of the vortex ring, where the rising air is accelerated by the vortex structure. In spite of the thermal bubble rising with 1m/s (200ft/min) the centre is producing climb rates of 2m/s which just balances out the descent of the paraglider. If it wasn't for this effect, and assuming a descent rate of -1m/s, the upper pilot would descend out of the bottom of the thermal bubble in 50 seconds (he was 50m higher than his buddy) – but instead he goes with it all the way to cloudbase!

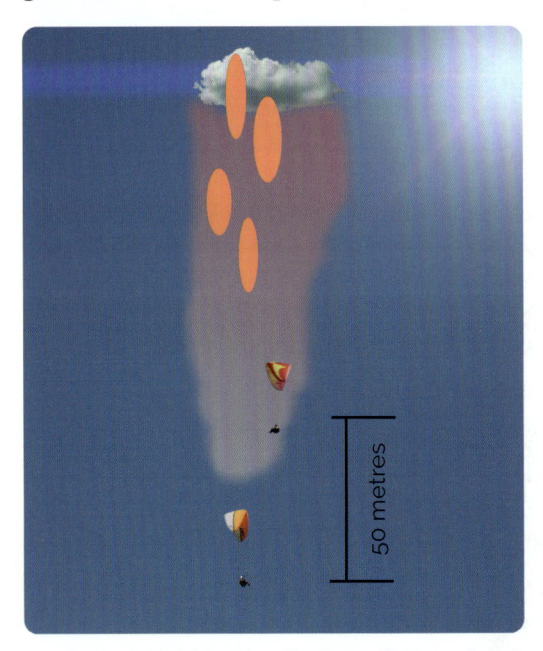

1.33 A cloud showing classic vortex shape. By looking at such clouds we can learn a lot about the structure of the invisible thermals

1.34 A thermal bubble rising. The lower pilot loses it early on, and searches in vain for the now much higher thermal. The upper pilot just makes it into the centre of the vortex ring, where he manages to remain. The lower pilot can only watch as his buddy becomes smaller and smaller. Within the thermal are several "hotspots" where the lift may be even better.

44

You should be safe in front of these impressive mountains because you are on the windward side Photo: Skywalk

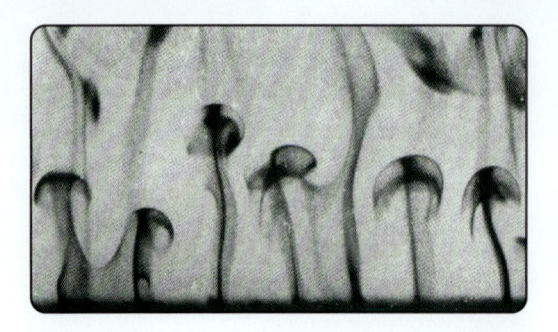

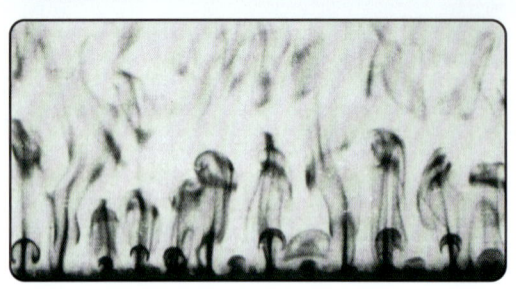

> **HINT:** Vortex rings are commonplace among isolated thermals with narrow cores. When the thermals grow large, as they do under cloud streets etcetera, the structure is rare.

Sinking air surrounding thermals

The good pilot is always trying to work out where in the thermal he will be. The air itself offers some valuable clues here.

Up high, and right on the outside of the thermal, we find not only increased descent but also a drift away from the thermal. To find it we need to turn against the drift. Down low the situation is reversed; the thermal sucks in surrounding air, which results in a light drift towards the lift combined with slightly reduced descent. We have seen that the available instability of a given air mass influences how high the thermals may go. But it also dictates the strength of the thermals, and where the best climbing may be found.

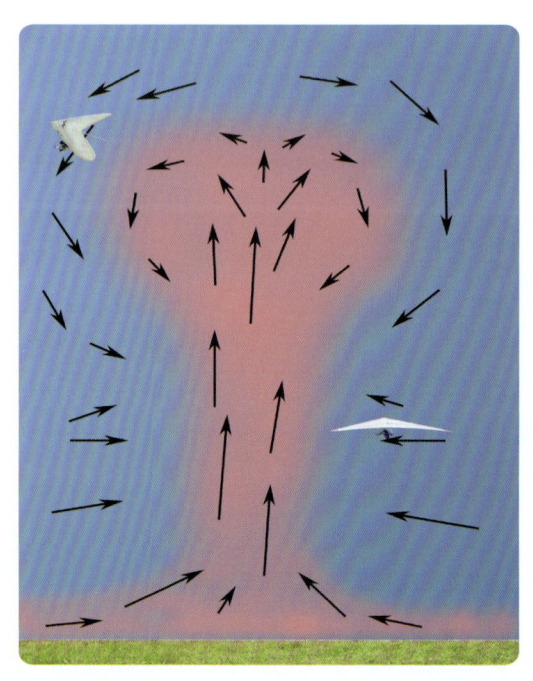

1.35 These pictures were produced by the University of Stanford in California (USA). They show oil being heated by a hot plate, with 'thermals' rising from the bottom. The top photo shows the ideal situation, with beautifully formed and regular shapes. The lower picture shows the same situation but now the hot plate has been turned up too high; the 'thermals' rise too fast and in a chaotic manner. This compares well to lee thermals or to air masses where the temperature gradient is too high.

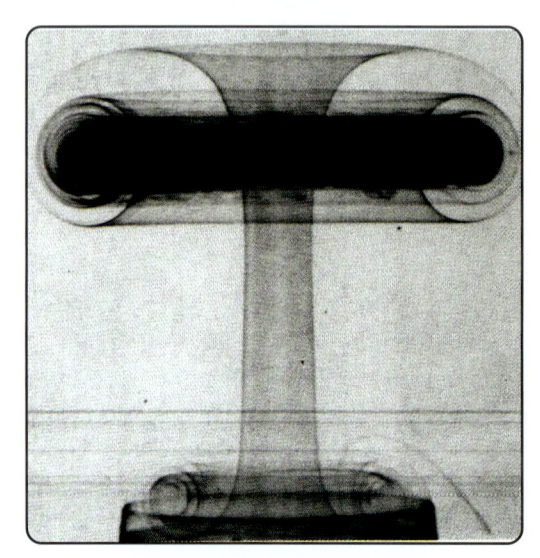

1.36 In this close-up of what is going on near the heated plate, the vortex structure is particularly visible

1.37 Air movement around a thermal. The higher hang glider is experiencing increased descent rates and a light tailwind component, whereas the lower one is being sucked in

46

Researching thermals

Scientific approaches to the measurement of thermals have often shown far more complex patterns than what we see in illustration 1.37. If we look at illustration 1.39 we can see an example of a thermal splitting up into two cores, where one reaches all the way to the cloudbase whereas the other suddenly stops. The reason is likely linked to the sinking air surrounding the thermal, where a part of it has managed to wedge into the lifting air putting a lid on some of it.

The paraglider in the illustration is not too far from the still-climbing hang glider. The former may think that he's continually dropping out of the side of the thermal but in reality his core has stopped climbing. His best approach is to move over to the hang glider, now above him, and continue climbing there.

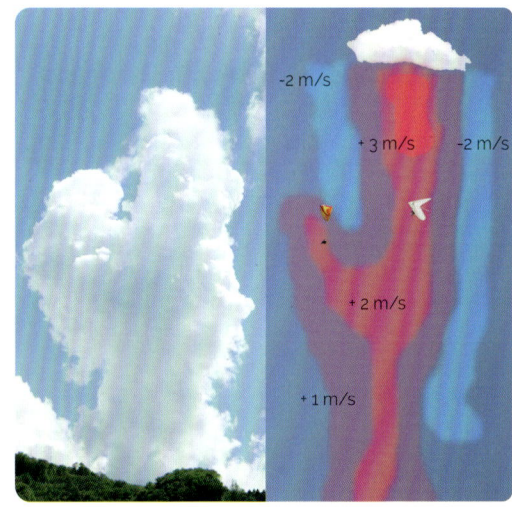

1.39 A sketch of a real thermal as it was determined during a test flight, with wings added for illustrative purposes. The hang glider has centred the better core whilst the paraglider is in a dead end. The picture on the right matches the illustration well – good for visualising what happens.

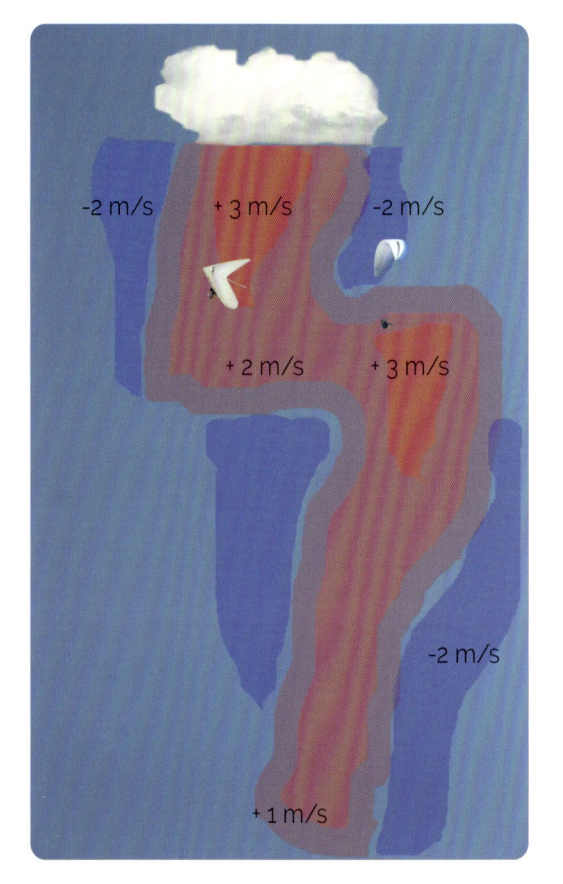

HINT Whenever I see proper cumulus clouds above me I know that there's a way to get up there. So when I find myself in a dead end like the paraglider in illustration 1.38 I simply increase my turning radius until I re-encounter the good core. I like flying alone a lot, but there's no denying that exploiting difficult thermals like the ones shown here is much easier when flying in a gaggle.

1.38 A thermal moving through a wind shear. Anyone remaining in the right-hand side will not be able to climb to cloudbase, as the thermal has been pushed to the side. By moving over to the hang glider the paraglider may still continue to climb. If we're alone, without other pilots around to show the lifting air, it pays to increase the centring radius in the direction of the drift.

The influence of air-mass (in)stability on thermal strength

We have seen that the available instability of a given air mass influences how high the thermals may go. But it also dictates the strength of the thermals, and where the best climbs may be found. These three examples are typical of what you will find.

Cloudbanks have a severe impact on thermals. Careful pilots fly around them if possible, as the chances of getting grounded by them are fairly high. Stubai Valley, Austria. Photo: Marcus King

The red line shows thermal strength as a function of altitude, increasing to the right

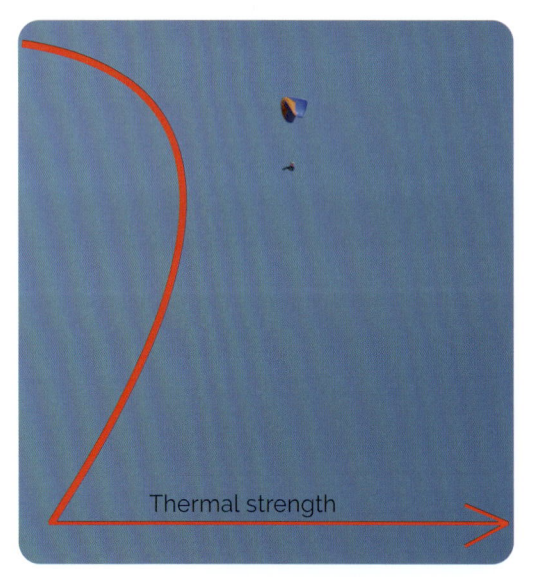

Thermal strength

Thermal strength

1.40 The air mass is basically unstable, but there's a high inversion putting a lid on things (see the red graph, indicating the temperature decrease with altitude). From experience we know that the thermal reaches its peak climb values in the upper third. Shortly before reaching cloudbase the thermal loses its momentum, and getting all the way to cloudbase is a patience game. That's why the risk of getting sucked in is minimal in this scenario. This is the most common situation in the Alps.

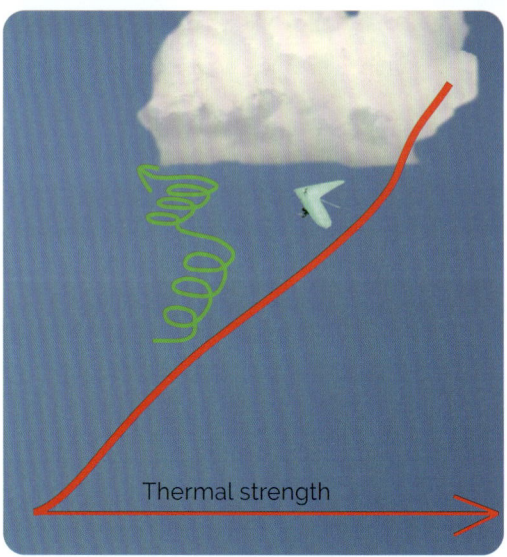

1.41 The situation shown here is the second most common one in the Alps. Instability continues way above cloudbase, which means that there's no inversion stopping the thermals from rising high. The climb rates continue to improve all the way to cloudbase and the clouds grow very big. It is easy to get sucked into the clouds and pilots should attempt to move to the edge of the climb well before reaching cloudbase (see the green line). Once at cloudbase it is easy to move away just as the first wisps of a cloud begin to appear.

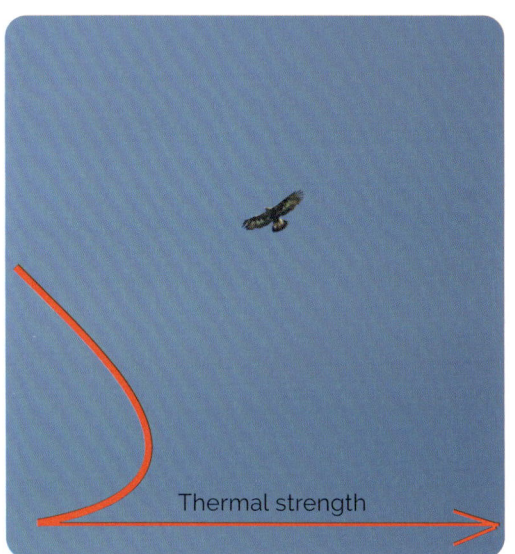

1.42 A stable air mass. This is a day that is not usually very good for us, or can be frustrating. The air is indifferently warm both high and low. If the sun is strong thermals may still form, but the stable air soon stops them. Birds still manage to get decent flights but they never get up very high. If you are in the valley it will be very hot. On days like these the trick is to get as high as you can into the big peaks before launching – take the longest cablecar or hike to the summit. Even then be prepapred to simply fly a big top-to-bottom.

1.43 Thermal dampening under a small cumulus cloud. The cloud is surrounded by cooler, sinking air. As it sinks this air warms up at around +1°C/100m, or somewhat more than the rising air inside the cloud cools down at -0.65°C/100m (see also chapter 9). The warmer air sinking around the thermal slows it down to the extent that cloudbase may remain out of reach for the pilot beneath! The first time this happens can be baffling – you're nearly at base, why can't you go any higher?! After V. Schwaniz.

Tactics for flying efficiently in different lift strengths

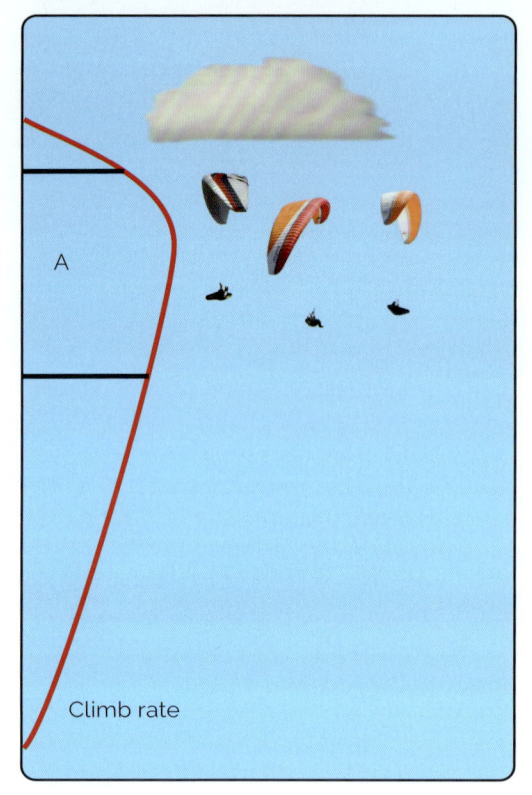

1.44 Climb rates are increasing as you go up. To fly quickly you should always try and stay in region A. The last few metres to cloudbase aren't really worth it, they take up too much time. On the other hand, if there's a large valley crossing ahead you should gain the last hundred metres. During flatland flying paragliders don't have the same range as hang gliders, due to different glide angles. Therefore you should always try and reach cloudbase even if it takes longer. The secret to cross country flying is to fly high, higher and still higher, at least for beginners. Maybe it's not the fastest style of flight but at least to begin with, it's the most effective.

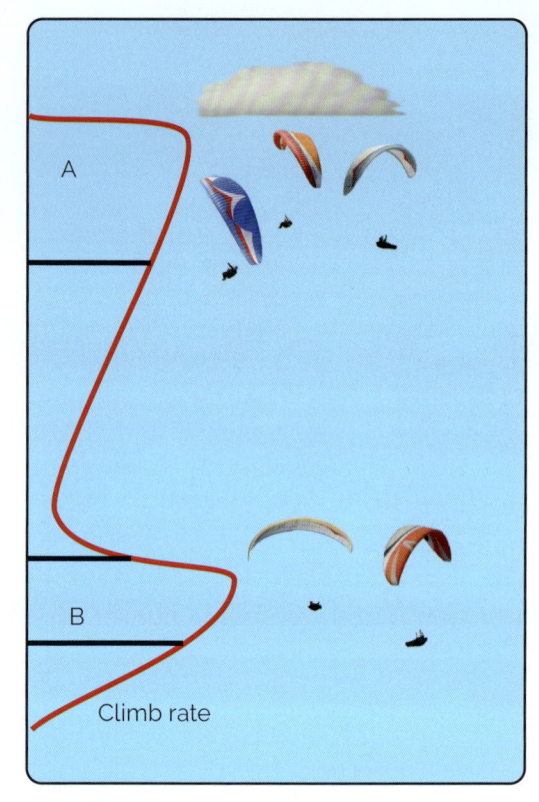

Photo: Jérôme Maupoint

1.45 Spring thermals with a weak inversion. Once you've made it into region A you should try and take every thermal you can get. Cross country pilots can easily make large valley crossings because in region B thermals are also strong. Above that you have to break through a weak inversion. This takes time, but the thermals are strong enough to make it.

Generally, thermal conditions remain constant during the day – if one thermal starts low then the next one will too. If it's difficult and you have to scratch your way back up again then you should really try and avoid sinking down low.

Low inversions at the beginning of the day will get burnt off with the sun, inversions higher up tend to remain. Then you will need a change of air to make climb rates improve. For example cloudbase in the middle of the Alps is usually much better than at the edge.

It's not a guarantee, but climb rates usually improve with height, and the higher cloudbase is, the better your climbs will be. For clouds of similar radius, you'll usually find better climb rates under the tallest cloud.

Thermal development in stable air – bullet thermals

The sun is strong and the day should be working, but the thermals still won't really form. This is a typical scenario in the late summer or early autumn, when a high-pressure system has been stationary for a few days (illustration 1.40).

Gliding close to the valley floor we suddenly encounter a small, turbulent thermal that is very hard to centre and only delays the inevitable for a few moments – and the climb rates deteriorate rapidly with the few metres of height gain we manage to make; we call these 'bullet thermals' and this is a classic state of affairs on a stable day.

Such days are really not very satisfying: the overheated air punches little thermals up that quickly lose momentum, only managing to stir up the air in an unpleasant way, enough to make it turbulent but never enough to get up high. Picture 1.21 shows such a day.

HINT Fly according to the day's quality. On days when the thermals increase in strength all the way to cloudbase I always try to remain as high as possible.

On the more common days where the thermal weakens a little right below cloudbase I only bother to go all the way up if I have a wide valley crossing ahead of me – otherwise I leave the thermals as they grow weaker and push on.

There are also days where the thermals are good down low, then around a certain altitude they get bumpy and weak, and above this layer they increase again. These days are easily recognised from the temperature gradient printouts (Chapter 9). On such days I try hard to remain above the inversion causing the slowdown as every visit below costs too much in time and tension battling my way back up.

It's like magic: cold advection

If the stationary high pressure is coming under the influence of a cold advection, where cooler air is pushing in at higher levels to replace the warm air present, the entire air mass becomes less stable and the thermal quality improves. If the influx of cold air persists into the evening we can have fantastic evening flights where the high peaks keep producing good thermals until sunset.

How to recognise cold advection?

In the Northern Hemisphere the high level wind usually turns 20-30° more to the right, in mountains even 30-40°, compared to the ground-level winds. This is due to ground friction. But when there's a cold advection happening the situation reverses – the high-level winds turn to the left instead (it works vice versa in the Southern Hemisphere).

By watching the high clouds we can learn to identify such a situation. In the Alps it is common with easterly winds, where the air influx is from the north and generally cooler.

1.46 Cold advection: When the high-altitude winds suddenly turn counter-clockwise (as opposed to the normal clockwise turning in the Northern hemisphere) we know that there is cold air flowing into the area up high. This means unstable air and good thermal development. We recognise it by comparing the drift of the high cirrus clouds (as in the picture) with the ground wind. Mount Lema, Switzerland, Photo: Nina Brümmer

HINT Cross country beginners should always try to remain as high as possible (remember to check if there are airspace regulations in your area). Doing so prolongs the flight and leaves more time for learning. Heinz Huth is a double world champion glider pilot. He has named it thermal hunting according to the Huth Model, or the 'Forest Theory'.

He compares the novice thermal chaser to a person running through the forest blindfolded. Every once in a while the person runs into a tree – sometimes a big one, sometimes a smaller one.

Fortunately the thermal development in the mountains is a great deal more predictable than that. It means mountain pilots and accomplished flatland pilots can learn to read the terrain and the clouds to the extent that at least part of their blindfold comes down. Now, instead of running blindfold through the woods the pilot at least has some idea of where they should be going.

1.48 High-Alpine flying near Fiesch, Switzerland. Plenty of big and strong thermals, but also smaller and weaker ones in between. If the pilot is in a hurry and has the skills he only uses the strong ones, but a novice or someone just out to enjoy the views should take every climb he finds.

HINT Experience has taught me that thermals will often show a great deal of similarity on any given day; if the last thermal was improving all the way to cloudbase, chances are that the next one will be exactly the same.

1.47 Flatland flying. The photo shows a planned route for a flight near Munich in Germany. The pilot takes every thermal as high as he can – in the flats staying high is even more important than in the mountains, where a ridge facing into the valley wind can often save the low pilot from a premature landing. This is almost never possible in flatland flying, which means that a lost thermal MUST be found again because we cannot just fly to the next expected lift zone – unless of course we can see other pilots, or birds, thermalling better within gliding distance.

Thermal spacing in the flatlands

Practical surveys have shown that an average thermal has a diameter of approximately 1000m up high – easy enough to stay in! But the core, where the climbing is good, is much smaller, maybe 50-100m across or even less. The distance between thermals in uniform flatland is generally 2.5 x height, which translates into the following little rule of thumb: The higher the cloudbase, the further to the next thermal! Smaller thermals between the proper ones may be found, but they often don't make it all the way to cloudbase.

All these values apply to homogenous ground on no-wind days. As soon as there is wind the picture becomes less schematic, and from only 15km/h wind lift bands under cloudstreets may begin to form.

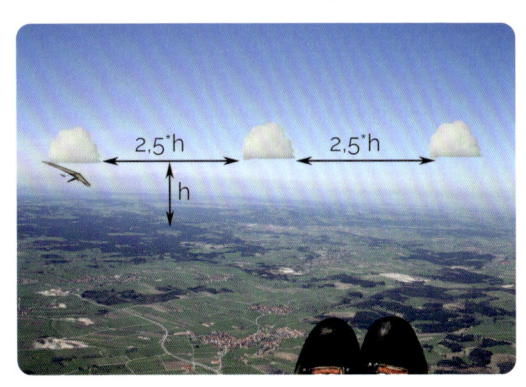

1.49 The distance between flatland thermals is generally assumed to be 2.5x their height above ground.

Rotating thermals

Contrary to popular belief the thermal rotation direction is not defined by the coreolis force. Thermals will often rotate, but in a random direction.

HINT Dust devils show the thermal rotation very clearly.

EXPERIENCE I experienced a perfect example of a rotating thermal in Bassano, Italy once: I was thermalling in a beautiful 3m/s thermal, turning left. A little leaf popped up next to me, also spiralling left. I increased my radius and kept the leaf in sight on my left wingtip, and 'we' continued to thermal together. But the leaf was climbing about a metre per circle faster than me and soon left me behind. The experience showed clearly how thermals are sometimes not only rotating inside out (page 43) but also around themselves vertically.

A second incident happened in Valle de Abdalajis in Spain. A number of plastic bags had been blown together by the wind on a little garbage dump, and the thermal triggered right off the crest of the dump, sucking in all the plastic bags. It was beautiful to watch the many colourful bags dancing left as they ascended.

1.50 Dust devils are rotating thermals being born. The picture shows the Babadağ launch in Ölüdeniz, Turkey. Empirical studies confirm that they turn randomly left or right everywhere on the planet. Photo: Nina Brümmer

HINT Some experienced pilots have speculated that thermalling against the thermal rotation will improve climb rates. If this is true then it would be good to be able to discern the rotation of a thermal before joining it. This is very hard to do, but there are some theories available that can help.

The flying meteorologist Sven Plöger has presented a usable hypothesis for mountain conditions. The rotation is determined by the release impulse.

An example could be a warm air bubble lying at the bottom of a north-south oriented valley, with the valley wind blowing from the north. According to this theory, thermals triggered near the west side of the valley or on the western slopes will rotate clockwise, on the east side they will rotate counter-clockwise.

I have yet to verify this hypothesis but will be observing it carefully to see if it holds.

EXPERIENCE Peter Karsten is a friend who has an office window facing a popular house thermal often filled with buzzards. Ever since reading the first edition of my book he set out to ascertain whether acknowledged experts like the buzzards had a preferred turn direction. In one year of studies he was unable to observe any tendency either way – indeed the buzzards would often reverse their turn direction! But I remain unconvinced that there is no benefit to turning against the flow in thermals, and will keep researching the subject!

HINT Pilot Graham Richards suggests flying against the rotation your groundspeed and, more importantly, your angular velocity will be lower. With a lower angular velocity and the same radius of turn, your bank will be less. Less bank means a lower sink rate. Sounds easy – maybe it is!

1.51 *Sven Plöger is a paraglider pilot and TV meteorologist who has a thermal-rotation hypothesis. He suggests that the triggering impulse determines the rotation direction so that when, in this example, the wind sets off a thermal on the far side of the valley this thermal rotates clockwise, whereas on this side it will rotate counter-clockwise. Sillian, Austria.*

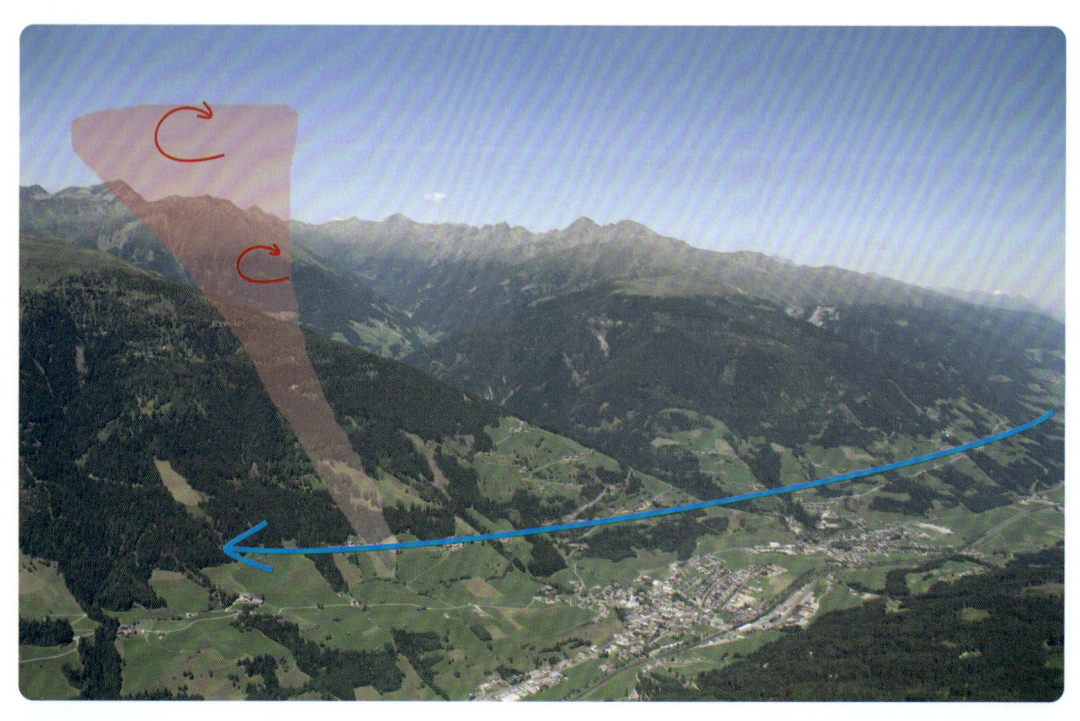

Thermal lifespan

The photo series shows a cumulus cloud indicating the life of a thermal. The wind pushes the warm air towards a triggering ground feature (here a forest edge) and it sets off as a thermal. A small cu is formed.

The cu grows as the warm-air influx from below increases, and eventually a semblance of a defined cloudbase is reached. After a while the cloud begins to dissipate, and later it is completely gone – the entire life span of a thermal made visible. Notice that the cloud looks similar in the forming and the dissipating phase – but flying under it is very different, as a dissipating cloud has only increased sink beneath it. As pilots we want to avoid heading for dissipating clouds and thus we need to observe our surroundings to be able to discern which clouds are forming and which are dissipating.

1.52 Six photos showing the life span of a cumulus cloud. In the first frame the cloud is just beginning to form, from photo 4 it is decaying again. It only pays to head for developing cu's as decaying clouds indicate nothing but increased sink. From the first to the last photo about 10 minutes went by.

HINT It is very difficult to assess clouds that are still forming. My preferred technique is the following: while thermalling I always watch the clouds in the direction that I'm going. A full circle takes about 15-20 seconds, and every time I have the cloud right in front of me I observe it briefly. After 4-6 looks spanning a few minutes I have a good idea of what the cloud is doing – much better than if I had been watching the cloud continuously during the same time. Don't think that this is easy though; the more clouds surrounding you, the harder it gets to pinpoint the interesting, growing ones!

HINT Observe your surroundings continuously whilst flying. Only by doing so can you build a picture of which of the Cu's around you are building up and which are dissipating. Track their development to get an idea of the life span of the thermals, and which ones have already been active so long that flying to them doesn't make sense.

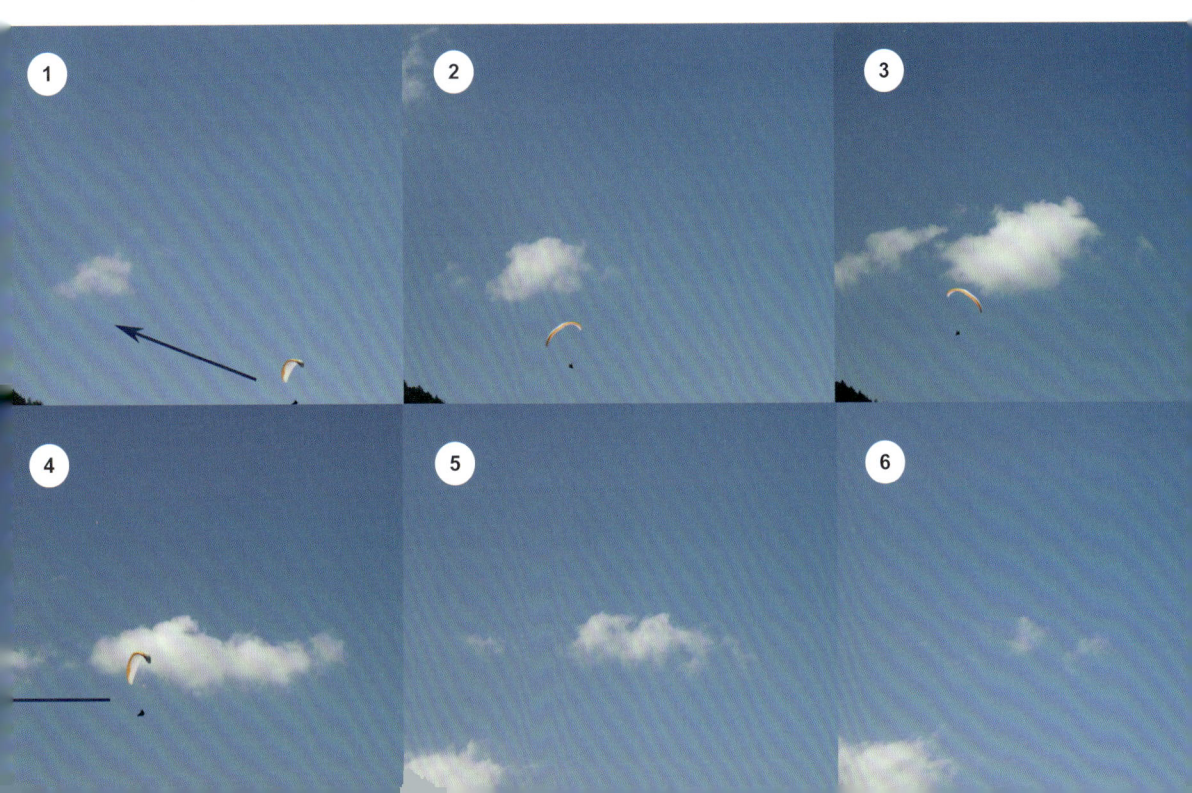

1.53 *In the first three photos the cloud is growing, then it begins to decay*

1.54 *Left of the first cumulus strands a second cloud is beginning to form. This cloud grows faster and taller – climb rates will be better here. Searching for better lift is often worthwhile, even when already climbing.*

1.55 *In this sequence of eight photos we can clearly see how several updraughts combine to form a big cumulus. Compare this set of photos with picture 1.12 on page 30.*

Large cumulus development in the hills of the Cauca Valley, a popular flying destination in Colombia
Photo: Skywalk

Wind influence on thermals

When the air is unstable and the sun is strong, good bubbles of warm air form, to rise as thermals. Once they begin rising, their path through the air is decided by the wind – the stronger the wind, the more they drift. When we approach a cloud expecting to find lift beneath it we must take this drift into account.

Large warm air bubbles can only form when they are relatively undisturbed by wind. This is the reason why leeside thermals are often stronger; they form in the lee where they are undisturbed by the wind, and thus trigger later than thermals coming off the windward side.

From wind strengths around 25km/h the warm air is continually disturbed and triggered into rising as undefined bubbles of lift, hardly usable by paragliders and hang gliders at least down low. Up higher the bubbles join into more defined thermals, allowing thermal flights even in strong winds. However, getting up there from a winch tow for example is generally rather difficult. Hang gliders being towed up by an ultralight aircraft have a definite advantage here.

Flying in mountain regions at such wind speeds is not recommended. The lee side of crests and ridges will produce very unpleasant and dangerous turbulence.

In the flatlands we may still carry out thermal flights at such wind speeds, because small local lees caused by hills, villages, forests etc. allow the thermals time to form and turn into usable lift. If the ground level wind is strong the thermals often don't trigger off their source but are pushed to more obvious trigger points, like forest edges, rivers, hills or even powerlines.

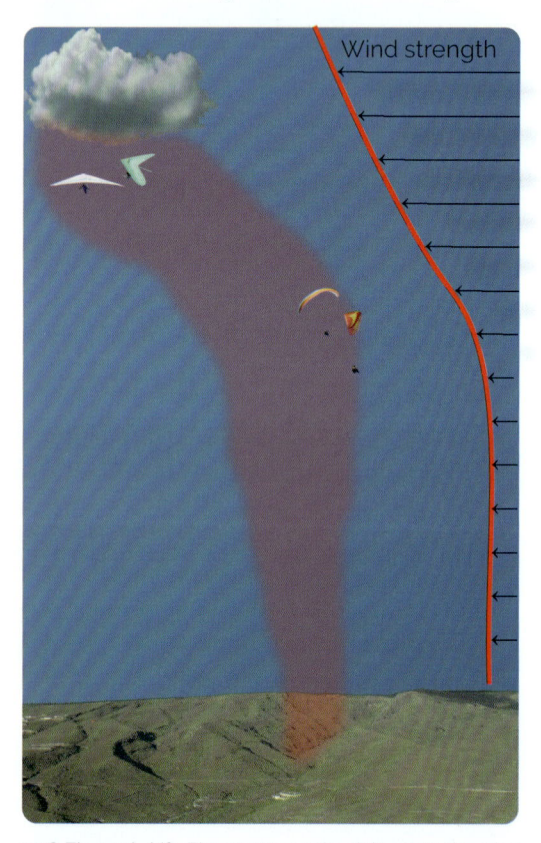

1.56 Thermal drift. The arrows on the right show the wind direction and strength – notice the increase with altitude. Low down where the wind is weak there is little drift and the thermal rises almost vertically. Up higher the wind increases and the thermal drifts with it – in this case at the altitude where the paragliders are. To remain in the thermal the pilots must follow the drift towards the left, or they fall out on the windward side.

1.57 This shows how the thermal drift increases with altitude. In the middle we can see a clear drift towards the left Photo: Bruce Goldsmith

HINT If the wind speeds increase dramatically with altitude (more than 20km/h per 1,000m) the thermals will be stirred to such an extent that flying for all practical purposes will become impossible. On such days it is better to remain on the ground.

HINT The same slope may produce both weak and strong thermals. To avoid the risk of getting blown back into the lee it is best to concentrate on the stronger ones. When thermalling in strong winds it is important to always remain near the windward edge, as dropping out here only causes us to descend back into the thermal, whereas dropping out on the lee side could mean sliding down the backside of the thermal unable to re-enter due to lack of groundspeed. More on this in chapter 8.

If the plateau behind the first crest has landing options we may opt to try coring even weaker thermals, thereby consciously risking a premature plateau landing.

Thermal drift over crests

Illustration 1.58 below shows the thermal drift over the terrain. Low down the warm air follows the slope in an anabatic flow, as seen in picture 1.5 on p26. Over the first crest the thermal is pushed still further right by the wind. Note that strong thermals are pushed less than weak ones!

1.58 The normal wind and thermal situation along the terrain when the wind is onto the slope. To avoid dropping out of the thermal when reaching the first crest the pilot must concentrate! Once higher he can allow himself to drift over to the higher ridge and either soar up or continue thermalling.

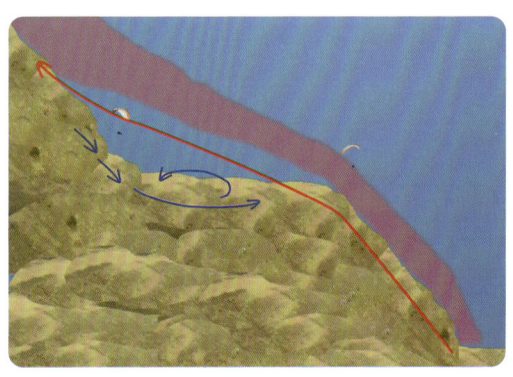

1.59 This illustration shows the problem from 1.58 even more clearly. The pilot on the right is thermalling near the windward side of the thermal whereas the left pilot tried to push back to the high terrain too early and now has to cope with a plateau landing in turbulent conditions.

Horacio Llorens and Juan Robles thermal together in Spain. Photo: Óscar Lagarrotxa / Ozone

2 Thermal generators and triggers

An amazing day in the Dolomites, Italy Photo: Skywalk

Chapter 2

Thermal generators and triggers

I often see pilots searching around for thermals in what I consider unlikely places, and pilots also often ask me why I have flown to a particular spot to search. Whenever the latter happens I have to stop myself from simply saying something like 'it looked good'. In fact, what makes a specific point in the landscape look 'better' than all the potential locations around it is a complex matter, and coming to a conclusion happens only via numerous deliberations. In the beginning these are all conscious but with experience they become increasingly subconscious until we cannot even say what caused us to fly there anymore!

2.1 A clearly marked thermal trigger point, the saddle above Schnalstal in the Italian Alps. Generally, the ridgeline will trigger the thermal (as seen in picture 1.4) but with a bowl like this facing right into the sun the areas right or left, depending on the wind direction, are also very good. In the middle of the bowl we can expect increased sink values.

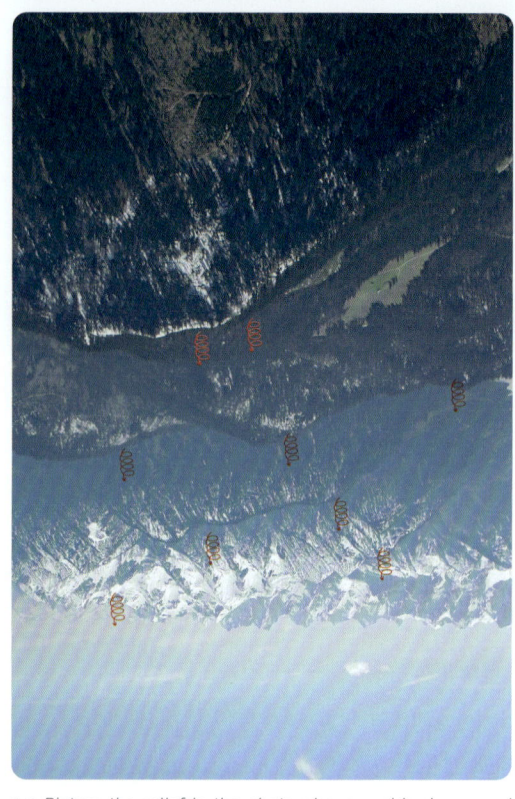

2.2 Picture the relief in the photo above upside down, and spray water over it. Where the water droplets build and fall off you'll find the release points for thermals. The positions are marked as examples in the photo.

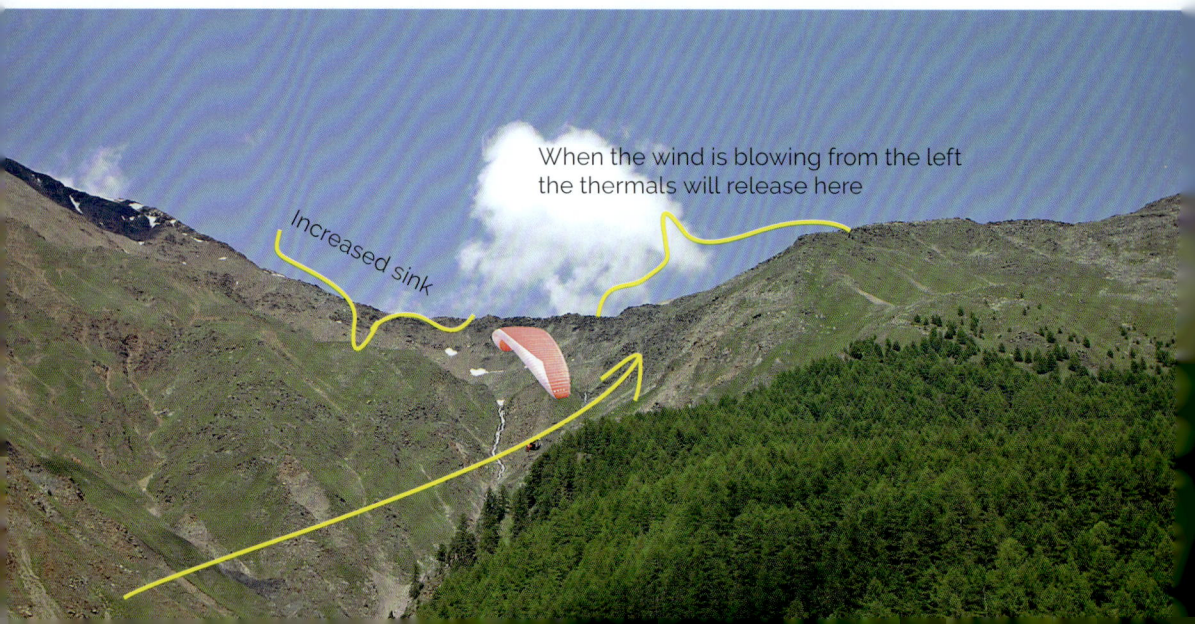

When the wind is blowing from the left the thermals will release here

Increased sink

Whilst learning we need to consider the following things:
- Which soil/ground heats well?
- Where would a thermal flow, coming from that patch of ground, taking into consideration the wind and the terrain?

We have learnt that thermals happen because the sun heats the ground, and the ground heats the air above it. Now let us take that one step further.

Albedo value, a measure for the 'heat-ability' of the soil

The albedo value indicates how much of the sun's rays are reflected by a given material. The higher the albedo value, the worse for thermal development because all the energy is reflected and not enough lingers to heat up the soil.

But the albedo value alone isn't the whole story. If the soil is soaked with water, energy must first be spent on evaporation before the heating can get underway. This process uses up a lot of energy, which then isn't available for thermal generation.

Finally a porous soil containing lots of air heats more easily than a more compact one.

Table 2.3 Albedo values for different soils

Surface	Albedo value
Dry grain fields	Extremely low
Asphalt	Extremely low
Black soil	Very low
Damp sand	Very low
Coniferous forest	Very low
Vegetation-free soil	Low
Grass	Low
Deciduous forest	Low
Desert, water	Medium
Dry sand	High
Snow	Very high

2.3 Snow's albedo value is very high, and very little energy is absorbed from the sun. Snow is the poorest possible thermal generator.

Factors to consider when evaluating the thermal generating properties of any given soil

- Damp soil absorbs much energy without releasing it again. For a moor to generate thermals we must wait until late in the day, when the surroundings have begun to cool down. The moorland will cool slower and sometimes allow us to linger in light lift over places where we are not accustomed to finding lift.
- Deciduous forests have a relatively low albedo value, but contain much humidity. This makes them less thermally interesting than coniferous forests where there is less humidity stored.
- Any surface oriented perpendicular to the sun's rays will heat better than surrounding, non-perpendicular surfaces. In the northern hemisphere this means east slopes in the morning, south slopes around noon and west slopes in the afternoon. Because the sun is higher around noon the south slopes can be shallower (on the Equator they can be horizontal) than the east and west slopes. In the European winter only steep south-facing cliff faces produce usable thermals.
- Surfaces with a high specific heat capacity (like rocks) take longer to

heat, but once warm they will continue to produce thermals even during short overcast periods. East facing vertical cliffs are the first to produce thermals in the morning, not because of the specific heat capacity but because they have been facing into the sun for the longest time.

- Desert surfaces and dry sand have high albedo values but are very porous. Further, deserts are often in regions with strong sunlight, and the porosity plus the strength of the sunlight combine to produce strong thermals in desert regions.
- Coniferous forest, and forest clearings in them, are good thermal generators.
- Wet green fields are no good, but newly harvested they are OK. If there's hay drying in a field it is probably good.
- Grain or potato fields are good. Corn fields only get really good in the autumn.
- Ploughed fields are better than untreated ones.
- And crowded parking lots or industrial expanses are always excellent thermal generators.

2.5 A farmer prepares the hay harvest. The pilot sees this and promptly flies there. The location is good, not only because of the low albedo value of grass fields, but also because the farmer in his tractor triggers all the accumulated hot air by driving around.

2.4 During the day, lakes, swamps and damp moorlands do not produce any thermals. Towards the evening, moorlands can release weak thermals, and lakes may produce reduced sink values. On a hillside next to a lake, only the flanks can produce thermals. Long flanks produce good thermals. Hillsides with lakes produce weaker thermals than those with dry ground in front of them. Lake Annecy, France. Photo: Jérôme Maupoint

2.6 Parseier Peak in the Inn Valley, Austria. The rocky, southeast-oriented slopes are perfect for generating early thermals. The hang glider pilot knows this and flies straight there. He has launched from the Venet, a north-facing launch that is uninteresting at this time of the day.

HINT The higher a site is above sea level, the quicker thermals will trigger. Thinner, clearer air is heated up faster by the ground.

HINT When a parking lot is full of cars it becomes even better, as more hot air may be trapped among all the parked vehicles. Thermals originating from full parking lots are generally both stronger and wider and thus easier to core.

HINT Thermals may come from any surface that is readily heated by the sun. For your mental picture try to imagine walking over the ground where you're flying. Wherever you feel the air getting warmer you can expect thermals to originate, whenever it gets cooler it is less interesting. This means that cool, shady and wet areas will always hinder thermal development.

2.7 Flying over the official landing at Brauneck, in the German Alps. This parking lot is an excellent thermal generator in spite of its location in the middle of a valley. However, the thermal will normally be offset by the valley wind and is often located right above the official landing, to the joy of the students training there. The instructors are less enthusiastic about it.

65

Thermal development delay

The time that passes between the sun hitting a given surface and the surface releasing the first thermal could be called the thermal development delay. This time differs from surface to surface.

Rocks have long delays but store the energy for a long time; coniferous woodlands and fields have shorter delays but stop working as soon as the sun stops hitting them.

Shade drawing in from the side triggers thermals, provided the air has been heated sufficiently, but once the thermal has released and risen the show will be over there until the shade is gone again.

Depending on the surface, some time will pass before a previously shaded area releases its next thermal after the sun has come out again. Readily heated surfaces will have the next thermal ready in as little as 10 minutes whereas areas consisting of soils with a high specific heat capacity, like rocks, take notably longer.

Thermal trigger points

Warm air, being lighter than cold, has the inherent tendency to rise. However a release impulse is needed to overcome the inertia. The following is a short and incomplete list of possible impulses or triggers:

- Terrain or vegetation changes, like forest edges, ridgelines, uneven slopes.
- Temperature changes caused by snow, shade or water.
- External factors, like moving objects or even acoustic impulses

The most obvious trigger point is always the peak, but the shoulder is no less important! In the Alpine spring the snow line takes over the shoulders' role.

More easily-identified thermal triggers

- Forest clearings
- Powerlines. In the mountains these are often located on shoulders (see picture 2.15) and this may partly account for their triggering capacities. But powerlines are also known to trigger thermals in flatlands, where there's no terrain to explain their effect.

2.8 Once the cloud shadow is gone it takes only a couple of minutes before the next thermal is ready.

2.9 A perfect thermal generator/trigger. Hopefully the pilot will arrive high enough to take advantage of it.

Above: Cumulus clouds have developed over the peaks, and over the valley the sky is blue. That's the way things should be! Cloud surfing above Plaine-Joux near Chamonix, France. Photo: Marcus King.
Below: Evening above Chamonix, no clouds, no thermals, no strong winds, no turbulence – wonderful. Photo: Ozone

2.12 When the main peak has a little shoulder in front, this will often be a more reliable trigger than the main peak. In this illustration the points A to C are the shoulders, and the mountain D has no shoulder. D is the best thermal generator (see arrow), E is the peak above shoulders A to C. If we're high we fly straight towards E, knowing that should it not work we can aim for A to C. Once high in either place the way to D is secured. This is the Valais in Switzerland.

2.10 An uninterrupted mountain chain, like the Pinzgau in Austria, will release thermals along its entire length. Once up bombing-out is almost out of the question.

2.11 Thermal flying along an exposed rocky ridge near Chamonix in France, west of the Mer de Glace. Thermals trigger directly from the ridge. Photo: Nina Brümmer

2.13 Such a distinct clearing in the woods is a very good thermal trigger. If the pilot is high he should fly to the crest above, but if that fails searching right above the clearing is a good strategy.

2.15 The electricity pylon is located right on the shoulder and we can expect good thermals to be coming off it. This is not one to use when you are low – only when you have height and can fly away. You do not want to land on an electricity pylon

2.14 In the mountains in spring the snow line is the most common thermal trigger. This photo shows April in the Alps, where the thermals are very good at this time of year. Thermals trigger exactly where the snow meets the exposed terrain. Photo: Ozone

Thermal triggers in flatland areas

- Look for large temperature differences, as found on lake and river shores.
- A forest edge or a tree line.
- Small hills – although these are difficult to see from altitude.
- Railroad tracks and roads.
- Active farming machinery, see picture 2.5. Harvesting is very often associated with excellent thermal development.
- Cloud shadow moving over the landscape – but beware! If the cloud is big and the drift slow the shade causes all activity to cease for a while!

HINT If the wind is strong, tree lines or forest edges may even be soared until a thermal is released. This trick is however an 'experts only' game, as coring thermals low down in strong drift is very tricky, and the chances of being dumped either in the lee or over unlandable woodlands are high. You need to hang on to the lift!

2.16 A lake or river shore is a very good thermal trigger. If the wind pushes the heated air towards the shore, the temperature difference will trigger it. Due to the thermal drift the lift will be located over the water.

2.18 The shade from the Cu moves over the landscape with the wind. As it progresses it triggers thermals in front of it. The black arrow shows the wind direction, and the pilot can fly with a tailwind from the cloud directly to the new thermal trigged by the cloud shadow. If the pilot has been flying on the upwind side of the big cloud (left) and the thermal has died, getting across the big shadow can be a challenge, but there's a good chance of getting up again if we can only reach the shadow border, where the next thermal is released.

2.17 A tree line is easy to see even from high altitude. When the wind blows against the line, even at an angle, the thermals will be triggered.

HINT A friend told me how he had once cored a thermal being 'pulled' up by a hot air balloon! It was the best thermal of the otherwise unspectacular day!

2.19 *De Aar, South Africa. It looked like a perfect day – but cloudbase was only 800m AGL and centring from low altitudes turned out to be difficult. It took four tows to finally get up to base.*

2.20 *Clouds indicate where the thermals are to be found. On this day the distance between thermals was unusually far, and cloudbase was not correspondingly high – which meant that we generally arrived really low in the next thermal! We found that industrial areas and villages were the best sources.*

Picture 2.21 *Ahh, to be towed up into the thermal and then release when the vario has been screaming for a few seconds.*

Cloud shadow as release impulse

By Volker Schwaniz

As soon as the ground becomes cloud covered, the surface begins to cool down. Due to this effect the temperature difference between shady and sunny is quite noticeable, and as we have seen before, temperature differences are reliable thermal triggers. Whether the thermal triggers upwind or downwind from the shade (cloud) is determined by the forward speed of the shady area, i.e. the cloud speed and thus the wind at cloud altitude rather than to the wind strength and direction at ground level.

In the mountains the thermal will normally be triggered to the upwind side of the cloud shade. The cool air from the cloud shade soon rolls down the mountainside in katabatic flow and pushes against the still active anabatic flow on the windward side of the cloud shadow, causing a very strong triggering impulse. This can be observed at slope launches susceptible to overshadowing; there's often a tailwind even if everyone is climbing happily only metres out from the slope.

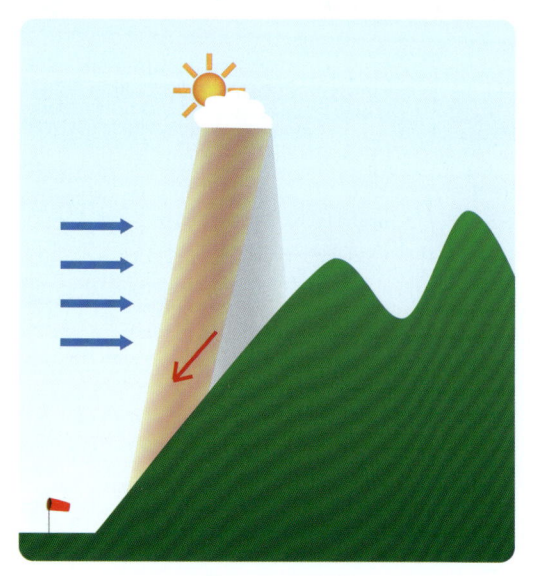

2.22 Cloud triggering of thermals in mountains often happens on the windward side of the cloud shadow.

HINT If the launch is getting cloud covered due to cumulus development over the launch mountain while the lower slopes are still in the sun it pays to get off quickly, before the katabatic flow sets in, causing a tailwind.

In the flatlands the cloud shadow triggers the next thermal on the downwind side of the cloud, see illustration 2.23. This is caused by the generally stronger wind high up causing the clouds to move faster than the winds at ground level can displace the warm air. The briskly moving cloud shadow thus 'pushes beneath' the warm air and triggers the thermal, which in turn is offset by the wind.

2.23 Flatland cloud shadow as a trigger. The thermals are triggered on the downwind side of the cloud shadow.

HINT In the flatlands cloud shadows should only be used as thermal indicators when we have a comfortable altitude margin, as coring below 300-400m is often difficult.

HINT When towing it pays to look out for approaching cloud shadows, as these increase our chances of hooking right into a good thermal, provided we get the timing right.

Thermal alignment with the wind

By Volker Schwaniz

Downwind of strong thermals we often encounter further thermals. They form in irregular intervals and are almost perfectly aligned with the wind. They are easy to see from the cumulus formation that they cause, which differs from cloud streets because they are further apart. Another difference is that neither a particular weather situation is needed, nor a specific wind strength. Whenever there's thermals and wind, this kind of alignment can be observed!

The precise reason for this is not entirely understood, but it is assumed that the peripheral, weaker parts of the mother thermal are offset more by the wind and drift further downwind, where they meet and join forces with new wafts of lift coming from beneath. Long rows of usable lift are generated in this manner, and they may live for as long as 30 minutes longer than the actual mother thermal.

Notice that the nature of the soil downwind of the mother thermal influences the extent of the phenomenon. Moist forest areas, wetlands or water inhibit it or stop it completely.

There's another hypothesis that attempts to explain the thermal alignment. It deals with the fact that the high-level winds are known to be brought into oscillations by flowing over strong thermals or well-formed cumulus clouds, setting up a wave pattern leeward of the mother thermal (see illustration 2.24).

In the upwardly moving sections of this wave pattern the air mass is less stable and more prone to thermal development. Glider pilots have been known to use cumulus waves to fly over strong cumulus clouds.

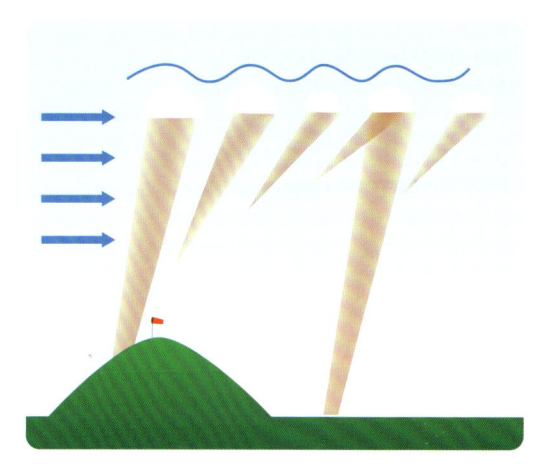

2.24 Downwind of strong thermal sources we often encounter further thermals and not only dissolving remains of the first, strong thermal.

HINT Inexperienced pilots often assume that the smaller cumulus clouds leeward of a big cloud are just dissolving remains of the big one, producing only increased sink. This is often not the case! Leeward of pulsating thermal sources we often encounter further, weaker lift. It follows that it pays to fly directly downwind from a good thermal, especially in the flats.

HINT Updraughts (thermals) and downdraughts go together like Red Bull and vodka, and just as the thermals tend to align with the wind the downdraughts will do the same. This means that the best escape route from widespread sink is perpendicular to the wind direction (provided the sink isn't caused by a lee zone).

HINT Thermal alignment due to wind does not depend on cloud condensation. This means that it is also found on blue days, albeit less visibly.

Two different route choices in a wide valley

As soon as the pilot decides to abandon one thermal and fly to the next, we can consider it XC flying. Here we describe two different choices (see picture 2.25).

First choice
The pilot flies from mountain shoulder to mountain shoulder.

Advantages are that he always arrives high enough to make it to the next west flank, where he can expect thermals to be coming up. Should no thermals be found he can glide down to land in the wide valley where he has plenty of landing options, instead of being forced into the high valley between the two ridges.

Disadvantage is that he soon finds himself under the influence of the valley wind system, where the strength of the wind is enough to disturb the thermals and make them difficult to use. This can often make it hard to get up high again.

Second choice
The pilot gains maximum altitude at A, then follows the terrain up along the flanks of the main summit until he is above the main ridge.

Advantages are that, provided cloudbase is high enough, he can remain above the main peaks, undisturbed by valley winds and with strong, consistent climbs. Our overall speed can be very good up here! Besides, the view is better than along the shoulders out near to the valley floor!

Disadvantages occur when he doesn't make it to the next climb above the ridge – then he could be looking either at a landing up high, or in a narrow side valley, or at least a long detour around the next perpendicular ridge. Even if this detour works it takes a long time, and because he arrives lower than he would have, had he come straight there, he must then battle

2.25 View of a wide, E-W oriented valley. On the left a massive, unbroken chain with wooded foothills reaching into the main valley, with narrow valleys between them. Two options for flying the ridge present themselves: either over the trigger shoulders near to the main valley or above the main peaks of the chain. In both cases we approach point A first to gain the altitude we need to continue. The photo shows the Pustertal, Italian/Austrian Alps.

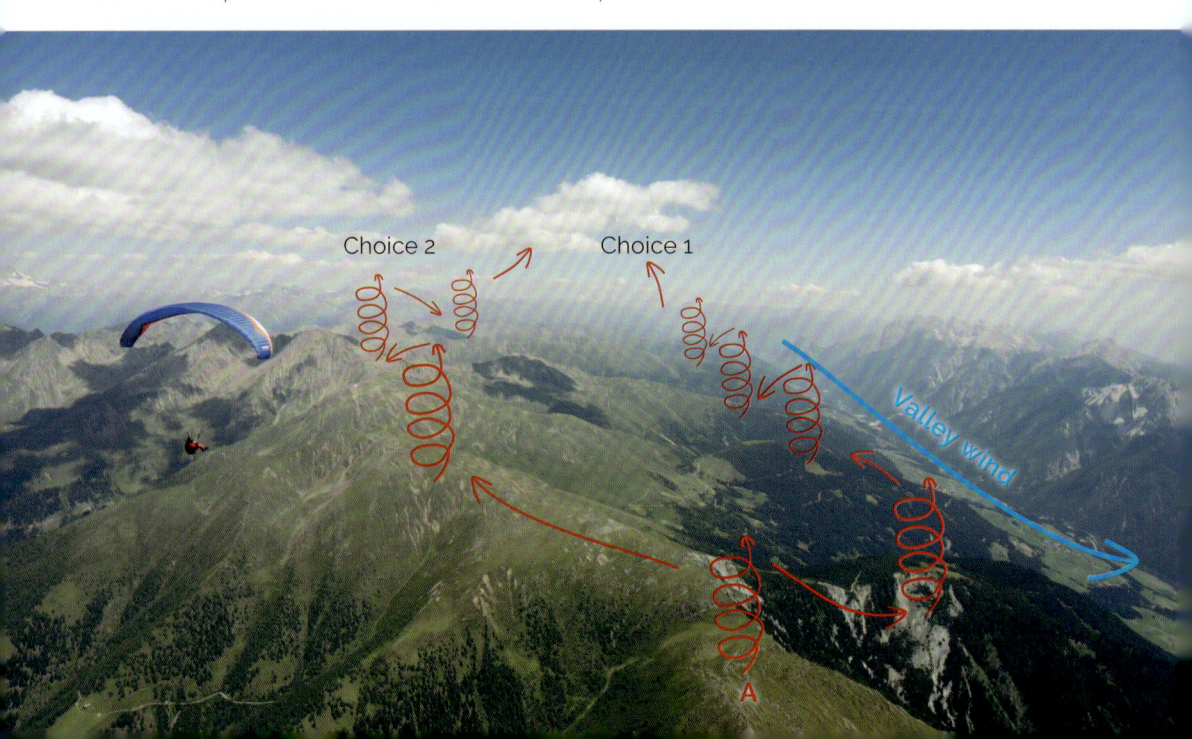

it out even lower in the valley wind to get back up high.

Preliminary conclusion
For the XC beginner it generally pays to remain above the foothills, or what we have called the 'shoulders'. The high route over the main ridge is only fast if there's no risk of not making it to the next thermal – otherwise there are large detours on the menu!

In the Alps these large E-W oriented valleys are plentiful, all very well suited for flying: in Austria we have the famous Pinzgau valley and the eastern end of the Pustertal, we have the Drautal (Greifenburg), the Inntal (from Innsbruck to Arlberg), and the Ennstal with Schladming and Werfenweng.

In Italy we find the Ahrntal in Alto Adige South Tyrol) and Feltre in the south east. Switzerland has the Engadin and the Valais, and all these valleys are renowned for their excellent flying conditions.

2.26 *Pinzgau, Austria. When cloudbase is very high, as in this picture, we remain above the main ridge. If against all odds we should fall out it will probably be right onto one of the shoulders seen protruding from the main ridge into the valley, and the chances of making it back up will be good. A further advantage is that we will not need to go into the narrow gullies between the mountains.*

2.27 *A similar chain to the one in picture 2.26, this time the Goms in Valais, Switzerland. This particular stretch of mountainscape is renowned for fast, reliable flying. The picture was taken from cloudbase, and the marked places all had (as indeed they generally do) very good thermals coming off them. On this day, cloudbase is insufficient to fly the high-Alpine route as indicated along the B arrow.*

Line B

Enjoying some good XC conditions in Westerndorf, Austria.
Photo: Daniel Gassner

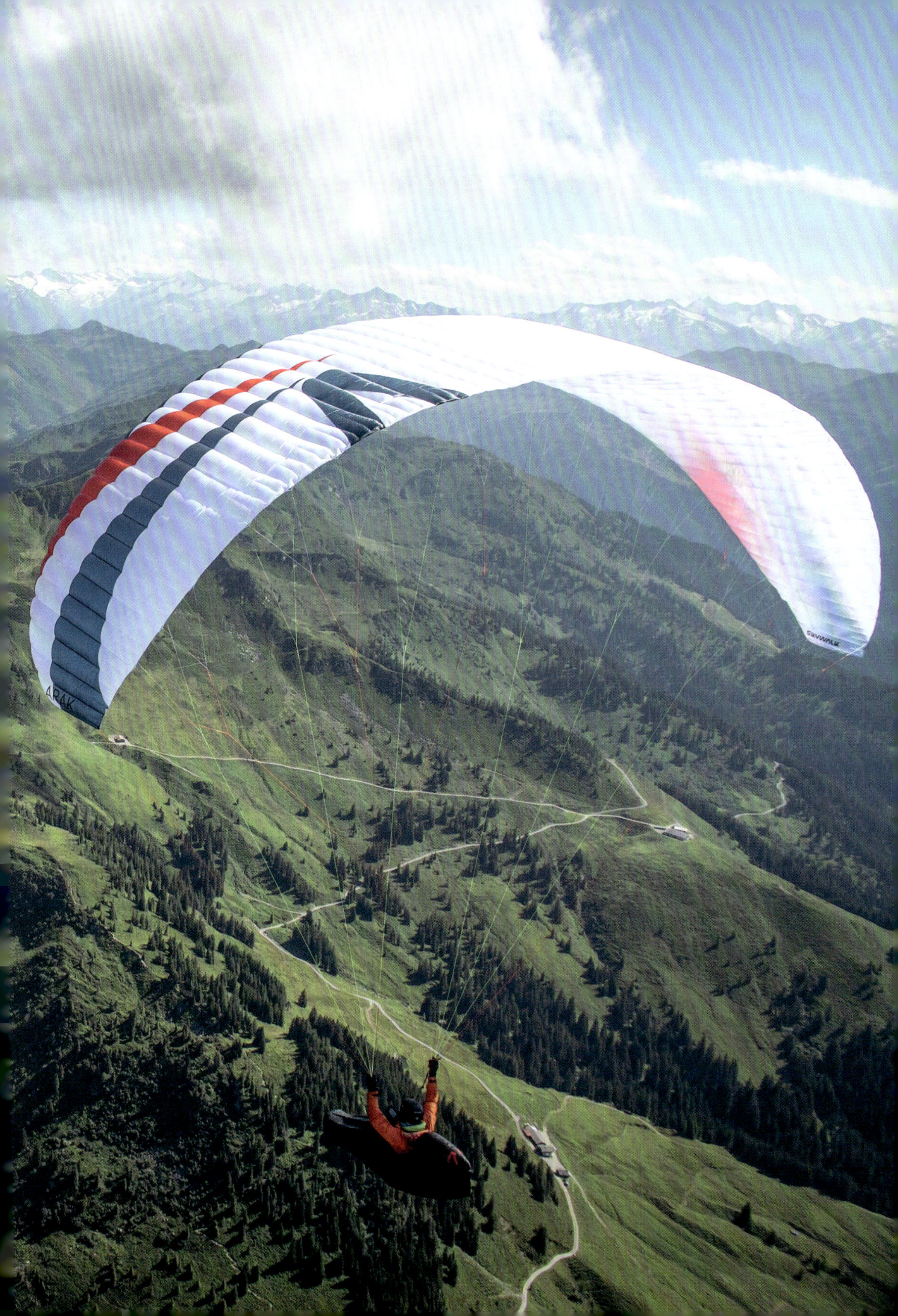
ARAK
SKYWALK

3 Flying in and around thermals

Flying in the high French Alps. Photo: Marcus King

Chapter 3

Flying in and around thermals

Turbulence

Turbulence is the pilot's natural enemy. The most well-known cause of turbulence is the lee, and I doubt that anyone enjoys flying in a strong lee. But since the air is rarely still it is a fact of life that we as pilots must get to grips with turbulence – avoid it as much as possible, but accept it where it is inevitable.

Leeside turbulence on a large scale may be found behind mountains, on a smaller scale behind other obstacles like trees and houses. 'Behind' in this sense is always 'on the lee side'.

Wind shears and even thermals are other causes of turbulence, as well as other wings passing upwind. Thermals bumping into inversion layers also cause turbulence. Generally, light winds and weak thermals mean less turbulence whereas strong winds and strong thermals cause strong, sometimes extreme turbulence.

In strong turbulence the paraglider may collapse and the hang glider may tuck. In extreme cases the pilot may crash due to these turbulence-induced disturbances. A mental picture could be the wave surfer, riding the crest of a wave – if he falls off he will be washed through the turbulent waters. But the air is invisible, so we need

3.1 Strong thermals cause strong turbulence. If the pilot falls out of the side of the thermal the wing may dive very aggressively. It is not dissimilar to a surfer falling off the lip of a wave.

3.2 The wingtip rotor (vortex) made visible in a wind tunnel test. Such a rotor is present behind any wing moving through air. The bigger and heavier a wing is, the stronger the vortex. Behind large aeroplanes the vortex may linger for several minutes and can still be strong enough to cause a paraglider to collapse.
Photo: Manfred Kistler / Skywalk.

to know the causes of turbulence to be able to avoid it; we cannot just look for it as the surfer can.

When watching aeroplanes landing, we can often observe the wingtip rotors (page 80). The vortex rings may be visible for several minutes after the plane has landed – but such rings may also linger in open air long after a plane has passed.

A large, heavy transport aeroplane creates extreme vortex rings and any hang glider or paraglider flying into them will be in for a big surprise!

As paraglider pilots we are familiar with wingtip turbulence from passing behind other pilots, especially when soaring small ridges with a group of other pilots.

The bigger the obstacle the greater the turbulence, and the stronger the wind the stronger the turbulence. With little obstacles like trees or rows of trees we should aim to land at least 100m downwind – if the obstacle is a house it is better to land off to either side.

Turbulence behind mountains

The strength of the turbulence depends on the terrain. Gentle slopes cause less turbulence than steep rock faces. If the wind is strong, the turbulence behind steep cliffs may stretch for several kilometres, but in flyable winds we use about one kilometre as a rule of thumb. The area closer to the obstacle is worse than further away.

Turbulence behind slope edges

Behind slope edges the strength of the turbulence depends on the inclination of the slope, the shape of the edge and the wind speed. The illustration shows a cross section through a typical soaring ridge, with the rotors drawn in. Pilots often top-land on such ridges, so here are a few tips:

Many mountain launches look similar to the one in picture 3.9. Sites in the Alps that come to mind are Aspres in France,

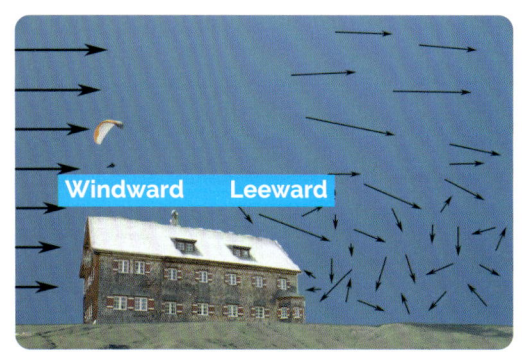

3.3 We encounter lee rotors 'behind' anything pointing into the airflow. This shows how the air may move on the leeward side of a house. The terms 'in front of' and 'behind' are linked to the wind direction.

3.4 Leeward side made visible. Notice that it is not very turbulent on the lee side, however the sink is greatly increased.

Windward The side facing into the wind. This is where we preferably fly.

Leeward The side facing away from the wind. We normally try to avoid flying here.

Laminar flow An undisturbed flow, comparable to water flowing smoothly out of a tap.

Turbulent flow A wild, unorganised flow comparable to the tap turned up to max.

See also Turbulence on p274

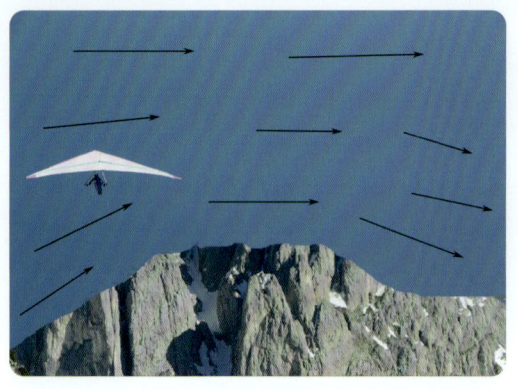

3.5 Behind gentle sloping peaks the turbulence may be all but nonexistent, but there will still be increased sink. This hang glider should stay on the windward side.

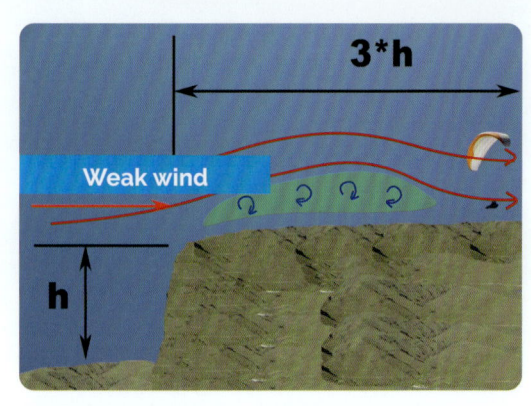

3.7 If the slope is steep, and the edge sharp, a rotor area will set up behind the edge (in green). In moderate winds it will normally be possible to land '3xh' downwind from the edge.

3.6 A flight along the famous 'Three Peaks' in the Dolomites. Behind such pointed, jagged peaks the turbulence may become dangerously strong, and we should strive to remain well away from them. This pilot should fly even further left.

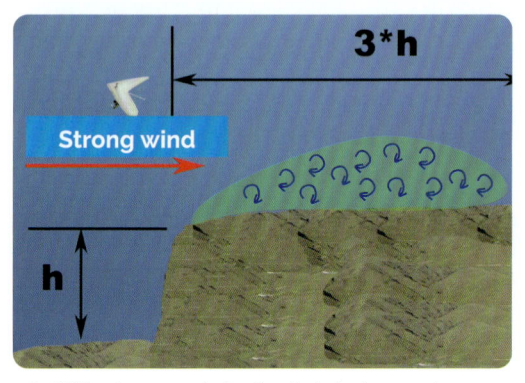

3.8 With stronger winds the turbulent area increases dramatically in size, to well beyond '3xh'. Top-landing will now be dangerous almost regardless of the distance from the edge.

Casteluccio, Meduno and Feltre in Italy. These flying sites are perfect for learning how to do top-landings.

General points for top-landing

- Weak winds mean less turbulence. That means top-landing is OK.
- The steeper the slope in front of the edge, the further the rotor area stretches downwind. As no one can exactly know *how* far, it is generally better not to top-land behind steep slopes.
- If the slope has thermals coming up we need to be extremely careful. If a thermal releases at the wrong time, and sucks in the air from all sides (even from the flat top where we are trying to land) things can get ugly quite quickly. It could be a case of tailwind *and* turbulence/rotor all at once, which might mean a fast, uncontrolled landing. This is when accidents can (and do) unfortunately happen.
- When you are top-landing, don't rush it. Take your time to assess the site, watch how other pilots approach it. Don't be fixated on getting it right first time – the aim is to do it right and smoothly, not stall the glider in.
- Get your feet down in good time.

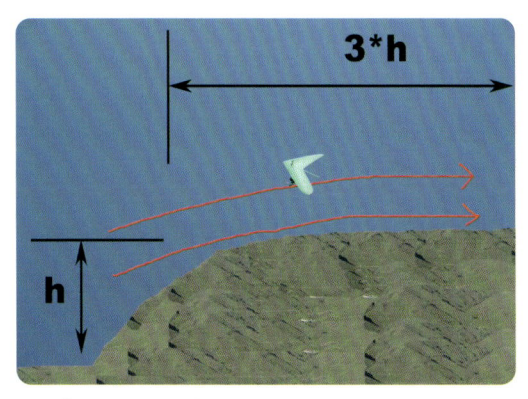

3.9 If the transition from slope/mountainside to plateau/mountain-top is gentle there may be no rotor formation at all. These are the soaring ridges where paraglider pilots can really play! Top-landing with no stress is guaranteed, see also picture 10.25 on page 254.

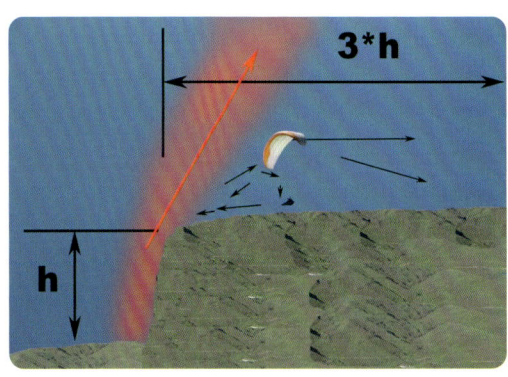

3.10 If the slope has thermals flowing up it, it is better not to try to top-land. The thermals will suck in air from all directions, causing a tailwind and switching winds on top while the thermal drifts past. You can end up landing downwind in turbulent air, which is never good

Antoine Girard top-landing in the Italian Alps on a vol-bivouac course. Photo: Marcus King

Horizontal rotors

Rotors are not exclusively vertical air movements. If the wind flows past obstacles there will be horizontal rotors behind the obstacles.

3.11 *A mountain with a horizontal rotor, drawn in yellow. The wind is not strong enough to flow over the mountain but flows around it instead. We must expect turbulence on the lee side, just like in the next picture.*

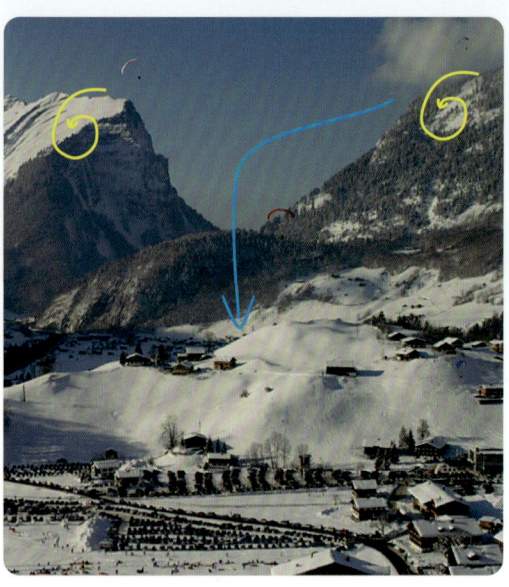

Picture 3.12 *As the valley wind blows through this venturi it increases quite dramatically in strength. It is still not strong enough to flow over the top of the mountains but will form horizontal rotors in the places indicated by the arrows. The picture shows the Diedamskopf, Austria.*

Observing clouds and how they move will reveal what the wind is doing at different levels. At this site in the south of France pilots often fly in the lee of an upper north wind, which can be seen in the clouds above. Photo: Marcus King

Using water to visualise rotor formation

Water and air behave in a similar manner when flowing around obstacles. This means that the observant pilot may learn about the invisible movement of the air by watching flowing water! Just as water flows around, and sometimes over, obstacles, so does air. By watching flowing water we can thus see exactly what is going on in the lee of mountains, behind valley constrictions, over the top of ridges etcetera. In the next three pictures the rocks symbolise mountains.

The examples are only a small selection of the lessons that may be learned from observing flowing water. Further examples on page 198.

3.14 A fast-flowing mountain stream. Possibly soarable on the windward side of the rock, behind the rock we can see the 'rotors' extending to approximately 5 times the height of the obstacle. Once past this area the water flow is laminar again.

3.15 The water is flowing down the 'lee' of a rock. Flow is fast and laminar. As it hits the bottom behind it turns very turbulent. It is comparable to a rounded-top mountain where the pilot may find himself in strong sink, only to encounter extreme turbulence right above the valley floor.

3.13 The water is flowing from left to right. If the rock had been a hill the centre would have been good for soaring, but closer to the sides the water is flowing sideways instead of up the slope. This is exactly what we observe when soaring – the best lift is found at the middle of the hill. Due to only moderate flow speeds there is hardly any turbulence behind the 'hill'.

3.16 In this photo the cloud formation shows the air movement. The air flows in the same manner on days when there's no cloud to make it visible. The site is Garland by Brauneck in Germany.

HINT Use the local brook to learn about the effect of slow and fast flows, of sharp versus rounded edges. Where are the rotors? How far 'downwind' do they stretch?

Turbulence caused by wind shears

Wind shear is when the wind direction and/or speed suddenly change at a particular altitude. The most common wind shear in the Alps is when the valley wind and the meteorological wind higher up are coming from different directions. The strength and extent of the turbulence caused by such wind shears depend on the wind velocity. Most of the times it is only noticeable as a light shaking but in extreme cases, where two strong winds meet, it can be quite rough.

Wind shears are common in connection with inversions because the wind direction is often different below and above an inversion.

Picture 3.18 *The picture shows a beautiful wind shear situation. The fog is being pushed against the ridge by the valley breeze but the wind is actually coming from the south (arrow). The south side was just soarable up until ridge height, where some turbulence announced that I had entered the realm of the valley wind coming from the north.*

HINT Inversions not only limit air movement vertically, they also influence horizontal air movement. It is not uncommon to experience a strong valley wind whilst the mountain top has no wind at all. This is one of several reasons why the speed bar should *always* be mounted before each flight – you never know when you might need it!

3.17 *The pilot is just about to descend into the very cold low-level air mass, often called a ground inversion. At altitude we had 15km/h from the south, whilst the wind at ground level was 10km/h from the north. The wind shear was nonetheless unspectacular.*

Flatland flying in Patu, near Quixada, Brazil

Windward and leeward thermals

When flying in the mountains it is important to know where the wind is coming from, particularly when using thermals.

Normally we fly on the windward side, and if there's no wind we aim for the sunny slopes.

- On no-wind days the thermals are easy to centre; they don't get torn apart by the wind and they don't drift
- Windward side thermals are almost equally nice as long as the wind remains weak
- Lee thermals are generally turbulent and thus best avoided

EXPERIENCE Once while flying the Laber near Oberammergau in Germany I went into the well-known lee on the south side of the ridge. I was descending with a steady -9m/s and thinking I would surely have to land at the Ettal monastery when I hit the thermal coming off this monastery – from there I climbed out with a steady 6m/s thermal! This means that I went from –9m/s to +6m/s within a very short horizontal distance – a difference of 15m/s (3,000ft/min) or 54km/h! Since then I have always avoided getting low south of the Laber!

3.20 Lee thermal development in Pustertal, Sillian, Austria. We recognise the situation by the big clouds being pushed into the valley from their point of origin on the higher slopes. The day was flyable, as the thermals coming up the face of the mountain were strong enough to override the wind from behind. The launch thus had wind coming up it, but it was turbulent and difficult flying.

Leeward thermals in the Alps are either on the south side of ridges near the northern boundary or in the leeward side of local valley wind systems. In the southern Alps the wind is generally local and south, since the mountains suck in so

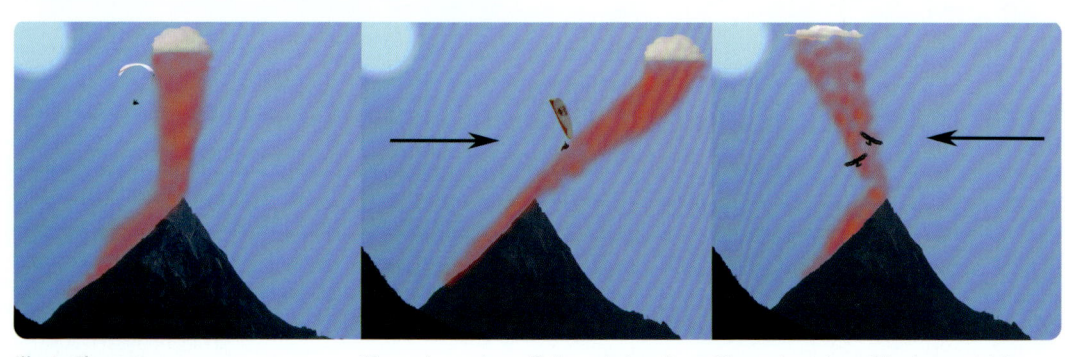

Illustration 3.19
Thermal formation in calm air

Thermal coming off the windward side

Thermal coming off the leeward side

88

much air from the flatlands that the wind on the sunny south-facing slopes is almost always on. This means nice windward-side thermals!

In strong winds lee flying must be avoided altogether. It can be extremely turbulent and dangerous.

Standing on launch it is not always clear if the wind we're feeling coming up the face is the 'real' macro-meteorological wind or just a thermal passing through, see illustration 3.22.

As a rule of thumb we can stipulate that in 'real' winds of up to 10km/h it is possible to use the thermal wind coming up the face to launch into, regardless of the wind direction. The thermals will generally not be too turbulent.

In stronger winds however, the leeside should be avoided altogether. In general paragliders cope well with turbulence, but we should take care to respect their limits (and ours too!). Deliberately flying in strong thermic leeside conditions with strong wind can create a problem.

3.21 Goms, Valais, Switzerland. On this day the wind was far too strong for flying. Compare the cloud formation to the picture on the previous page.

3.22 The sun is shining from the left (west, afternoon) but the 'real' wind is coming from the right (east). The sun causes big, strong thermals to flow up the west face, and it is easy to assume that all is well, if we are not observant. But by watching the windsock for a bit longer the real wind direction should become apparent and warn us that we're subject to lee thermal conditions. St. André-les-Alpes, France.

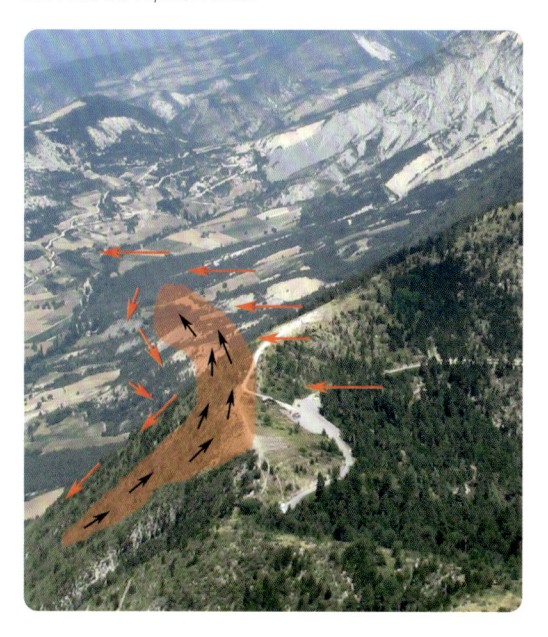

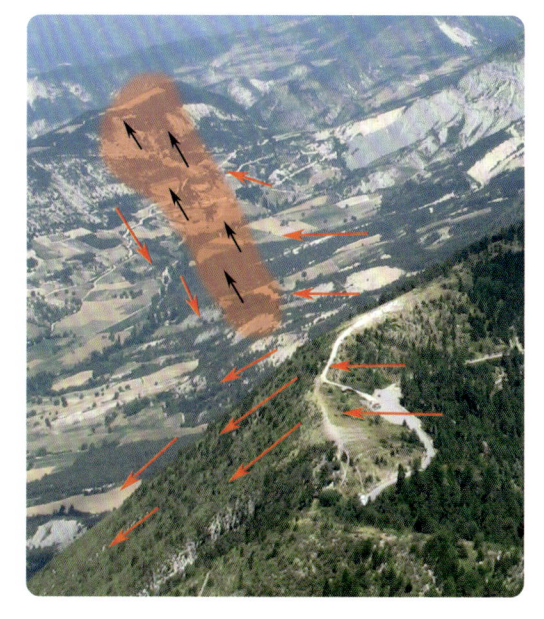

Leeward side – flyable or not?

The road to heaven is paved with good intentions; and one of these is to not fly in lee. However, if we don't find any lift on the windward side, maybe we'll get lucky over on the leeward side?

To do this in relative safety we must understand that lee isn't just lee. Illustration 3.23a depicts a lee situation on a stable day. It could be an autumn day in the north Alps, with high pressure and a strong inversion. The temperature hardly decreases with altitude, in this example only about 1°C per 1,000m, or a temperature gradient (see chapter 9) of 0.1°C/100m.

If the wind is on the face of the mountain it may still be soarable, and the air mass being pushed up over the mountain will still cool down dry-adiabatically, i.e. with 1°C/100m (3°C/1,000ft). Once the air mass reaches the top, parts of it will be 9°C colder than the surrounding air, and very much heavier. On the lee side of the mountain the cold, dense air rushes violently back down, causing extreme turbulence on its way. Flying here is not an option, even for pro's.

To illustrate the violence of such a leeside air movement we only need to consider that thermals begin to rise by temperature differences of as little as 2°C – a thermal stemming from a temperature difference of 9°C would be very extreme indeed, probably showing climb rates well beyond 20m/s.

In illustration 3.23b, you see the same mountain, now surrounded by extremely unstable air where the temperature decreases dramatically with altitude. Again, air is being pushed up over the mountain by the wind and getting chilled dry-adiabatically – but this time the temperature decrease just matches that of the surrounding air since the surrounding air is 11°C at ridge level, and the rising air mass has been cooled down to 10°C on its way up. It will still sink back down on the lee side, but with the low difference in temperature the movement will be much more benign. Anyone flying into this lee still needs to fly actively, but it is fully feasible and survivable, as opposed to the previous situation.

Both illustrations assume weak winds and are consciously drawn more extreme than reality would normally be, but the example serves the purpose of explaining the differences between leeside flying on stable and unstable days.

The examples dealt with the turbulence caused by the downrush of cold, dense

3.23a In stable conditions the temperatures in the valley and around the peaks are almost equal. The air mass being pushed over the ridge by the wind is adiabatically cooled to a temperature much lower than the surrounding air. On the lee side the supercooled, dense air rushes down very violently.

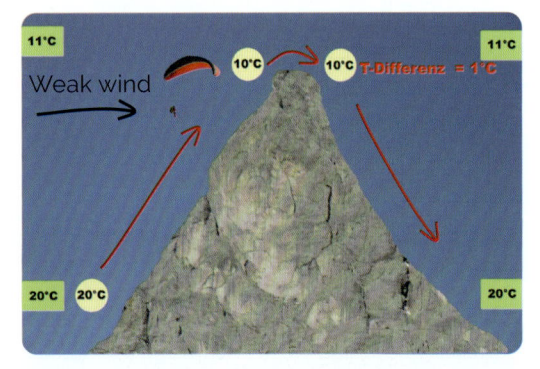

3.23b The same mountain in unstable conditions. The air mass being pushed over the mountain decreases 1°C/100m, just as in the previous example, but this time the surrounding air is cooling almost as much with increasing altitude. Turbulence on the lee side remains within flyable limits.

air due to pressure differences. The turbulence caused by the wind flowing over the obstacle adds to the complexity of the picture but again we can assume that it is proportional to the wind strength.

> **HINT** I consider leeside flying in moderate winds and unstable conditions to be fully doable by experienced pilots, but I personally still seek to avoid it. If I see that leeside flying is inevitable on a cross country flight, I try to balance the risks with the possible rewards. Is the wind really not too strong? Is the air mass unstable? If I can say yes to these two, and there are emergency landings available I may decide to do it – but the landings are important because if I don't find anything I'll be on the ground soon due to the increased sink in the lee.

Waves and flying in them

Wave flying is really something that is best left to the sailplanes. Reichmann (see the literary references in the back of this book) has described wave flying in detail and reveals that sailplanes have reached altitudes of well over 10,000m in waves, flying at wind speeds of more than 100km/h (54kn)!

However some waves, appearing at far more reasonable wind strengths, *can* actually be flown by hang gliders and even paragliders.

> Research into the formation of wave clouds has revealed that some or all of the following conditions are needed:
>
> **Landscape**
> - The lee side of the lee-triggering ridge should be steep
> - The entire mountain should be smooth
> - The ridge should be long to ensure that the air doesn't flow around instead of over
> - The ridge should be oriented perpendicular to the wind
> - Downwind of the primary wave trigger, at a distance matching the wave amplitude, a secondary ridge should be found
>
> **Weather**
> - Stable air mass – thermal turbulence disrupts the wave formation
> - Wind strength at least 30km/h (16kn)
> - The wind direction should remain uniform all the way up to the top of the stable air mass The wind speed should increase with altitude

In the weather forecasts for glider pilots the meteorologists frequently state things like "winds insufficient for wave formation" or "wave conditions setting up on the north side of the Alps"; when the latter is the case we should leave the air to the sailplanes and stay at home!

But a few waves, for example the so-called 'Thüringer wave' appear at wind speeds low enough for them to be flyable for us, and Chrigel Maurer from Switzerland flew a short XC in wave in 2004. The story is pretty amazing, as Chrigel was getting groundspeeds in excess of 100km/h (54kn) during his flight.

3.24 Evenly spaced and shaped, lenticular clouds are a sure sign of wave formation. They also indicate wind speeds way beyond what we normally should be flying in.

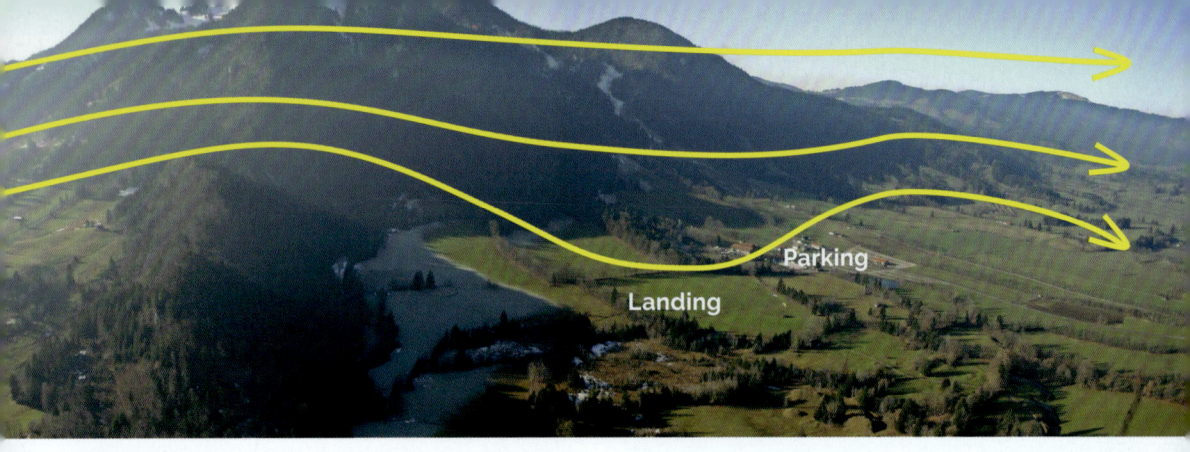

3.25 Wave next to the Brauneck in the German Alps. The little hill on the left triggers the wave, which sets up right over the Brauneck parking site. It happens in south winds of approximately 25-30km/h on stable days.

EXPERIENCE I have flown in wave at my own home site, the Brauneck. Most of the conditions from the previous page were fulfilled in that the air was stable and the wind was around 30km/h. The wave trigger was the little 150m high hill SE of the Brauneck, and the wave set up 400-800m downwind. We were all flying right above the valley parking in smooth gentle lift of app. 1m/s. The landing, right beneath the wave, was slightly turbulent.

EXPERIENCE I flew one of my most memorable XC flights on a blue day. I had good climbs of around 5m/s and large, well-mannered thermals. There was no risk of overdevelopment, no clouds disturbing the thermal formation – a great day. Since there were no clouds I could always fly to the best thermal sources without worrying about clouds growing bigger and shade and shadow stopping the thermals before I got there.

Blue thermals and clear air thermals

Blue thermals are just thermals without cumulus clouds to top them. Blue days are days when the air is too dry for Cu's to form, and there is an inversion somewhere beneath the condensation point stopping the thermals before they reach their condensation level (see chapter 9). The condensation level is the altitude where a thermal reaches a relative humidity of 100% and the cumulus begins to form – cloudbase is always at condensation level.

In desert regions the inversion can be very high and still the day remains blue – this is due to the extremely dry air found here.

It is obviously harder to locate thermals on blue days when no Cu's show us where they are. On such days we must base our route decisions on the terrain and simply aim for likely thermal sources and triggers, or we must watch for other hints. Birds, dust, grass, butterflies or even pollen are good markers, as are other pilots. Blue thermals are as diverse as normal thermals; they may be big or small, strong or weak, smooth or turbulent.

3.26 Blue day in the Dolomites. Photo: Skywalk

Launch above the clouds. To fly thermals you first have to descend to under cloudbase. Volcano Villarica, Pucon, Chile.

HINT Many flying areas are very remote to fly. I have friends in Australia who always fly along roads so as to avoid landing too far away from civilisation.

HINT There's no reason to think that a blue day is less turbulent than a cloudy day. Blue thermals come in all shapes, strengths and sizes.

HINT Magic air can also be found over the sea. I once experienced this in Monaco, where the cold air was flowing down the mountain around sunset, triggering a very smooth and gentle thermal right from the shoreline, allowing me another half hour flying over the water – fantastic!

EXPERIENCE I once finished an XC flight with an extra 30km flown solely in magic air over the valley floor. It was the first time I had experienced stronger, somewhat turbulent magic air, and this was only the case down low. Up high it was as gentle as ever.

Magic air and reverse thermals

When the sun begins to get low and one side of the valley is already in shade we sometimes get to experience one of the greatest phenomena of free flight. In English we call it 'magic air' because it feels so truly magic – but first things first, here's the explanation.

As the air cools down over the shady slopes of the valley a katabatic flow down the slopes sets in. This cool air pushes under the warmer air on the valley floor, triggering it. This may happen some time during the afternoon and is the first stage of the magic air phenomenon.

The thermals are offset towards the still-sunny side of the valley. The sunny upper slopes on this side are producing their last thermals at this time – soon these parts will also be in the shade, and the katabatic flow sets in on this side as well.

The two air masses now meet at the valley bottom, and since there's nowhere to escape to, the air begins to rise from the middle of the valley – the second stage of the magic air is in place. Thus, it begins on the sunny side of the valley and gradually moves into the middle as both slopes fall into the shade.

The climb rates are not high (mostly) but the lift area is big and gentle (mostly).

To experience this we must try to remain

3.27 It is soon time for some magic air flying. The high west-facing slopes are just releasing their last thermals and the east-facing slope is in deep shade, with cold air flowing down from it.

3.28 By now both sides of the valley are in the shade and there's cool air flowing down from both sides. It meets in the middle of the valley and rises gently. The hang glider pilot has noticed it and heads out with maximum altitude.

airborne in the last real thermals of the day. Only when these finally stop do we glide straight for the middle of the valley. The higher the mountains around are, the better the chances of magic air.

Magic air occasionally even produces cumulus clouds, very feeble things appearing over the valley late in the afternoon and into the evening. It is also responsible for many extra XC kilometres flown late in the day and therefore an important thing to know and understand if we wish to go far.

3.29 *Magic air on a spring evening in the Isar Valley, Germany. The healthy-looking cumulus clouds indicate strong lift in the middle of the valley.*

3.31 *The last wisps of magic air have caused light cumulus clouds above the centre of the valley. The wisps may help us locate this elusive lift at the very end of the day.*

3.30 *Not convergence, but thermals over a cooling tower on a stable day. The cloud is separating and re-forming at altitude. Cooling tower thermals can be good on weak days.*

3.32 *The best evening launches are those that are high enough to allow us to connect with the magic air releasing from the valley floor. Photo: Advance*

Convergence

When two air masses meet there's nowhere for the air to go, except up. We call this phenomenon 'convergence' because the air masses converge to create bands of lift that we may exploit.

Flying convergence lines is great fun – generally not very strong, but mellow and reliable. Sometimes a convergence line may allow us to cross an entire valley without losing any altitude. This is clearly a great advantage for XC!

Just as was the case for magic air, there are clouds that can help us find and use convergence lines.

For example, two valleys meeting in a pass will normally both have air flowing up towards the pass. Once in the pass the air converges and rises as lift – depending on the meteorological wind the convergence line may be offset to either side of the actual pass.

If we want to switch valley sides we're obviously interested in finding this convergence to minimise our altitude loss, and if no local pilots are available to tell us where it is we have only the clouds to look at. This only works when there are cumulus formations.

3.33 Typical convergence clouds. Convergence clouds are formed by air condensing as it rises, forced higher by converging winds. However, they tend to have much less defined bases, and are often ragged in appearance.

3.35a Convergence in a pass. Both valley breezes are equally strong and the convergence is found directly above the pass. The pilots have found the line and are exploiting it to cross the valley.

3.34 Convergence clouds in Val Sugana on the way to Bassano. The strong north wind that had accompanied us all the way from home meets the humid air from the Po plains. A great sight, because it means it is flyable in Bassano in spite of the N wind. The convergence is marked by little Cu's.

3.35b The convergence clouds here are forming straight across the Puster Valley in Italy and clearly indicate the location of the convergence line. The Puster Valley is one of the largest longitudinal valleys in the Alps. It separates the Southern Limestone Alps from the Central Eastern Alps.

Above: Heading to a classic convergence cloud just north of St André-les-Alpes in France. Air coming up two valleys meets, causing an area of lift on a north-facing slope where you wouldn't normally expect lift. Convergence is more common than many pilots think, and understanding how it works in an area can allow great flights to be done.

Below: Gréolières in the south of France faces south, with a valley running from the sea to it. When the wind comes from any other direction this can cause convergence. On this day a light NW wind was blowing up high creating areas of convergence and allowing pilots to get high despite a stable air mass. The ragged, wispy clouds at the top, left of centre, are the clues to look for.

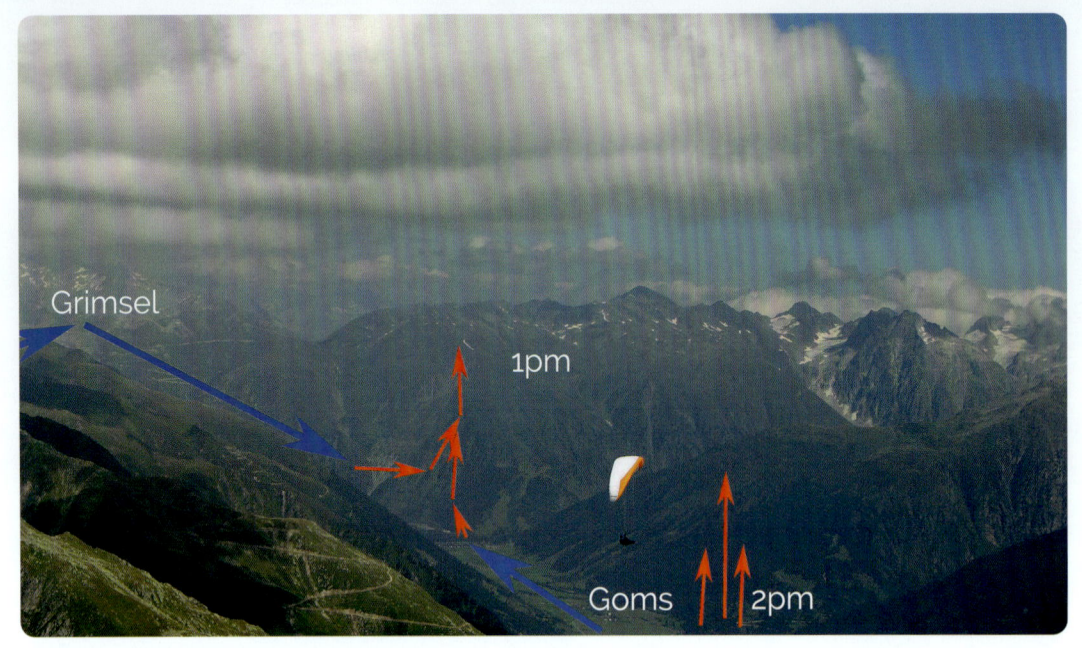

3.36 Convergence in the upper Rhône Valley, Valais, Switzerland. The valley breeze coming over the Grimsel Pass is so strong that it pushes the convergence line ever further into the main valley. At 2pm it may be 10-20 km down from the Grimsel in Goms, in the middle of the valley.

Further convergence examples

1. **The Gerlos Pass**, in the famous Pinzgau Valley in Austria, often sees convergence. Pilots often switch valley sides here and obviously have an easier time when they can locate the convergence line.
2. **The Grimsel/Goms** convergence in the upper Rhône Valley, Valais, Switzerland (picture 3.36). Since the Grimsel wind is stronger than the normal valley breeze coming up the Rhône Valley, the convergence line gets pushed progressively further into the main valley as the conditions improve. Around 4pm it is often strong enough to reach down to the main landing in Fiesch.
3. The convergence near the north end of **Lake Como, Italy**, is also well known (picture 3.37). The lake has a distinctive bend here, and both sides of the ridge produce valley breezes.
4. **Over the sea** we can often observe a cloud wall, formed by the convergence of a meteorological wind blowing offshore and the sea breeze. The wall remains stationary and could probably be used for altitude gains but it is a bit of a gamble.
5. When **cold air masses from the sea** are blown under warmer air over land they trigger a line of lift. The distance from the shore depends on the wind strength. It is not uncommon to observe conditions where this first line of lift produces Cu´s – further inland it may be completely blue again.
6. **The Inn Valley** in Austria and the **Rhine Valley** in Switzerland both have valley breezes. These winds meet and converge somewhere in the Arlberg region. The resulting convergence is often easy to spot due to the Rhine Valley air being more humid than its eastern counterpart, causing two different cloudbases within a few kilometres of each other. Identifiable by a visible 'step' in the cloudbases.

HINT Convergence is great to fly when we're high, but nearer the ground we may encounter strong turbulence. This is because the winds lower down are colliding with each other. The result is wind shear and turbulent air. Try to set yourself up so you approach known areas of convergence high to avoid fighting down low.

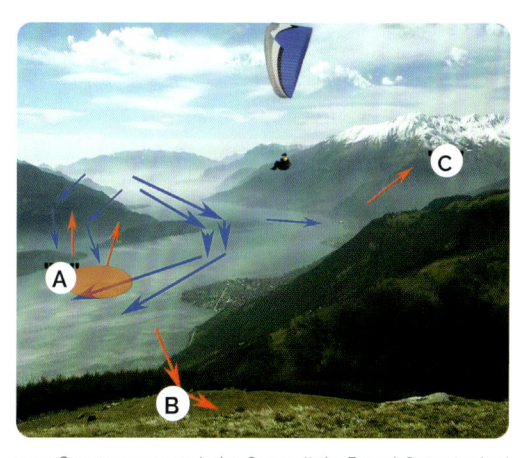

3.37 Convergence on Lake Como, Italy. B and C are typical dynamic soaring ridges, with C being the Monte Mezzo launch. The interesting spot is A, where the valley breeze follows the bend in the valley. But a small part of it goes over the little promontory and falls back into the valley, meeting the valley breeze again and getting pushed up by it. The area marked in red indicates the convergence, with an area of approximately one square kilometre and lifting to an altitude of 300m above the lake.

Picture 3.39 Over the sea there is a cloud wall that looks like a convergence. What it really is, is moist air condensing over the ice cold water. During the day the cloud wanders offshore, in the evening it returns. Soaring the dunes near Torra Bay, Namibia

Picture 3.40 The sea breeze comes inland. Here on La Palma, the mountains force it upwards and produce a good and easy to use thermally active cloud line. A similar effect happens over the north German flatlands. Sea breezes push inland and produce a thermally active convergence cloud line, but it's not quite as regular as over La Palma or Tenerife.

3.38 An interesting convergence developing west of the Tschirgant in the Inn Valley, Austria. The Tschirgant ridge runs for about 10km from east to west. On the north side, the valley wind from the Fernpass flows off to the west. On its south side, the Inn Valley wind also blows to the west. At the west end of the Tschirgant a convergence of these two winds builds a long stretched-out cloud out towards the Venet mountain. If the convergence is working well, you can often fly for several kilometres without height loss.

3.41 When two valley breezes meet, and one is much more humid than the other, we get staggered cloudbases as seen here, where the group is flying from the higher base towards the lower clouds.

HINT Some convergence clouds are caused by the meeting of different winds up high. They look like the ones we have learnt to identify at convergences lower down but bring us no usable lift, as they happen above the levels where we fly. See picture 3.42.

Lower cloudbase in mountain foothills

3.42 High convergence clouds. Of no value for paragliders and hang gliders as they are above our flying altitude.

Compared to areas deeper into mountain ranges, the foothills have a significantly lower cloudbase. If a mountain range is oriented perpendicular to the prevailing wind direction the foothills will also get above average precipitation levels due to the air masses getting blown against and over the mountains by the wind. During high-pressure meteorological conditions, most of the moisture in the air comes from water trapped in the soil-bogs, wetlands and green fields.

Near my home, right on the northernmost edge of the Alps, cloudbase is often 500-1,000m lower than only 15-20km further south. Though the valley bottoms are also higher in the central Alps the workable altitude span is still far greater deep in the mountains.

The difference is caused by the larger amount of moisture found in the flatland air, and the higher temperatures in the central Alps (more about this in Chapter 6, Valley Breezes).

3.43 Big jumps in cloudbase are common in the Italian Dolomites. South of the Plattkofel peaks is the dry high-Alpine Fassa Valley, north of which the humid air from the Eisack Valley affects the cloudbase.

HINT When varying cloudbases are present, it is often possible to fly next to, and not under, clouds. From my home site, the Brauneck in Germany, I often fly west to the Benedict Wall where the cloudbase is generally considerably higher. From there I continue to the Jochberg above the two lakes; Kochelsee and Walchensee.

The area around the Kochelsee is very wet and the cloudbase there is much lower again – sometimes I approach the next cloud from above rather than from below, or from the side! If the sun is shining on me and then down on the cloud beneath me, a Brocken Spectre appears, one of the prettiest sights in free flying (picture 3.44).

3.44 Brocken Spectres appear when we fly between sun and clouds. The thicker the cloud the clearer the spectre becomes. Photo: Advance

3.45 The clouds creeping over the mountain range which borders the Valais in Switzerland to the south look just like a Föhn wall, but they only indicate a light southerly wind and a far higher humidity on the south side of the range. The Valais remains perfectly flyable, but going south is not possible. On the north side of the valley, cloudbase may be 1,500-2,000m higher than what we see in the picture.

Ground-level inversions and ground fog

Normally, temperature decreases with altitude. When the temperature decreases fast the conditions are unstable; when the decrease is less significant the conditions are more stable.

Sometimes we even see a temperature status quo or slight increase with altitude, and this is called 'inversion' because it is the inverse situation of the normal one. Thermals struggle to rise through inversions.

There are various types of inversions, distinguished by their height above the ground. The rapid cooling of the ground during the night causes inversions at ground level; the cold earth cools the overlying air, and a ground-level inversion is formed.

The cold air is heavier than the warmer, overlying air so in the morning we encounter a 'sea of cold air' in the valleys. In the summer this is best noticed due to smog trapped under it, in the autumn and winter fog forms to cover entire valleys (see picture 5.18, page 158).

Such days are great for those going above the inversions, where the skies are clear and the views over the fog-covered valleys magnificent. It is possible to fly over such 'seas of fog' but only when there's either a landing above the fog, or there are holes big enough in it that we may reach the ground safely.

> **HINT** Fog layers fluctuate in thickness so to fly safely above them the landing must be well above the upper limit of the fog. Flying through them whilst relying on GPS courses is not advisable – they'll often begin right at ground level, which means that visibility remains almost zero all the way to the ground.

> **HINT** There will often be thermals coming off the upper slopes of mountains whose valleys are still deep in ground fog (see picture 3.47). When we wish to fly before the sun has burnt off the fog we must simply launch higher and make sure we do not descend down. Once the sun burns off the fog the thermals will gain strength, as there will then be more land exposed to the sun, heating the overlying air masses.

3.46 Summer in the Inn Valley, Austria. Our feathered friends are already thermalling but we'd better wait an hour or two before launching, as the valley is still covered in the ground inversion. The first cu's are forming over the high peaks.

3.47 The Krippenstein launch, Hallstättersee in Austria. Flying may be possible but landing in the valley is out of the question as thick fog obscures everything. But the pilot is still looking forward to her flight!

3.48 *Whenever the fog is not thick, and great gaps are to be seen, the flying becomes particularly scenic. Care must always be taken to stay clear of flying deep into the cloud, or losing track of your way. The Brauneck flying arena, Lenggries, Germany.*

3.49 *The clouds here in Passy, France, indicate the height of the inversion. Above, the air appears to be warmer, otherwise much higher clouds would be expected. This inversion is formed due to a high pressure weather system. Photo: Jérôme Maupoint*

Summer inversions in the foothills

Summer time is inversion time along the foothills of mountains all over the world. The inversions appear in connection with stable high-pressure systems setting in, where the air from ground level up to great heights is slowly heated to a very homogenous temperature. There's hardly any mixing happening, and the smog from cars, industry and other pollution sources is trapped under the inversion layer. When this situation sets in along the north side of the Alps, thermal flying all but ceases. The conditions are great for learning to fly, as there is hardly any turbulence and whatever there may be is very weak.

The dirty air is easily observed when looking over the flatlands from the mountains, see picture 3.51.

A good place to escape to, when the foothills are totally covered by inversion, is the central mountain regions, where the inversion problems decrease as we approach the highest peaks.

3.51 Summer inversion on the north side of the Alps, little or no thermal development. The picture was taken from the Waidringer Rock Plateau in Austria, looking north into Germany. The smoggy air is clearly visible along the horizon. The small cumulus cloud in the left side of the picture may be caused by the Landshut nuclear power plant.

HINT Thermals rising up to meet an inversion become turbulent at inversion level. If we prefer to avoid turbulence it is best to leave the thermal before reaching this level – only 100m lower it is less turbulent. However, on some days a strong thermal may push through the inversion and with some persistence we may go with it through the bouncy part, and enjoy the clear air and spectacular views above the inversion layer.

3.50 Summer inversion in Bassano del Grappa, Italy. Different rules apply here, as it is often possible to thermal up to the top of the inversion level. These have been called the 'Bassano wonderthermals'.

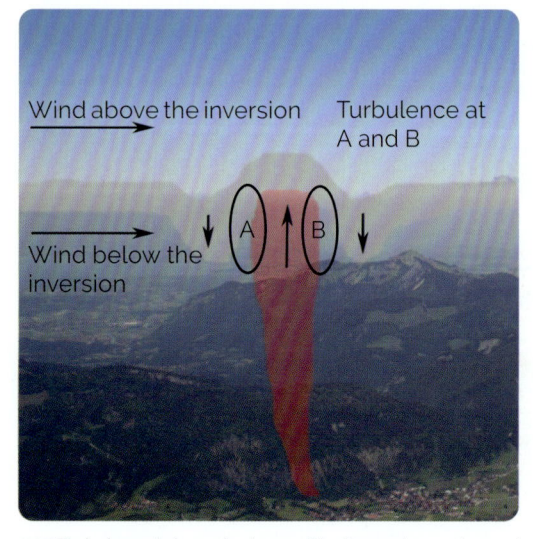

3.52 Turbulence in inversion layers. The thermals are stopped at the inversion, and the wind shears caused by different wind strengths and directions above and below cause the turbulence, marked A and B in the illustration. After Volker Schwaniz.

A low layer of cloud clearly indicates the existence of an inversion. Site: Chamonix, France. Photo: Skywalk

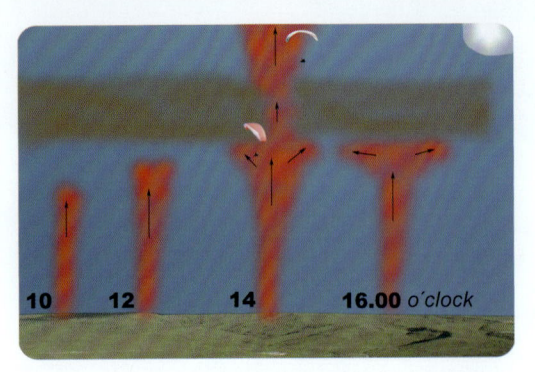

3.53 Around the time when the thermals are strongest we sometimes find a thermal that is stronger than the rest, and thus able to punch through the inversion. If we're lucky there'll be more of these around, and we may continue our flight above the inversion rather than descend through it again.

Inversions at mid-level and how to climb through them

We often encounter inversions as thin layers at mid-altitude on otherwise unstable days. On such days most pilots are forced to fly beneath the inversion whilst a few happy guys make it

3.56 A mid-level inversion is stopping the thermals just under peak altitude. Above and below it is unstable and flyable. Cloudbase is high but the inversion won't let us through. Once through, the upper-level instability would allow us to continue flying high. There are two ways through, either as described in 3.53 or by getting in really close to the mountain sticking up through the inversion. Here, the anabatic airflow seeps through the inversion but the pilot must be prepared to, and able to fly close to the terrain.

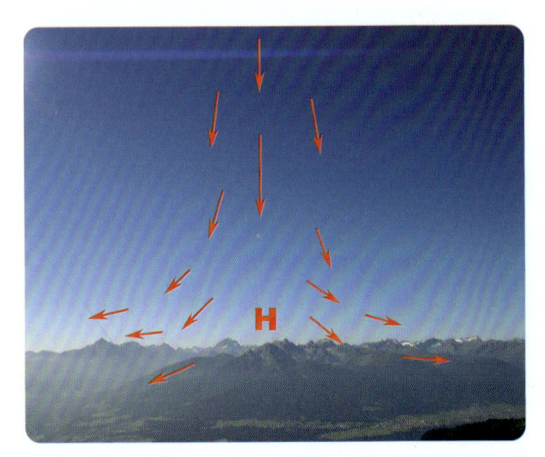

3.54 and 3.55 In the Italian Dolomites we often encounter mid-level inversions. To get through these we actually soar the anabatic winds flowing up the terrain – you have to tuck in close. Once through, we fly thermals in the normal way.

3.57 During high-pressure conditions air sinks down and gets compressed, creating a subsidence inversion. It forms at mid- to high-altitude first because the air nearer to the ground can escape to the sides. The slowly sinking air moves at several centimetres per second.

through and fly around above wearing a big grin on their faces – looking down on other pilots is always a good feeling!

There are two ways of breaking through such inversions and joining the smirking crowd (illustrations 3.53-3.56).

High-pressure subsidence inversions

During high-pressure conditions a subsidence inversion forms at mid-altitude (see illustration 3.57). The mechanism behind it can be compared to a bicycle pump; when we pressurise air it gets warmer. This happens first at mid-altitude because the air closer to the ground can escape by flowing off to the sides.

Once the mid-level air is heated to a temperature that is higher than the air below it, we have a subsidence inversion. As the high pressure grows older this inversion sinks, progressively decreasing the usable vertical range.

The typical progression of this high-pressure subsidence inversion is depicted in illustration 3.58. Once the high pressure is replaced by cold air flowing into the higher areas the air mass becomes unstable again, and the last day of a high-pressure period may again be XC suitable.

We all know that during high-pressure spells the cumulus clouds dissipate after their brief lifespan. If this wasn't the case, the sky would soon be covered and no more sunshine would reach the ground.

But why do the Cu's dissipate? The sinking air from above pushes the cloud down, thereby compressing and heating it. Warm air can hold more moisture than cold, so the cloud disappears! Mixing with the surrounding air due to turbulence and wind speeds up this process.

If you're into arcana you might want to know that the sink rate of the subsidence inversion is in the order of magnitude of around 1/100 of thermal climb rates.

The development of subsidence inversions over several days is as follows:

Day 1: Right after the trough/cold front passage the air is humid and the cloudbase is low. A high-pressure ridge is approaching.

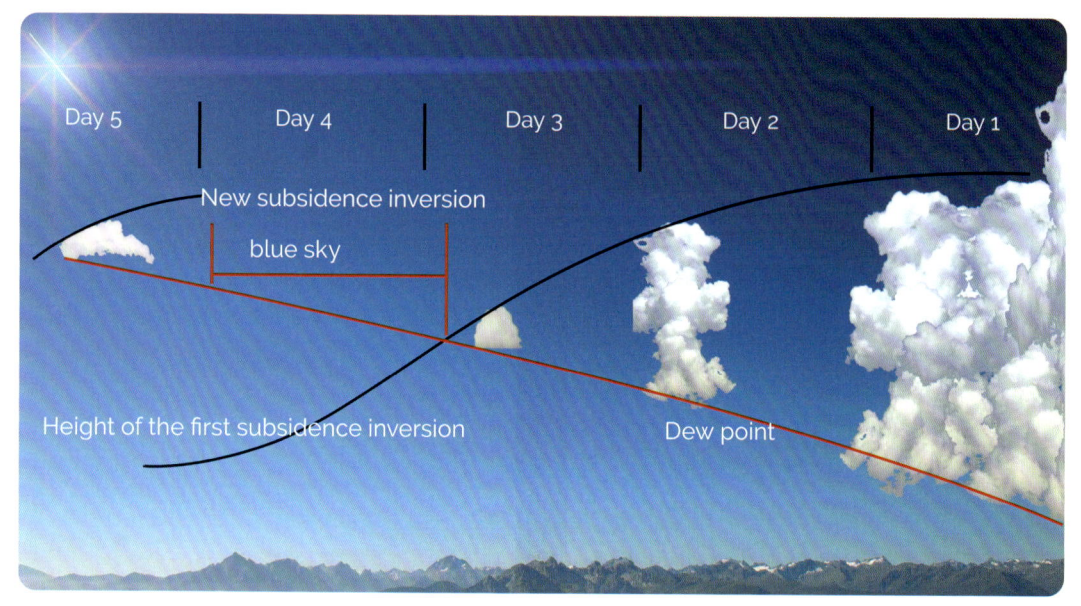

3.58 High-pressure inversion development seen over the course of a few days. The red line is the dew point where the rising air reaches 100% relative humidity and clouds begin to form. The vertical growth of the clouds is decided by the inversion altitude (black line). The further these two lines are apart, the taller the clouds may grow. Once the inversion sinks below the dew point, the skies become blue.

Early on the inversion is still very high, and the Cu's can grow tall – sometimes we even get showers and Cb formation.

But the situation is rapidly stabilising and cloudbase is getting progressively higher – the clouds grow flatter. Such days are great for XC flying over the flatlands, but in the mountains the clouds tend to congest, especially if there's wind, and the rain persists for another day.

Day 2: From now on the flying conditions in the mountains are very good. Cloudbase continues to rise, the air is drying and the subsidence inversion is sinking down, reducing the risk of overdevelopment. Expected climb rates are as in illustration 1.41 page 48. This is a good day to act on those plans to go big – they call them "Hammer Days" in the Alps.

Day 3: Early in the day we may still see minor Cu development, later the inversion sinks below the dew point and the day goes 'blue'. Still good flying and XC conditions with climb rates as in illustration 1.40.

Day 4: By now the inversion has sunk so low that flying is hardly possible. Climb rates as in illustration 1.42.

Day 5: By now the subsidence inversion

> **EXPERIENCE** One of my longest flights ever was done in conditions like the ones described under day 2, with the clouds growing worryingly tall in the beginning of the day. In fact many pilots opted to land for fear of overdevelopment, but I kept observing the clouds and detected a tendency towards dissipation. I flew on, and managed a flight long enough to win me the German XC title.

is almost at ground level. If no major perturbation occurs a new inversion may begin to form up high. If the sun is able to burn off the ground inversion the day may become very good for flying, with a very high cloudbase due to the low moisture content in the air.

Note that all this is an idealised model, and that nature has many variations up her sleeve. The entire process may take as few as two or as many as eight days to complete. However, a basic understanding of the cycle makes it easier to predict and understand flying conditions.

> **HINT** It is common for south-facing launches in the northern Alps to have a tailwind setting up around noon on thermally active days. In many places this is a good thing, as there are also north-facing launches available. I have noticed that as soon as the first wafts of tailwind set in on the southern launch it is no longer possible to climb out from there, even if launching is still possible in the lulls. But the valley wind lee creates a smooth but strong sinking bubble where unlucky pilots descend with 3-5m/s until they land.
>
> This means that if we didn't get off before noon, it is best to wait another hour until the thermals have begun rising up the north face, and launch here. These thermals do not originate on the north slopes; they are warm air from the flatlands below being pushed up the north face by the wind.

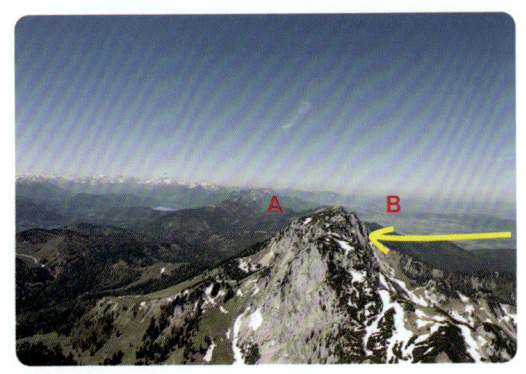

3.59 Once the valley breeze (yellow arrow) is fully on, we limit our thermal search to the north (B) side of the ridges. But early in the day, before the valley winds grow strong, we use the south (A) side. The picture shows the Benediktenwand above Lenggries, Germany. This is my first destination when flying west from my home site.

Flying in the lee of mountain chains

If the macro-meteorological wind is not strong, it is perfectly possible to fly on the lee side of a mountain chain. In the Alps we often fly the south side in weak northerlies, or the north side in weak southerlies.

As soon as the valley breezes set in, it is important to know which side of a mountain to approach when crossing valleys. In the northern Alps the valley wind systems, once active, often reach high enough to overflow the ridges and cause leeside conditions on what from a macro-meteorological viewpoint should be the windward side! Thermals are first offset towards the south, and then when they push through the wind shear they are offset back towards the north.

The question we must ask ourselves in such conditions is: "Will the valley breeze be strong enough to push over the top of the next ridge?" If the answer is yes, we must approach the north side (where the valley wind comes from) to avoid finding ourselves in the lee. If the answer is negative we approach the south side.

Thermal lunchbreak in the foothills

Thermal activity begins in the late morning, and it is not uncommon to see a number of early pilots circling in the still weak lift. But suddenly the thermals die and the pilots slowly descend out – we call this the 'thermal lunchbreak'.

> **HINT** On weaker days the thermal lunchbreak may last even longer, whereas on strong, unstable days it may be all but indiscernible. In the central Alps, far from any flatland influence, I have never been able to discern the existence of a thermal lunchbreak with any certainty.

The mechanism is as follows: In the mountains, and the mountain foothills, the thermals begin working earlier than in the surrounding flatlands. But as the thermals grow stronger the mountains begin to draw in colder air from the surrounding flatlands, where it suppresses the thermal development for a while, until it has been heated sufficiently to begin rising as thermals. This process takes around 30-45 minutes and generally no usable lift is found during this break.

Thermal lunchbreak near the sea

The oceanside lunchbreak is caused by very similar mechanisms to the foothill one. Here, the cold air being drawn in by the beginning sea breeze effectively stops thermal development, which is also the reason why the best thermalling close to the sea is generally early in the day. Once the sea breeze sets in the thermals become weak or nonexistent and at the very least the cloudbase lowers due to the humid sea air.

One advantage that coastal sites have is apparent in the winter; due to the often warmer sea the air doesn't cool so drastically during the night and the ground inversion in the morning is thus

3.60 *The beginning of the sea breeze effect is the cause of the oceanside lunchbreak. In the mountains the onset of the valley wind systems has a similar effect. In this picture the pilots fall out collectively in spite of good thermals only shortly before.*

3.61 *The lunchbreak effect has advantages too. In Monaco it is often flyable long after storm development has effectively put a halt to any flying only a few kilometres inland. The same is the case in the picture in Australia where there are no clouds above the sea but overdevelopment 20km away. Soaring the cloud-free coast is possible and safe, but keep an eye on development behind you.*
Photo: Tex Bex

less dramatic. Combined with a low sun heating the slopes, this is often sufficient for usable thermals to form. The popular winter site at Monaco is a good example of this.

A second advantage that coastal sites have is on very unstable days, where storm cells form inland and drown any hope of flying; but near the coast the weak thermals don't have the energy needed for storm development and the flying may continue long after the inland sites have been shut down.

Thermal lunchbreak in hill country and flatlands

Even in flatlands or low hills we may experience the thermal lunchbreak phenomenon, albeit caused by entirely different mechanisms. The cause this time is the wind, and the wind may also help the hill-country pilot to stay in the air during a thermal pause, by allowing the soaring of small ridges.

On days with any wind the ridges or low crests are often the thermal triggers in low country. The wind pushes the warm air along the ground, and when it reaches a terrain protrusion it is triggered to form thermal columns. This mechanism is quite reliable in hilly to nearly flat terrain, but when the wind abates it gets more complicated.

But why would the wind suddenly abate? In a high-pressure region the wind blows towards the low pressure. Near the ground the high inversion funnels this wind, but as the day grows warmer the inversion

3.62 *In the flatlands and in low mountains a brief thermal break will generally see us on the ground. To avoid this, XC beginners should only launch after the thermal lunchbreak, often around 1-2pm. As always, beginners should avoid flying during the strongest time of the day. Site: Rioja, Argentina.*

Coastal soaring in Madeira. Photo: Skywalk

lifts; the wind has more vertical space to move in, the funnel (or venturi) effect is reduced, and the wind at ground level abates. Note that this only happens when the macro-meteorological wind is not particularly strong.

Dust devils

Pilots fear them and spectators are fascinated by them. Dust devils occur when the air mass is over-adiabatic, i.e. when the air near the ground has been heated to temperatures where it should have risen as thermals long ago, but there hasn't been a triggering impulse yet.

When the triggering impulse arrives, for example in the shape of a gust creeping over the crest from the windward side, the thermal rises with a vengeance, rotating and forming a dust devil as it goes.

When the air is particularly unstable, mountain regions often have dust devils forming off sunny lee sides. On such days pilots either launch into the wind on the windward side, or into the thermal breeze on the leeward side. The launch at Babadağ in Ölüdeniz in Turkey is renowned for its dust devils. It is an example of the situation described above, where the south-facing launch often has wind from the north – a virtual dust devil recipe.

> **EXPERIENCE** Once I saw a paraglider complete with harness taking off in a dust devil and looking almost normal until about 20m off the ground – shortly thereafter it was nothing but a bundle of cloth and lines. And at the Babadağ launch in Turkey, mentioned above, one pilot getting ready for launch got picked up by a dustie and did a full loop from standing – luckily his injuries were only minor.
>
> When launching from dust devil-prone launches it is highly recommended to wait until one has gone through, thus releasing the overheated air. Right after a dust devil has gone through, the probability of another one forming is much reduced. Flying into dust devils at low altitude is very dangerous.
>
> I was towing in Australia when a sudden dustie came my way. As I was only 150m above ground I decided to release and escape. I was back on the ground in no time, battling my flapping wing in a bundle due to the +40km/h winds. Since that little incident my flying suit has some very decorative holes in it. The locals later told me that they often fly into dusties as long as they are more than 300m above ground – lower than that and even the most hardcore of them steer well clear. I wouldn't recommend flying into dusties at any altitude, but as this story shows some pilots do. See also page 274.

3.63 *Kobala launch, Slovenia. The wind was light easterly and the launch faces into the strong afternoon sun. This is dustie heaven, as the photo shows. Compare with the picture 1.50, page 53.*

HINT Dust devils are also thermals. When encountered at an altitude, good pilots may choose to fly into them to climb. When doing so it is always best to enter against the turn direction as this will have the wing pitch back – less dangerous than flying with the rotation direction and have the wing diving forward upon entry. I always advice against dust devil flying due to the strong turbulence often associated with it – experts only!

Smoke and dust as thermal markers

If you observe two smoke trails drifting towards each other chances are that there'll be a thermal rising from where they meet. Thermals suck in air from all around, and the effect is easiest to observe on windless days. If the two smoke or dust trails are drifting away from each other there's no thermal.

Using smoke to learn about inversion levels

Smoke stacks are also handy for judging the stability/instability of the lower levels – and if the smoke rises high we can even use it to learn about air movement and stability at higher levels. If the smoke is rising vertically we know that there's no wind, and when the smoke rises to a very well defined level only to be spread out along it we know that there's a strong inversion at this altitude. When this phenomenon is visible along the valley floor we can expect very calm conditions.

3.65 Rising smoke meets the inversion and spreads out horizontally. From this picture we can't say anything meaningful about the possible turbulence at higher levels, but beneath the inversion there's not going to be any turbulence at all.

3.64 Two smoke trails drifting towards each other. Where they meet (red patch) there's a good chance that a thermal is releasing. The hang glider pilot has noticed it and is aiming right for the thermal. Low down the lateral drift is stronger. This means that two pilots thermalling at different altitudes in the same thermal column will experience differentiated drift, with the lower pilot drifting more!

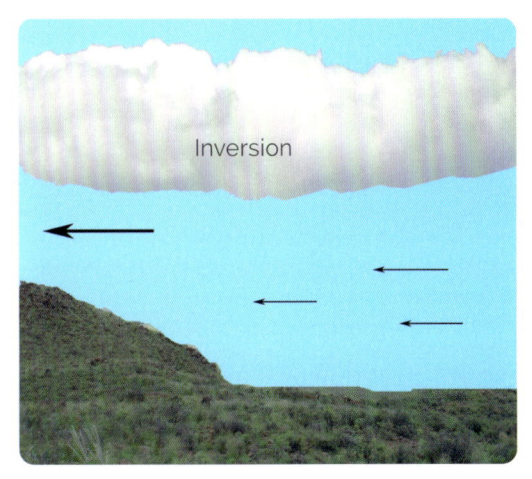

3.66 Inversions often magnify venturi effects. As seen in the drawing the hill and the low inversion combine to make the wind stronger at hilltop level.

Systematic thermal hunting

In the long run thermal flying should cease to be a matter of chance. To achieve this the pilot must learn to search for lift in a systematic manner. Here are some tips, in order of importance.

- The single most important factor is **the wind**. Where is it coming from? If the wind is coming from the north the pilot should concentrate on searching north, northeast or northwest slopes.
- Second most important is **the sun**. The best thermals originate from areas oriented perpendicularly to the sunshine direction, especially if they have already been exposed for a long time.
- Where are **the trigger points**? Are there any obvious triggers given by the terrain? Remember that the most important trigger is the mountaintop! If this isn't usable (low cloud or shade all around) then look for snow lines, streams or rivers, motorways, and don't forget shadow edges! Whenever a cloud shadow is moving over the terrain with the wind, the upwind shadow edge is the best potential trigger point.
- And all the **other considerations**: What kinds of ground do we have available? Forest clearings are better than deciduous forest, rockslides are better than the surrounding coniferous forest (see picture below), mountain pastures, especially those surrounded by woods, are always good. The good pilot always attempts to take the wind drift into consideration when basing the search on ground sources.
- **In the flats** it is less straightforward. The thermal sources are less obvious, but some good examples are grain fields, ploughed fields, sandy soils, earth embankments, tree-breaks, highways, junctions and riverbanks.

3.67 A pilot glides to a hillside looking for the next thermal. Where the steep forested slopes end with clearer shallow slopes above are likely to be good for releasing thermals. The most promising spot is the rock outcrop just to the left of the pilot's wing. Photo: Marcus King

This ridge, the Aravis in France, is easy to fly once you're up above start height. Thermals trigger along the entire ridge face
Photo: Jerôme Maupoint

Thermal hunting in hill-country and low mountains

By Volker Schwaniz

The albedo value of the ground is very important for the heating of the air – but it doesn't reliably tell us where the thermal actually can be found. In real-life flying we will often experience situations where a mass of warm air is pushed along by the wind until it meets a trigger point, where it releases as a thermal.

This is the reason why flight routes going over large expanses of homogenous terrain are less promising than routes following valley sides, where there are often tree lines, power lines etc, to trigger the thermals.

This is particularly true when the wind increases in strength – then trigger points overtake ground sources as our number one thermal search locations.

> **HINT** On no-wind days we use our understanding of albedo values to locate the thermals. There's no wind to push the overheated air away and against a thermal trigger, so we have to depend on the thermal releasing from its actual source.

> **HINT** When the wind is light we look downwind from the best heating areas (the ones we were using above). If the wind is really light the thermals may come from both the actual sources and from just downwind of the sources.

> **HINT** As the wind gets stronger our focus shifts towards trigger points downwind of the most easily heated areas.

3.68 Cloud distribution is a good thermal and day-quality indicator. This April day had weak winds, polar air influence and low base. The soil was very dry. Notice that in spite of the ideal terrain for thermal development in the flats, thermal quality is still far better above the hills.

3.69 This is the same day and the same location as picture 3.68 but taken from a different angle. Again we notice the more promising-looking cloud picture over the hill country compared to the flats. Even the small hill closest to the camera is triggering a thermal – note the small Cu above.

Searching for flatland thermals low down

1. Where's the wind coming from? Flatland flying means fewer leeside worries, but even a small hill may cause a serious rotor.
2. Is there anywhere where the landscape is oriented better towards the sun?
3. Where is the best soil for heating?
4. Where will the thermal be triggered?

This brief checklist can be summarised into an even briefer sentence: First look for easily heated soil, then try to visualise where the thermal will release!

HINT To summarise the mountain search pattern rules: stay out of the lee and aim for thermal trigger points.

3.70 *A dark field is a good thermal factory*

3.71 *When thermal hunting over relatively even ground there's less reason to worry about lee. But if we're low enough to discern hills (like the one behind this pilot) we should generally aim for them, as they are often good thermal triggers. It is hard to make out hills from higher altitudes – the higher you get, the flatter the landscape looks below you. This is flying in Patu, Brazil.*

Searching for mountain thermals low down

The checklist is the same as in the flats, but the order of the points is different;

Point 1 is even more important in the mountains, as leeside flying should be avoided. But since we generally find mountain thermals where they are released rather than where they are produced, we must go straight from point 1 to point 4. If this happens to be downwind of a location of warm air production then we made it.

Point 3 can generally not be taken into account once we find ourselves low in a valley. Remember: our main concern in the mountains is to stay out of the lee.

If you have a choice between deciduous and coniferous forest choose the latter. If around noon you have a choice between a steep mountainside and a rounded knoll choose the mountain. Note that neither of these choices is common in real-life flying!

Searching for thermals from high altitudes

Once we are high life is much easier; there are many more options and we have plenty of time to search for, find and use thermals. Furthermore, flying high allows us to use the clouds as thermal indicators.

We fly towards cumulus clouds that are still building and avoid decaying ones, and we remember to keep observing our surroundings whilst thermalling, especially in our intended flying direction. By doing so we may notice new wisps of cloud forming and observe them long enough to know if they are worth aiming for.

We will explore clouds and what they mean in more detail in the next chapter.

3.72 An abundance of thermal triggers near Chamonix, France. The snow line, rocky outcrops and borders of forested areas will all trigger thermals – just make sure you stay on the windward side of any relief. Photo: Marcus King

3.73 Once we have made it to cloudbase we use the clouds to direct us from one thermal to the next one. Aim for Cu's that are still forming and avoid decaying ones. All pilots should practise visualising where the thermal is coming from – this helps us to improve our thermal hunting when down at low altitude. At mid-level we must learn to aim right between the source and the cloud to find the thermal. This is flying over an unseasonably green landscape from distance-mecca Quixadá, Brazil.

4 Clouds

Mauricio Orozco flatland flying in Colombia. Photo: Cody Tuttle / Ozone

Chapter 4

Clouds

Clouds, and especially cumulus clouds, used to be simply annoying when I wanted to get some sun on my face. Nowadays I look at them from a different point of view, in fact I am practically ALWAYS aware of the clouds above me and when they look good I immediately start dreaming about flying. My studies of the skies are more than a pleasant pastime though – cloud observing helps me to become a better pilot.

Forming, dissipating

Our beloved cumulus clouds are made of tiny water droplets. To understand them we need to look briefly at how clouds form.

The sun heats the ground, which in turn heats the overlying air. The air expands and becomes lighter, and eventually rises as a thermal. While rising the air cools down adiabatically, which means about 1 degree per 100m altitude. The cooling is primarily caused by the expansion of the air and only on a very small scale by mixing with the surrounding, colder air.

To explain adiabatic cooling/heating consider the following example: When we use a bicycle pump we are familiar with the fact that the compression of the air causes it to heat up. The opposite is also the case; when air expands it cools down. This is what is known as adiabatic temperature change, which simply means that it takes place with no external influence and no energy is added or deducted, and no mixing with surrounding air masses occurs.

The rising thermal contains the moisture present at ground level, but as it cools down the relative humidity increases as the temperature drops. If it continues rising up to the dew point the humidity condenses – the cloud starts forming. The cloud continues to grow as long as there's still new warm air, and thus humidity, being added from below.

In a high-pressure system (where the air pressure is high at ground level) the air is always sinking slowly. The sinking motion happens at a rate of centimetres/hour, whereas thermal climb rates are measured in metres/second or feet/minute.

But the slow sinking of the air is enough to push the clouds downwards as soon as the thermal ceases, which in turn increases the pressure of the general air mass. And the increased pressure causes the temperature to rise so that the relative humidity decreases – the cloud dissipates.

Adding to this effect is the mixing that happens with the surrounding, drier air. Once the cloud has disappeared completely the sun may heat the ground again, and the process repeats itself.

Cloud coverage

When we talk about cloud coverage we use the term oktas, or increments of 1/8. A blue sky with no clouds has 0/8 cloud coverage,

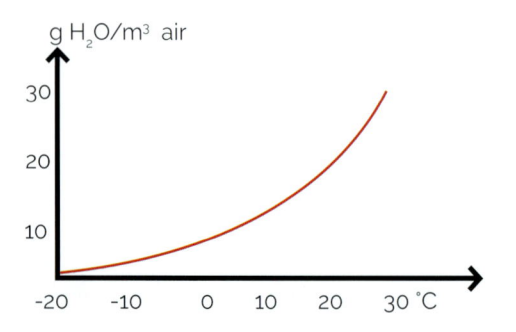

4.1 *Maximum water absorption per cubic metre of air, as a function of air temperature. The warmer the air becomes the more water it can hold. At 10°C air may hold about 10g of water per cubic metre. We saw in the previous chapter that air in high-pressure systems is perpetually sinking. This means that the air containing the clouds is also sinking, and getting warmed up, which eventually leads to the dissipation of the cloud.*

whereas a completely covered sky is referred to as 8/8. In the weather forecast it may be given as in Table 4.2:

Table 4.2 Cloud coverage

Oktas	Description	METAR abbr.
0/8	(Sky) Clear	SKC
1-2/8	Few	FEW
3-4/8	Scattered	SCT
5-7/8	Broken	BKN
8/8	Overcast	OVC

4.3 Scattered clouds (3/8) in the Pustertal, Austria

Locating the area of best climb under a cloud

Once we're high we may use the clouds to locate the best climbs. Normally these are found under the thickest part of the cloud, which is where the cloud looks darkest when observed from below. It takes time to learn how to read the clouds like this.

When approaching a cloud it pays to do so in a way that brings us directly to the thickest or darkest part of the cloud. To do this we must also consider the wind direction at cloud level, as the best climbs are often found on the upwind side.

4.4 Climb rates under clouds are generally best under the thickest part of the cloud. When approaching a cloud, fly straight for this area. From beneath it can be located by its dark grey colour.

4.5 Cloud streets will also have thicker, darker sections indicating where the best climbs are found. This hang glider has noticed the most promising looking section and aims straight for it

HINT Flatland thermals often set up in rows following the wind direction. For the flatland pilot this has the benefit that when exiting a thermal the most likely location of the next one is directly downwind – just as the cloud streets indicate. Notice that this is also the case on blue days!

If we must fly crosswind it follows that our best strategy is to fly perpendicular to the wind direction until we have connected with the next cloud street (or thermal line, on blue days), then follow that for a bit downwind until we make the next jump perpendicular to the wind. Flying at any other angle between thermal lines increases the distance between them, and our risk of landing while crossing the gap.

123

4.6 Cloud streets over the flatlands. Photo: Volker Schwaniz

4.8 The cloud tail hanging down indicates where the strongest climb rates can be found.

4.9 The best climbs can be found under the darkest area of the cloud.

4.7 Cloud street formation over De Aar, South Africa, with thermals and the wind direction drawn in

4.10 An aerial view of cloud streets

4.11 Cloud street formation over the flatlands. Similar to picture 4.7, but with four cloud streets. Compare these with the situation in illustration 4.44 on p138

4.12 Wind-sculpted cumulus cloud. The wind is coming from the right and the best climbs can be expected under the windward/right-hand side of the cloud. If at all possible we approach this cloud in a way that takes us straight there without leading us through the increased sink just downwind of the cloud (on the left)

4.13 On the left-hand side the cloud has already begun to show signs of dissipation. If there is still climbing to be found it will be under the right side. However, since the cloud has no clear cauliflower structure it is probably already dead

Sometimes the wind speeds decrease again above a certain altitude – in these cases the best climbs may be found on the side facing away from the wind. If the cloud is already showing signs of dissipation (picture 4.13) the climb has most likely abated here – in these cases it is imperative to aim for the areas still unaffected by the dissipation. These signs are generally not as clear to see as in the example shown here.

HINT When flying cross country we generally approach all clouds straight on, but if we're aiming for a cloud in a headwind we must first fly through the increased sink on the downwind side of it. In these cases it may often be worthwhile to fly a large curve around the sink area – this costs less altitude than a direct approach.

Cloud associated dangers

Paraglider and hang glider pilots are not allowed to fly into clouds, but at times it can happen before you know it! Inexperienced pilots often get so excited about their thermal flight that they forget to remain alert and maintain a safe distance to the cloud above them. Here are some of the problems with cloud flying.

- Getting sucked in can cause instantaneous loss of orientation. Some pilots actually deliberately fly into clouds when on XC flights, in order to gain extra altitude before a big valley crossing etc. In my view this generally doesn't pay off as the loss of orientation frequently leads to panic and thus to inability to follow the best route even with GPS.
- Big, thick clouds often impede signal reception to the extent that the GPS loses its bearings, and then you're *really* lost. If you regularly fly near cloud, get a ball compass for your flight deck and learn how to use it in clear air.
- Danger of collision with other pilots
- Danger of collision with mountains
- Danger of collision with IFR-approved aeroplanes.
- Inability to watch out for cloud overdevelopment, and the risks involved in flying in or near cumulonimbus clouds
- Hypothermia or freezing to death; blacking out at high altitudes; getting struck by lightning.

4.15 *If the lightning begins and you're still in the air you have made a wrong decision somewhere. Even full-sized passenger aircraft avoid thunderstorms, so it is no surprise that we must be extremely careful with them when flying our flimsy craft. Photo: Tex Bex*

The larger the cloud grows the bigger the risk of getting sucked in becomes – and once inside we have no way of knowing if the cloud is turning into a cumulonimbus (Cb). An example: suppose that we have a cloud base at 2,500m, and the inversion putting a lid on cloud growth lies at 5,000m. This means that the cloud may grow 2.5km thick – from beneath, such a monster looks dark and dangerous!

The climb rates right beneath such clouds may easily double compared to the rest of the thermal. This great increase in lift is caused by the energy released into the system through the condensation process, where heat stored from the evaporation is

4.14 *Big cumulus cloud. Flying under such clouds involves a great risk of getting sucked in. Make sure you fly towards the edge of the cloud well before reaching cloudbase.*

4.16 *Similar to the cloud from 4.14 but this time photographed from a distance. From beneath the cloud in the centre of the picture the view will be just like in picture 4.14. These are the kinds of clouds that overdevelop and grow into cumulonimbus.*

> **HINT** The closer you get to cloudbase the further out towards the edge of the cloud you should fly, preferably on the upwind side if there are no obstacles around. In the mountains, and on days where cloudbase is beneath the peaks, you aim for the valley side of the cloud, where a brief visit inside is less consequential. See picture 1.41 on page 48.

released again. This extra heat accelerates the climbs right under, and inside, big clouds. There is more about this mechanism in chapter 9.

A pilot coring a steady 6m/s thermal all the way to cloudbase may suddenly encounter 12m/s right under the cloud – a real problem if the pilot hasn't remembered to move close to the edge in time. I recommend the spiral dive (for paraglider pilots) to escape such a strong lift, but bear in mind that many pilots have reported difficulties initiating spiral dives when they were in a strong lift. A hang glider cannot reach these sink rates but may more effectively outrun the strong lift by diving for the edge.

Note that big, shallow clouds do not have the same extreme climb rates associated with them and are thus easier to avoid. Only when the cloud's vertical expanse goes beyond maybe 1000m do we have to be aware of the development, both to avoid getting sucked in and to see if it turns into a Cb. Gliders may fly around Cb's where paragliders and even hang gliders would find themselves in deep trouble.

4.18 Large but shallow cumulus clouds. These clouds indicate excellent thermal conditions with no particular dangers. However, anyone flying under the middle one would still probably encounter strong lift and surely see a great and dark cloud overhead.

4.19 After a few minutes inside a cloud the condensation will start running down the lines. The brake line becomes a small river of water, the water soaks first the gloves, then sleeves and back of the pilot. If it is cold the water freezes and ice may form. You should fly towards clear air and let the glider thaw out and then dry out. Photo: Mads Syndergaard

4.17 Interesting sky. Everything is overdeveloped on the right, while on the left we still see blue thermals and a clear sky

Gust fronts

Another cloud-related danger in the air is the so-called gust front preceding showers, originating from overdeveloped cumulus or cumulonimbus clouds.

A gust front behaves like a small, local cold front by expanding in all directions and pushing the surrounding air up and away. Gust fronts may extend to upwards of 30km from their source, but even small showers coming from overdeveloped cumulus clouds will often have their own little mini cold fronts preceding them.

The cold air of a gust front wedges in under the surrounding air and lifts it up (just as happens on a larger scale when real cold fronts come through) and may trigger extensive thermal development in their path. This may sound just great, and you may even see pilots take advantage of this sudden abundance of 'lift everywhere', but the turbulence caused by the strong cold wind mixing with the surrounding air is not for the faint of heart.

4.20 In this picture, clouds form in the lee of the mountain – it almost looks volcanic. You could soar on the windward face. Lee clouds form due to slightly reduced air pressure on a mountain's leeside, which aids condensation. Generally when lee clouds form, the wind is too strong on the windward side for paragliders to fly. Photo: Jérôme Maupoint

4.21 A fully formed thunderstorm seen from a distance of about 30km in Bassano, Italy. This one caused immense gust fronts to come through at Bassano, a clear indicator of how careful one must be with these phenomena. A few daredevils were seen flying backwards at around 10km/h, so we can deduce that the wind speeds were in excess of 50km/h – remember this was at least 30km from the cloud. Wind around storms is nearly always dangerous for pilots

4.22 All these photos show clouds that are good indicators of a very unstable atmospheric situation. Visible storm clouds are the least of our problems – we should go and land before it is too late – but embedded in thick cloud cover, or hidden by smog or poor visibility they are far more unpredictable.

Top row, left to right: clouds like this early on mean the air is unstable and you will likely get storms later; strong vertical development with wind up high; strong development over the mountains in the distance.

Bottom row: an isolated cloud developing, one to watch as it grows during the day; haze obscuring cloud development over the back; haze obscuring storm cell development out in the flats. The south side of the Alps often sees hazy conditions like this.

4.23 On a day like this in the Jura, when a strong inversion a few hundred metres above cloudbase stops any overdevelopment, the clouds will remain small. Right beneath these clouds they may still look somewhat dark but there is no risk of overdevelopment. The day may turn blue later if cloudbase rises further and goes above the inversion. Photo Jérôme Maupoint.

4.24 A local overdeveloped Cu dumping rain. The gust fronts caused by this kind of very local shower are not as strong as some but the dangers associated are the same.

4.27 This pilot has cut it a bit too close and landed just as it started to rain. Luckily the gust front was weak, otherwise they would have had a difficult landing.

4.25 Embedded cumulonimbus are storm clouds that are part of wider cloud cover. Unlike the big storm cells out on the flats or the heavy and dark cu-nims at the head of a valley they are invisible to the pilot below because of the thick cloud cover. Consequently they are far more dangerous than visible storm clouds. They can develop when the air mass is extremely unstable. Extra care must be taken on days when embedded cu-nims might be present.

Stable

Unstable = thunderstorms likely

4.26 An impressive cumulonimbus (Cb) in southern France. Thunderstorms are typical in the region in summer and will build through the day. This shot was taken at about 3pm. The storm will continue to develop through the afternoon

No thermals without sun, but are there still dangers?

By Volker Schwaniz

Inexperienced pilots will be excused for thinking that as long as the sky is overcast and no sunlight is seeping through to feed thermals, there will be no danger from overdeveloping clouds. They may think that without the influx of energy from the sun to the ground there will be no thermals, and with no thermals there will be no clouds suddenly growing alarmingly big. This deduction is quite reasonable at first glance, but it is wrong.

Stratus layer clouds are often the visible indicator that the atmosphere is severely unstable; so unstable in fact that even the diffuse light making it through the cloud cover may be enough to feed overdevelopment and turn it into showers and cumulonimbus clouds!

Besides, the stratus layers may make imminent weather changes, like the arrival of a cold front or a trough, invisible to the pilot observing from beneath. Any of these scenarios adversely influences the flying conditions, often to a dangerous degree – and the cloud layer keeps it invisible to the observer!

In mountainous regions air getting pushed over elevations by the wind will be cooled down and heat will be released, and if the air mass is sufficiently unstable this extra energy influx will be enough to trigger cloud overdevelopment and so-called orographic showers or Cb's.

4.28 An orographic storm brewing above the stratus layer. Danger!

The unexpected thunderstorm: learning from mishaps

By Volker Schwaniz

Some time ago I received an email from a pilot who needed an explanation to an incident he had gone through.

The pilot had been flying a soaring site on an overcast early summer day. After a while he noticed that the skies at the opposite end of the lake in front of him were growing darker and he decided to land.

However, as he was approaching the lakeside landing he noticed that there were already whitecaps forming. Suddenly gusts of 40-50km/h were blowing through. It was a gust front and he was still in the air – he'd been caught out.

He was lucky and survived the unavoidable crash with only minor injuries, but he was understandably looking for an explanation as to what had happened.

The pilot's mistake was that he underestimated the instability of the air mass he was dealing with. The air mass would have been unstable to the extent that even without direct sunlight, storms could still form, while

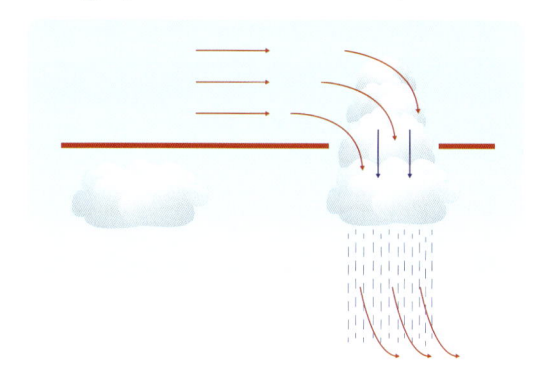

4.29 On the left a normal cumulus cloud that is being stopped from overdeveloping vertically by the high-pressure inversion (see chapter 3). On the right an unstable situation combined with high humidity in the air. The inversion is too weak to stop the vertical (over)development and the Cu rapidly turns into a Cb.

remaining hidden from his view by the cloud cover. The dangers are caused by the rain (wet paragliders often behave in an unpredictable manner) and gusting winds, which are known to be particularly vehement on days with tall clouds and a strong wind up high.

In this example the pilot 'only' had to deal with the gusts originating from the embedded storm, and not rain or hail. But sometimes it may be more than that.

4.31 *We have summer storms, cold front storms and also orographic storms as described in illustration 4.28.*

4.30 *Summer storms may brew fast but nonetheless they don't just materialise out of nowhere. The reasonable pilot lands before things get critical. If you ever find yourself thinking 'This is easy, there is lift everywhere', then that is a clue! Photo: Bruce Goldsmith*

4.32 Beautiful cumulus castellanus are fantastic to watch but indicate a high likelihood of storms later in the day. It could be in an hour, it could be in five, but almost certainly it will come. The pilot must remain alert. When this photo was taken it was still flyable.

Escaping from clouds

Generally pilots should avoid touching cloudbase. This is best done by repeatedly looking up while thermalling, always attempting to estimate the remaining distance to the cloud. This is not easy in the beginning! If you're unsure of how far you still have to go, fly out on the upwind side of the thermal or cloud and get a look from a different perspective – if it turns out you still have a good margin, you can always fly back in. By doing so you will be slowly approaching the cloud at your own pace, and you'll be learning lots about assessing cloud distance.

Sometimes novice thermal pilots find themselves getting overly enthusiastic about the whole endeavour and suddenly end up uncomfortably close to a fat Cu sucking like a vacuum cleaner. The best trick is to hightail for the edge of the cloud, possibly even with the ears tucked in and stomping the speed bar as hard as conditions allow. If it looks like you will be sucked in, note your direction and use your instrument and/or compass to keep flying in a straight line.

Spiral diving straight down may help, but typically you will just spiral down and still be in strong lift. Note that if you're doing these things together with a group of other pilots you must make sure you're not colliding with anyone whilst battling the excessive lift.

The hang glider pilot has an advantage in this situation, as he may simply pull the bar in and dive out at high speed. Should he miss that point he'll be in a worse place than the paraglider though, as he'll find it even harder to maintain a steady heading *and* he may even find it hard to avoid suddenly flying upside down.

The paraglider is better in this respect as the pilot is *always* beneath the canopy. The hang glider is not so lucky and will be more careful next time!

4.33 Big Cu over the Zugspitze, Germany. With clouds this big the pilot must be alert in order to make sure he flies out of the strong lift and towards the edge in time.

4.34 In order to escape from clouds sucking too much, the paraglider pilot pulls in his ears and pushes the speed bar, and the hang glider pulls in and dives out.

4.35 Large cumulus clouds being fed by strong thermals often develop concave domes at their base. The hang glider in the picture knows that the dome indicates strong lift and flies there.

HINT If you notice a cloud with a dome forming you can be sure to find strong lift under it. IMPORTANT: do not take the thermal all the way to cloudbase!

EXPERIENCE When the air mass is very unstable the summer storms may arrive as early as around noon. I once sat on take-off inside a cloud waiting for a window to launch in. After 45 minutes the window finally appeared, but by then we didn't dare to launch anymore as there was no way of knowing how big the cloud had grown in the meantime. It turned out to be an excellent decision as the lightning began only five minutes later!

Cloud domes

Illustration 4.35 shows a cloud dome as they frequently occur on the base of strong, fat Cu's. The dome may be up to 150m deep, i.e. the edges of the cloud are 150m lower than the centre. The dome develops because the condensation process is somewhat delayed in fast rising thermals. If the pilot remains in the thermal long enough to go up into the dome (illegal in controlled airspace) then the only way out is through the lower edges of the cloud. See also picture 1.12.

Inversion domes on blue days

Flatland pilots have reported dome formation into inversion layers when flying on blue days. The strong thermals make dome-shaped indentations in the inversion layer, and when there is smog these domes are visible from the side (not from beneath). The higher the pilot is the easier it is to see the domes and use them as thermal markers. Picture 1.20, page 34, shows an inversion where domes will be easy to notice.

4.36 'Blue domes' occur on smoggy blue days with strong thermals. They can be recognised by the wisps surrounding them, which are excellent thermal markers

4.37 Here is another nice domed cloud. The cloud is active and very large. As soon as you fly closer to the domed part, take care not to get sucked in. Fly out to the edge well before you get to cloudbase otherwise you will find yourself in the 'white room'

Cloud shadows can help you determine the size of the clouds around you. Photo: Jérôme Maupoint

Judging cloud size

Once we have climbed to cloudbase or thereabout it becomes very hard to see how big an adjacent cloud is. To get an idea of this we need to use another trick, by looking at the cloud shadow on the ground. If the shadow is full of holes it is safe to assume that the cloud is already dissipating and that it is of no use to us any longer.

4.38 We judge the size of a cloud from the air by looking at its shadow on the ground. The picture shows the Valais, Switzerland.

HINT Judging distance correctly in the air is very difficult and the pilot in front of us who looks as if he is already approaching the opposite side of the valley may only be searching for a thermal a bit further out from the ridge. It is important to train the eye to become more accurate in distance assessment – not easy, but experience helps. And it makes it much easier finding the lift that someone else indicated and then left.

Judging cloud distance

Cloud shadow is useful for judging the distance you need to reach the next cloud. You need to take cloudbase and the sun's position into account. If you are at base, look down at the shadows on the ground.

On clear days clouds will look closer – this is a phenomenon that is well known by the residents of Munich, as strong föhn days where the air is completely clear always make it look as if the Alps, 70km (43 miles) to the south, are literally on the outskirts of town.

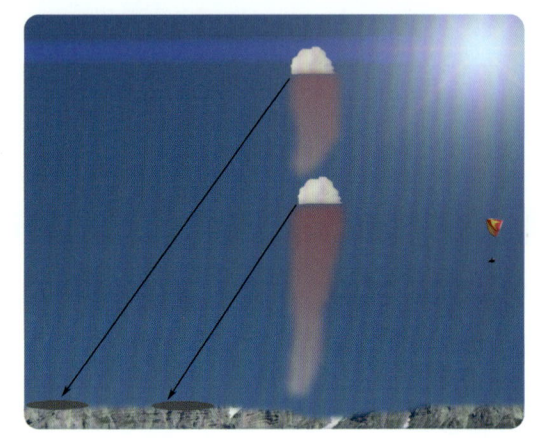

4.39 By watching the cloud shadow on the ground you may attempt to assess the distance to it. In this illustration both thermals are at the same distance. The pilot sees the shadow and attempts to connect it with the right cloud. The higher the cloudbase, the further away the cloud shadow will be (provided the sun is not in zenith). The lower the sun sinks the more distinct this effect becomes.

4.40 Low clouds are easier to connect to their shadows on the ground. The higher the cloudbase, the harder it gets to estimate the distance to the next cloud. Big winter thermals in the Isar valley, Bavaria.

Flying in broken cloud conditions

Plenty of clouds in the skies are not necessarily a sign of plenty of thermals too. If the high-pressure inversion is weak it takes longer for it to dissolve all the clouds forming, and they may remain in the skies long after the lift has died.

The same thing happens when the air is very moist: the clouds last long after the thermal has stopped. On such days the challenge is to identify the clouds still working, where the feeding thermals are still active.

4.41 and 4.42 Many big clouds in the skies, and sadly also many that are not marking lift. It is much easier to fly when the clouds dissipate as soon as their thermal dies.

Cloud streets in the mountains

A long sun-facing ridge may have an almost uninterrupted cloud street sitting above it for hours. XC pilots love this view, because it means fast going with little or no need for thermalling for long distances at a time.

Picture 4.43 An impressive looking cloud street in the Inn valley, Austria. Every sun-facing slope produces lift, and every thermal has its Cu. Over the valley the skies are completely clear.

Dolphin-flying under cloud streets

Dolphin-flying, or dolphining, is the fastest and most efficient way to make some distance when flying XC. When dolphining the pilot simply flies straight, braking in lift and accelerating in sink. The trick is to adjust the speed exactly so that the net altitude remains the same over time, and this is something that takes a lot of practising.

Near cloudbase we speed up and increase our sink rate so that we avoid getting sucked in. Lower down we may choose to fly closer to minimum sink in order to get the most out of the lift at hand. By constantly changing the amount of speed bar we push or even the amount of brake input we attempt to remain roughly within the area of the best climbing, normally quite close to the cloudbase. Once we have this dialled in we can experience some very satisfying flying.

Approx. distance 2,5 to 3 H

Convective boundary layer (H)

4.44 and 4.45 *Here is a more in-depth explanation of dolphining and how to do it. Under the darker cloud areas we reduce speed (and climb) to take advantage of the lift, and if we get too close to cloudbase we speed up again.*

When there's no lift we fly at the speed for best glide (hands up). If sink increases we speed up even more by using the speed bar; when we again meet lifting air we slow down, but we don't thermal. We only start thermalling again when we have lost contact with the good lift band and need to get back up to where the best lift is.

Sailplane pilots use dolphining to optimise their distance/time ratio, just like we do. But they go further whilst doing it – flights of more than 3,000km have been logged using dolphin-flying techniques in wave conditions.
Blue line: flying at minimum sink
Red line: flying accelerated

Cloud streets over the flatlands

If the conditions are right, cloud streets form over the flatlands. Just as in the mountains these are the days when the lucky pilot can go really far in a short time. All the distance world records have been set in the flatlands using cloud streets.

Necessary conditions for cloud street formation in the flatlands are:
- While the wind direction must remain pretty constant at all levels the wind speed should increase with altitude.
- The wind strength should be highest in the upper 1/3 of the space between the ground and the top of the cloud.

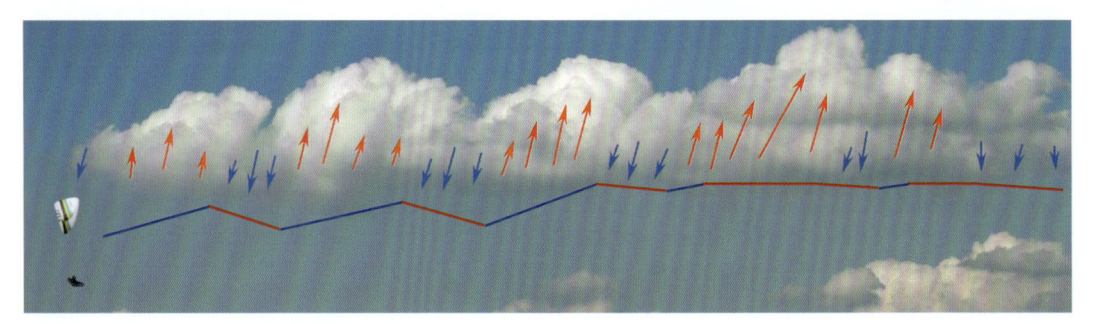

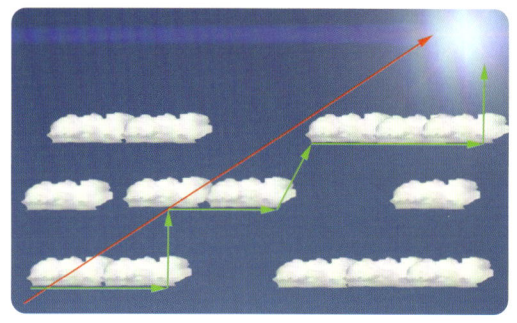

4.46 The planned direction (red) and the most efficient line (green). The gaps in the cloud streets are used to change streets and move in the desired direction. Big gaps in cloud streets are also better negotiated by changing street than by attempting to cross large blue holes.

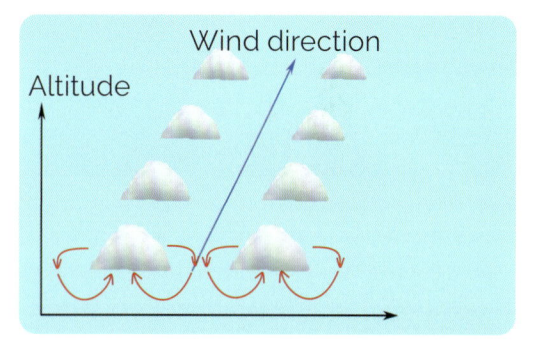

- There should be an inversion present at an altitude corresponding to the top of the cloud; the clouds must have vertical room for a healthy development but they cannot be allowed to grow too big. An inversion around 1,000m above the condensation level is probably right.

When all these conditions are met we can expect the distance between the cloud streets to be 2.5 to 3 times the distance ground-cloud top. If the clouds grow to 3,000m above ground the next cloud street will probably be approximately 7-9km away, and the cloud streets will be aligned with the wind.

4.47 Compare this illustration to pictures 4.10 and 4.11 on page 124, a simplified illustration of the air movement around cloud streets. This illustration also serves to illuminate why the jump from one cloud street to the next should always be done at right-angles to the wind direction (as shown in Illustration 4.46) – to avoid spending more time than needed in the sink between the streets. In the air this can feel counter-intuitive, especially when flying downwind, so you need to learn this technique and put it into practice. Your drift will naturally carry you downwind as you fly across.

HINT The distance to the pilot you are looking at is much shorter than you think! As a rule of thumb they are half as far away as you think, and then closer still! Try this at base: pick a pilot and estimate how far away they are. Fly to them and measure the distance on your GPS. See? Told you!

HINT Two things to consider when using cloud streets to fly in the flatlands:
- If the gap between two clouds in a street is greater than the distance to the next parallel street it is probably wiser to change streets,
- If your bearing is at an angle to the cloud streets it pays to go as far as possible along the streets and change street when a gap in your current street appears.

What else can clouds tell us?

Cloud spotting should become a passion for the keen pilot. It helps us when assessing lurking dangers but it also tells us a lot about the quality of the day.

You should start to look at the clouds and try to interpret them while you are still in training school, that way you can take advantage of your instructor's knowledge.

Get into the habit of looking at clouds whenever you are not flying too and you will soon develop some skills. It is one important thing that you can do when you are not in the air that will genuinely help you develop as a pilot.

4.48 *These two pictures were taken within two seconds of each other. Notice how far the cloud has drifted in the second shot by looking at the treetops at the bottom. The wind is far too strong for flying, and if it is still quiet at ground level it is only because the wind has not come down there yet. Cloud drift tells us a lot about wind velocity and direction.*

4.49 *It is not often that the wind direction is so easy to tell as in this shot. Strong vertical development on a windy day.*

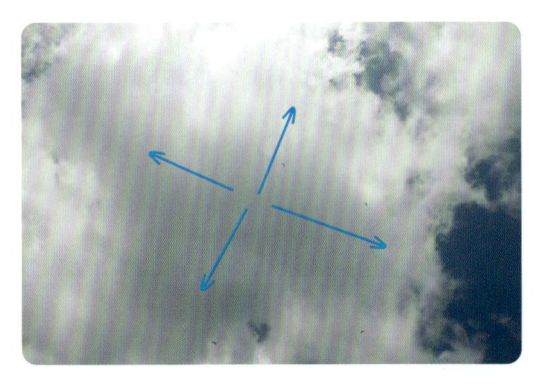

4.51 *Forming cumulus clouds expand in all directions. If we only watch a part of such a cloud it would be easy to misjudge the wind direction! It is important to know that the cloud expansion has nothing to do with the wind direction – this is seen from the cloud drift!*

> **HINT** Try to become accustomed to watching clouds form and dissipate. Train yourself by keeping an eye out for cloud wisps and try to predict if they are forming or dissipating when you see them. Keep watching the wisps to see if your prediction was correct.

4.50 *Observe the wind coming from the left from the little rotor cloud at the top of the main part of the cloud on the left.*

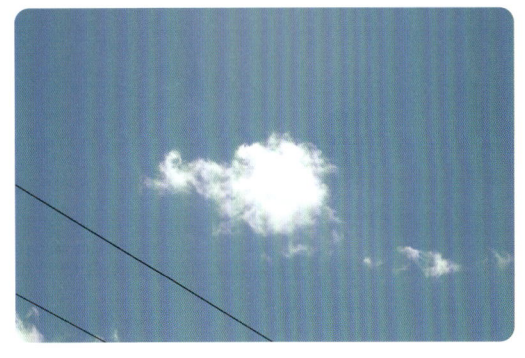

4.52 On thermally active days the first cumulus start forming around 8-9am. If there are plenty around earlier than that, the day will be too unstable and probably overdevelop early. There's still a chance that the flying will be good for a few hours before the overdevelopment sets in, but we must watch the conditions carefully.

4.53 On good days the clouds will form, then float for some time before they dissipate. Clouds that are in the process of either building or evaporating will look fringy and puffy. Good cumulus have a flat bottom and a cauliflower top. If all the clouds in the sky look torn and uneven it means that the wind is strong and is 'shredding' the thermals. It could well be too strong for comfortable flying.

4.54 When the day is not blue, thermals will be topped by cumulus clouds. It follows that areas with no clouds will also have no thermals! If you're flying along a mountain ridge with clouds lining it all the way and you come upon a place where there is no cloud it is highly likely that you have found the place where the ridge is being flushed by the valley wind. To cross such sections you need to climb as high as possible in order to have sufficient altitude to get across. Once you descend down into the wind the sink gets unbearable and there's nothing to do but change valley side ASAP to soar up on the other side, where the valley wind hits the ridge.

4.55 Dolphining is not only for cloud streets – on long ridges it may be possible to speed up the XC flight in a similar manner. You simply fly fast along the ridge, and climb at the end

4.56 One should always attempt to connect the cloud and the cloud source. Among other things this will give you a better understanding of the thermal-generating properties of diverse soils. The tropical pilot will have an easier time of that since the sun is more vertically overhead. On no-wind days the cloud shadow will thus be covering the area that produced the thermal!

HINT Never stop observing clouds: sunbathing, working in the office, whenever! It is interesting, and it'll make you a better pilot. When you are earth-bound you generally have more time to follow the life cycle of the clouds you are observing – once airborne this is much harder. Ask yourself, how long does the cloud last from the moment you notice it till it has disappeared again? And equally important: how long till the same area produces the next cloud?

HINT In order to determine whether a cloud is growing or collapsing I use a special technique. While thermalling I look in the direction I wish to continue. If there is a cloud there that looks promising I check it out briefly, then I continue my circle without looking at it again. Only when I'm again facing the same cloud in my circling (15-20 seconds is pretty normal for a full 360 in a thermal) I check it again. After a few turns I have a good idea of how it is developing.

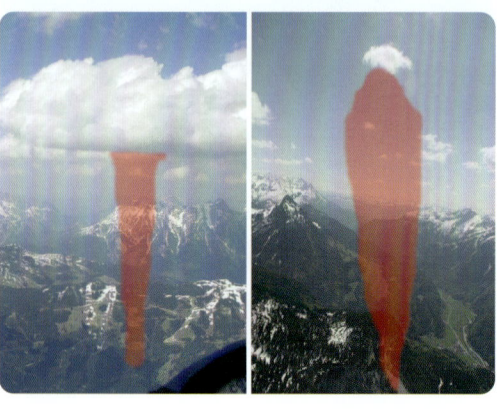

4.57 Does a big cloud always indicate a hefty thermal? And does a hefty thermal always have a big cloud? No, a small Cu may have a strong thermal beneath it, and if the conditions favour the growth of the clouds even a small thermal may be topped by a monster cloud, as on the left.

4.59 An evening shot (9pm) of the north-west facing ridges in the Ötztal in Austria. Notice that the clouds indicate continued thermal activity even at this late hour. At this time of the evening the whole landscape will be releasing energy, and the climbs will likely be smooth, mellow and go high.

Picture 4.58 Judging the distance to other pilots flying ahead is extremely difficult. One thing is for sure: they are closer than they appear! The better we become at judging distance the easier it will be to find the thermals that the other pilots recently left.

Picture 4.60 Turbulence made visible. The clouds tell us that there is a rotor turning left.

HINT On any given day the lifespan of a cloud tends to be roughly the same. This must be taken into account when we have reached cloudbase and are aiming for the next cloud or thermal. We always try to identify a good growing cloud that is still in the early phases of development, ideally only visible as wisps when we commence our glide – this cloud will then be at the peak of its life when we reach it.

When I was less experienced I often found myself aiming for beautiful big and mature clouds only to find that they had died once I finally got there, and got only increased sink for my troubles.

Always try to keep an eye on the clouds in the vicinity while you are still thermalling and *before* you reach cloudbase; from cloudbase visibility is never great, and the decision should already have been taken earlier.

If you notice a new cloud forming nearby, and you're not busy with your own great thermal, it usually pays to go straight for the new cloud – there will almost always be excellent lift under it.

Clouds with a well defined base indicate a relatively longer lifespan. This may then be an indicator that the thermal feeding is not just a bubble but a regular column that has been feeding the cloud for a long time.

4.61 This glider has got wet and needs drying – a pleasant pastime for windy days. That the day is windy can easily be seen from the cloud in the background.

4.62 A leeside thermal being broken up by the wind. The cloud shows the air movement, with a lee rotor right and another rotor turning the opposite way on the left.

4.63 A handsome lee vortex formed by föhn wind blowing over the Alpine main ridge. Nice to look at, not to fly in!

4.64 The E-W oriented Inn Valley in Austria is not very good when the wind is from the North. The south-facing slopes are in the lee and get turbulent. The clouds overshadow the very slopes which should produce the thermals we need to get high, as clearly seen in this photograph.

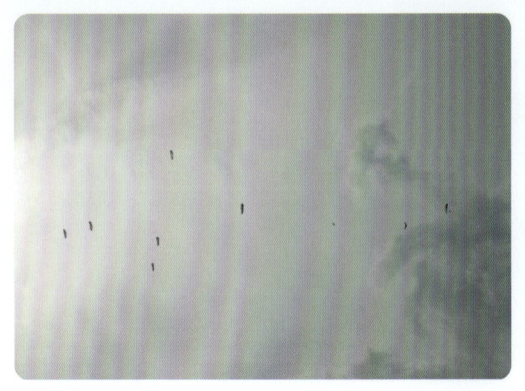

4.65 If the air mass is very unstable, thermals may form even under overcast skies. This shot was taken during the Bavarian Open in Berchtesgaden, Germany. One hour later the storm arrived.

4.66 How would you fly to get to this cloud? The sun is shining from the right onto the slope and the upper wind is also blowing from the right. Both indicate that the cloud should be approached at its right end (arrow).

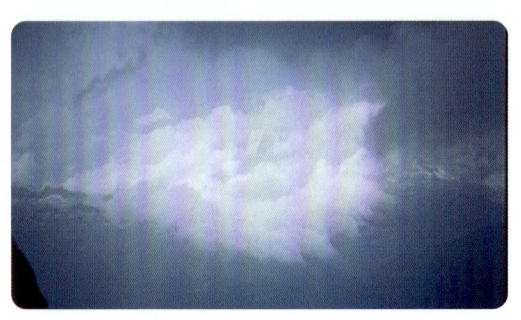

4.67 A cold front pushing through a pass. It goes fast, and it is only really visible once it is too late. Within minutes the conditions become unflyable. On this day the wind was suddenly gusting to 70km/h at the landing site.

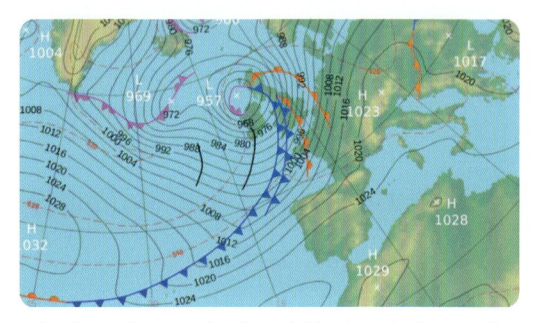

4.67a Learn to recognise the cold front symbol on weather charts: pointed triangles, often blue. To remember easily what they mean, think of the triangle as a mountain (cold). Warm front symbols are semi-circles – like the sun.

4.68 Clouds which are wider at the bottom than the top generally decay. In addition, the cloud on the left is getting rather frayed at the edges – a good indicator that it is no longer active. The cloud on the right has better definition and is still growing.

4.69 This contrail shows the wind at altitude is blowing from right to left! Contrails will often spread out across the sky.

4.72 Pulsating thermals – only the left one is active. The rest are dying out and drifting to the right on the wind.

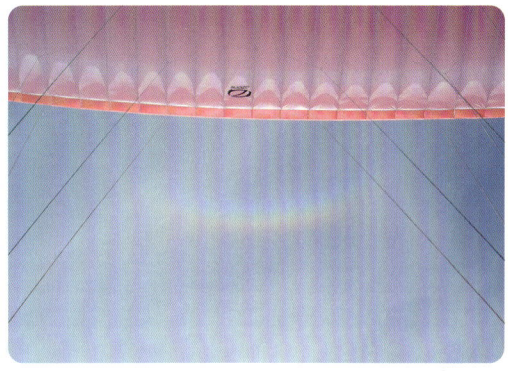

4.70 Halos indicate moist air at altitude – possible signs of an approaching warm front.

4.73 Active, unstable air behind a cold front. Cloud streets have formed over flatlands with almost full snow cover.

4.71 If you are already close to cloudbase, then choose your route according to the clouds. Active cumuli don't drift too fast with the wind, but decaying cumuli do. Sometimes you just can't seem to catch up with a cloud, even though it seems to be close. If this is the case, the cloud is probably already decaying and it's usually better to take a U-turn and look for the next pulsating thermal upwind. A small vulture showed me a thermal here in Brazil.

4.74 In a natural bowl on a hillside the air is relatively undisturbed and can heat up nicely in the sun, producing good strong thermals. Out on the exposed flanks of the mountain extending down to the valley floor any warm air is often blown away by valley winds, meaning you will have a harder time trying to find a thermal. Any lift you do find will drift along the slope, taking you with it. Your track will show you 'crabbing' sideways along the mountain as you climb.

4.75 *Hexagonal thermal distribution in nil-wind in the desert.*

4.76 *Some pilots like to push their luck. Just 10 minutes after this photo was taken in the Pinzgau Valley in Austria a big thunderstorm gust front blew through. Danger from thunderstorms includes the strong wind, often with an abrupt change in direction, rain or hail, and very strong lift.*
Photo: Nina Brümmer

4.78 *Cloudbase at different altitudes. Big differences in the Fassa Valley, Dolomites – damp air from the Grödner Valley in the north condenses up to 1,000m lower down. The damp southern air can sometimes condense even lower – if you're above the Marmolada, you can sometimes look down on cumuli in the south!*

4.77 *Every good thermal mountain ought to have its own cumulus cloud in thermal conditions. If this is true for all except one, then the mountain is probably directly in the path of the (usually valley) wind and should be avoided. In the afternoon, northerly winds from Obersdorf blow over the top of this peak, the Jöchelspitze, into the Lech valley.*

4.79 *This line of mountains is really working well and will allow pilots to fly fast along it. The development is capped, so the clouds are not developing too fast or too high. Out in the valley the sky is blue, except for a few tiny wisps, meaning all the active air is above the mountains. This is a classic day in the Alps and you should be able to fly far.*

Drying out after rainfall

With input from Volker Schwaniz

To be able to judge how soon conditions will turn favourable again after a rainy spell we need to know something about the new air mass replacing the rain. If it is a dry, warm air mass it can absorb very large amounts of humidity in a very short time.

If the high pressure travels fast and replaces the trough very quickly the drying of the soil and air happens fast.

However, when this occurs we can often observe the rising humidity getting caught under the inversion and creating a cloud cover, so that the best conditions are still a few hours away.

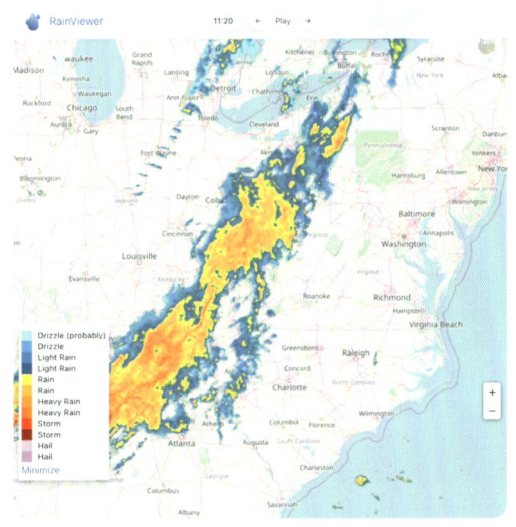

HINT When after a rainy spell I find myself driving towards a flying site I always try to estimate how much precipitation the area has received. From my home I can reach the Ennstal or the Arlberg, both in Austria, in about two hours, and I always try to go for the one where the least rain has fallen, as this is the place where the drying will be faster.

4.81 A radar image showing precipitation quantities for the eastern USA. Most weather sites provide these animated images in 'real time' and for the past few hours, so you can get an idea of where most precipitation has fallen. Image: rainradar.net

4.80 Lots of post-frontal moisture in Valais, Switzerland. The high pressure is already there and the shape of the clouds indicates a light northerly flow. Around 1pm we were already at 2,500m – this area dries faster than the north side of the Alps.

The time for the drying process also depends on the geographical location. In the Alps for example the following applies. These trends are probably applicable to most mountainous regions.

Northern Alps

After rain we often get what we call post-frontal weather, with NW flow pushing the air up against the north side of the Alps. On the first day after a frontal passage the cloud cover is thick and there may still be showers on and off. On the second day after the front the conditions will have dried out sufficiently for flying.

The High Mountains

The weather improvement sets in sooner than on the north side but it still takes a while for the moisture to evaporate from the valleys. On the second day of the high pressure the conditions are back to normal.

Southern Alps

The NW flow pushing the clouds up against the flanks of the Northern Alps creates a föhn-like effect on the south side of the Alps. This very dry air removes all moisture very quickly, and the conditions may be good-to-great right from the first day after a frontal passage, in spite of heavy rainfall. Beware of the north wind: if it gets too strong the conditions become dangerous.

If there's no north flow the drying will take longer, similar to the process in the abovementioned regions.

Flatland versus hill country

If there is some wind to help with evaporation then conditions may already be fine on the first day after heavy rains. Cloudbase remains relatively low due to the high water content in the air, but small XC flights should be possible. On bigger hills we may observe a similar effect to the massing of clouds on the north side of the Alps, with overcast skies and some tendency towards rain, but it will be on a smaller scale.

EXPERIENCE The Drautal/Greifenburg in Austria is renowned for developing good flying conditions in spite of having thick, deep cloud in the morning. I have often seen cloudbase hover around the bottom of the ridge in the morning around 8am, only to rise to 1,800m at 11am and have us laughing out loud from 2,700m at 2pm!

4.82 The Zillertal, Austria, after rain. The moisture in the valley is evaporating, forming small, low clouds.

4.83 The same arena as in picture 4.82 but three hours later. It is rare to have the conditions dry out so fast after a frontal passage, and in spite of the promising looks the day was pretty average. Even at its peak the valley wind reached only 20km/h in places where it is often twice as strong.

A classic example of föhn cloud in Austria. Warm, moist air is piling up on the southern side, breaking over the mountain passes and drying out as it descends. Föhn winds were first identified and studied in the Alps, but can can form in all mountain ranges and have local names: Chinook in the Rockies; Ghibli in Libya; and Zonda in the Andes of Argentina.
Photo: Marcus King

5 Clouds and weather

High above Frutigen in the Bernese Oberland, Switzerland. Photo: Jérôme Maupoint

Chapter 5

Clouds and weather

In order to practise paragliding in a safe way some weather knowledge is essential. Knowing a little about clouds, and what they tell us about the current weather situation, is particularly important.

If we can read the clouds correctly we can often tell if the weather is suitable for flying or not, but only the very experienced can predict something meaningful about the development over the next 12 hours just from watching clouds. For this reason understanding basic clouds does not replace the glider forecast, it does however supplement it well.

If my book can help you to become more attuned to the reading of clouds much of what I set out to do with it will have been fulfilled. The WMO Cloud Atlas is a great resource online: cloudatlas.wmo.int

Cloud formations and what they tell us

Cirrus (Ci)

Cirrus occurs when there is turbulence at high altitudes. The turbulence could be caused by large differences in wind direction at different altitudes or by the lifting of one air mass over another as happens when a warm front approaches.

5.1 Isolated cirrus formation.

5.2 Cirrus approaching from the west and covering the skies indicates the arrival of a warm front.

In the Alps the occurrence of isolated Ci coming from easterly directions, as shown in picture 5.1, indicates that the current high pressure influence will remain, or even strengthen in the near future. If the Ci fields are thicker and they are approaching from the west

5.3 Cirrus coming from the southwest. If we look to the north we will see a situation like in picture 5.4. Two days later it was raining on the south side of the Alps and there was a light föhn influence north of the Alps.

5.4 At Speikboden, Alto Adige, Italy. This picture goes with 5.3 and shows the view to the north from the same observation point and time. Photo: Michael Wiedenmann

Table 5.1 The 10 most important cloud types

Name	Abbreviation	Altitude	Remarks
High Clouds	**Prefix 'Cirro'**	**6-11 km**	**Made up of ice crystals**
Cirrus	Ci		Isolated ice-crystal clouds
Cirrocumulus	Cc		High piled (cumulus) clouds
Cirrostratus	Cs		Layer cirrus clouds (stratus=layer)
Mid-level clouds	**Prefix 'Alto'**	**2-6 km**	
Altostratus	As		High layer clouds
Altocumulus	Ac		High piled (cumulus) clouds
Low clouds	**No prefix**	**0-2 km**	
Stratocumulus	Sc		Layer clouds with Cu development
Stratus	St		Layer clouds
Cumulus	Cu	bis 6 km	Thermal cloud
Clouds with great vertical expansion		**0-11 km**	
Nimbostratus	Ns		Rain clouds (nimbo = rain)
Cumulonimbus	Cb		Storm clouds

(picture 5.2) it means that a warm front is approaching, or that we'll soon (within 12-36 hours) find ourselves sitting right under an occlusion. If we have access to a barometer we will also see a decreasing tendency for the air pressure, and finally the increased humidity will cause the cloudbase to lower.

A thick cirrus cover approaching from the southwest means that the high pressure is being replaced by a trough and may indicate the transition to a situation where there will be increased cloud cover on the south side of the Alps and föhn on the north side within the next 24-48 hours.

Cirrocumulus (Cc)

Generally Cc clouds precede warm fronts. They are caused by the general lifting of the oncoming air mass up onto the present one, or by a thickening of already present Ci clouds.

The arrival of Cc clouds indicates an increasing instability in the air mass. As such they may be the first warning of upcoming thunderstorms. They may however also dissolve again and allow the high-pressure situation to remain. If they

5.5 The occurrence of Cc in the skies is a good indicator that the air mass is unstable.

153

appear isolated the latter is the case.

When thick, wavy Cc layers approach from the west a weather deterioration within the next 6-12 hours is on its way; if it is a cold front it may come even faster.

Cirrostratus (Cs)

Cirrostratus forms when a humid air mass gets lifted up, or when cirrus clouds grow thicker.

It generally announces the arrival of a warm front.

Halos can often be visible around the sun or the moon, or you might see a secondary 'sun' next to the normal one (picture 5.8, also called sun dogs) are signs that there will be precipitation soon. If you see a sky like this you can expect the front will arrive in the next 12-24 hours.

Contrails/condensation trails

Contrails are a combination of water droplets from the combustion and sooty particles, produced by jet engines, which form iced particles. Both are necessary for the enriched surrounding air to condense. Caused by the aeroplane as it moves through the air at a certain height band. Humid surrounding air allows the contrails to grow, whereas in dry air they will dissolve rapidly again.

If the contrails remain in the sky long after the plane has passed, and maybe even grow, it is a clear sign that the atmosphere is getting increasingly humid, and that the weather is about to change for the worse. On days when the contrails form, then disappear rapidly again, the high-pressure situation can be expected to continue.

5.6 *In the foreground there are some thin cirrostratus clouds, progressively getting thicker with depth.*

5.8 *Secondary sun visible on the right Cs cloud.*

5.7 *Rapidly thickening cirrostratus clouds are a sign that rain is on the way.*

5.9 *If contrails dissolve again after being formed then this is a sign that the high-pressure influence will continue.*

Altocumulus (Ac)

Altocumulus clouds form when a warmer air mass pushes itself up onto a colder one, through convection or through turbulence in extremely unstable air layers. They may occur when rain clouds dissipate and transform into altocumulus.

The most important thing to know is that Ac fields spreading out are a sure sign that the weather is about to change for the worse. However, if they appear near the perimeter of an intermediary high-pressure they may mean nothing at all!

Minor Ac fields passing through due to the winds at altitude have no impact on the local weather apart from a passing weakening of thermal strength as the ground is shaded out.

Altocumulus lenticularis, lenticular clouds (pictures 5.11 to 5.14 on the next page) are a different kettle of fish altogether. They are the classic föhn indicators. On the north side of the Alps föhn is generally followed by a trough with rain and bad weather, whereas on the south side post-föhn may mean fast improvement.

5.10 *Altocumulus or mackerel sky. As pretty as they are, they are generally messengers of an imminent weather deterioration. This is particularly the case when they are as thick as in this photo, where they indicate a lot of instability at their altitude. The term 'mackerel sky' refers to their fishscale-like appearance.*

5.11 Spectacular lenticularis clouds high above the Alps, from the Kaiser Range, Tyrol, Austria. Direction of view is southwest

5.12 Altocumulus lenticularis

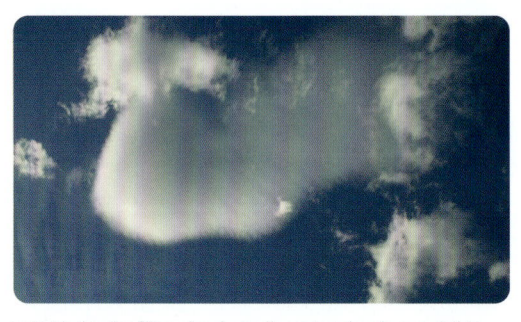

5.13 Under the föhn cloud smaller rotor clouds are visible.

5.14 The lenticular clouds are surely some of the most impressive cloud formations in the skies.

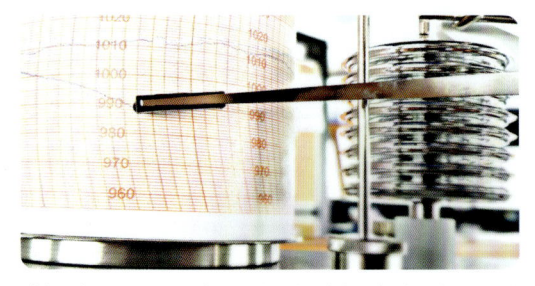

If the air pressure on the north side of the Alps begins to sink rapidly with otherwise sunny weather, this is an indication of föhn winds.

5.15 A cold front announces its arrival with a line of As coming from the NW. In this case a prefrontal föhn situation is keeping the front on hold, but it is a losing battle.

Altostratus clouds (As)

- Signify arrival of cold fronts. The cold air mass pushes under the warmer air already present, causing the warm air to lift and humidity to condense.
- Thick altocumulus may also turn into altostratus.
- Dissipating nimbostratus goes through an As phase before disappearing completely.
- The same goes for decaying cumulonimbus.
- Large fields of incoming As may have been formed elsewhere and blown in by the high-altitude winds.

As a general rule, As clouds indicate the arrival, or the presence of, a poor-weather spell. Thickening As layers are a good indicator that there will be precipitation within the next few hours.

Stratocumulus (Sc)

Stratocumulus clouds form when there is either convection or turbulence in saturated layers at mid levels. They may also be remainders of other cloud forms (nimbostratus or stratus), or they may be Cu's overdeveloping horizontally.

If they look as in picture 5.16 they indicate an oncoming weather

5.16 Stratocumuli indicate a weather improvement with rising pressure and general drying tendencies. In this case the clouds have formed in the warm, humid air behind the receding warm front. Although they look really promising the lift under them will not be sufficient for thermalling as the thermals are very weak.

157

5.17 Bands of stratocumuli. In this case they are the precursor to an approaching cold front.

improvement. There is still plenty of excess humidity around, the cloudbase is low and the thermals still too weak, but the situation is improving.

However, if they look more like the ones in picture 5.17 then there are showers, or at least overcast skies, where they are. Depending on the direction the weather is travelling it may or may not influence our own situation.

Stratus (St)

- High fog fields, as seen in picture 5.18, develop when the ground cools down through radiation, and the overlying air follows suit until the dew point is reached. In the winter this effect may last for days in the Alpine valleys, but above the high fog it may be perfectly flyable!
- Ground-level fog develops in the same way. The only difference is that the fog remains earthbound.
- A cloud shrouding a mountain may also be a stratus cloud.
- Sinking stratocumulus layers (Sc).
- Not a bad sign itself. For the day to turn into a really good one the sun must burn away the stratus fields so that thermals may form.
- If the stratus fields arrive from somewhere else, or if their origin is the sinking of stratocumulus, the weather will deteriorate further and rain will prevail.
- Very thick stratus layers will turn into nimbostratus.

5.18 Stratus layer. In this case as high fog in the Alps. Fog like this can develop and last for days in winter! You can fly safely above it, but visibility will be poor if you sink into it.

5.19 Ground fog, also known as radiation fog, forms due to air being cooled by a cold soil. When the dew point is reached the moisture in the air condenses and fog forms.

Nimbostratus (Ns)

No need for long explanations – it is raining, and the rain will last. Nimbostratus follows days of altocumulus formation caused by the arrival of a warm front. During stationary lows the total nimbostratus cover is the most common view.

5.20 Nimbostratus means rain – and lots of it for longer than we dare to imagine.

5.21 Cumulus clouds. The one in the background already has a well-formed base whereas the front one is still in its forming phase. The eagle shows the way, the pilot follows, with 4m/s (800 ft/min) integrated climb rate.

Cumulus (Cu)

Cumuli are thermal clouds (picture 5.21). Warm air rises, reaches the dew point and moisture condenses to form the cumulus cloud. The drier the air, the higher the cloudbase. When the air contains much moisture the clouds will grow big and wide, and if there's no inversion to stop the development vertically, thunderclouds will form.

Cumulonimbus (Cb)

A cumulus cloud gone mad, continuing to grow because there is no inversion above the dew point to stop it. Thunderstorm clouds also occur along cold fronts where the triggering impulse is the cold air pushing under the warmer air around.

In a way, summer thunderstorm Cb's are a sign that the weather is nice! For some brief moments while the cloud is dumping, flying is absolutely out of the question.

5.22 A summer storm. As the cloud dumps its large quantities of rain or hail, strong vertical wind movements occur. The downdraughts are caused by the falling precipitation hitting the ground and spreading out radially from the impact zone as strong gust fronts with associated turbulence. The cold air pushes under the prevalent warmer summer air and triggers very large areas of lift, possibly forming the next thunderstorm cell. Flying near such clouds is dangerous, both due to the turbulence caused by the gust fronts, the extensive lift and the risk of new Cb's forming right over one's head.

Once the rain has stopped and the Cb dissipated, the weather is usually fine again.

Frontal storms indicate the arrival of a cold front. Cold fronts travel fast and bring strong turbulence, hail, wind and general misery for any pilot still in the air. Picture 5.23 shows one of the wildest cold front arrivals in recent years.

5.23 One of the most powerful cold fronts to hit my home town in recent years. It brought with it extreme hail and strong wind. The only place to be when the sky is like this is on the ground, it's not a good day for flying.

5.24 The transformation of a Cu into a Cb. At the moment the only danger is getting sucked in from beneath, and anyone watching from a distance like the photographer is still perfectly safe. But this may change in minutes.

5.25 A summer storm developing on the east coast of Australia. This shouldn't pose a problem really, as no-one should be in the air with conditions like this. However, if there is a mountain ridge between you and the storm and you can no longer see how it is building, then there's a problem.

Paragliders are insignificant compared to the forces of nature. Always be aware of what weather is building. Photo Tex Beck

What can we learn about the weather from observing the wind?

As a supplement to the personal weather forecasting the winds can give important hints as well.

In the Alps, low clouds coming from the south and high clouds from the northwest indicate a warm-weather spell.

The opposite situation, with low clouds from the northwest and high from southwest, indicates a cold spell.

During high-pressure spells along the northern perimeter of the Alps it is common to have winds gusting with variable strength from the east. If these winds prevail during the entire day the high-pressure will remain in place, but if the wind direction turns to west a period of changeable conditions is due. A decreasing easterly wind at night is a good sign, dry air from Russia with high pressure is coming. But remember,

5.26 *Sustained gusty winds from the east in the northern Alps indicate a prolonged high-pressure situation.*

5.27 *The pilot is waiting for wind to take off. It would be nice if the valley wind reached up to the launch site.*

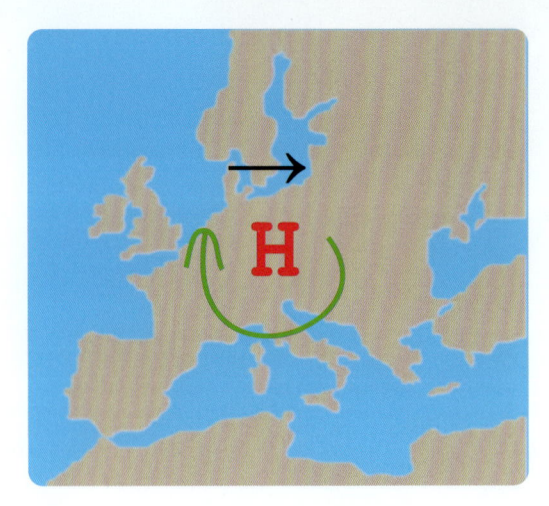

5.28 *The high-pressure travels from west to east, and the wind directions follow clockwise around the centre of the high-pressure. In the Dolomites for instance the winds start around the north turning first east, then south. This entire process takes a couple of days.*

normally east wind days are also turbulent.

During high-pressure days the valley winds will characterise the mountain regions and the sea breeze the coast.

If the wind in the northern hemisphere turns left during the day the weather is about to change to the worse. If the skies clear during this process the situation is defined as an intermediate high-pressure, which rarely lasts very long.

> When we know where the wind is coming from we can also come up with an idea about where the air mass is coming from – and use it for our own forecast.

- The wind strength increases with altitude due to wind gradient. The Coriolis effect causes the wind to turn to the right (northern Hemisphere), by as much as 30-40 degrees in the mountains and 15-20 degrees in the flats.
- So when the wind is turning right, from west to northwest, it means that there is drier air arriving and the skies are about to clear.
- If the wind turns even further, from

5.29 *In the Dolomites the direction of the high winds reveals cloudbase altitude. North and east means dry air and high cloud base whereas southerly directions mean lower cloudbase and imminent rain.*

northwest to north to northeast, we get cool dry air from Russia. Prolonged periods of nice, flyable weather!
- Further turning to the right, from east to south, means the intrusion of humid Mediterranean air. The clear spell is drawing to an end and the cloudbase gets lower.

The Coriolis effect
Named after the French physicist C.G. de Coriolis (1792-1843) who described it in 1835, the Coriolis effect is the observation that an object moving perpendicularly to the rotation of a sphere (for example, moving north or south on the earth which rotates east-west) will not travel in an apparent straight line, but will curve in a specific direction. This is called the Coriolis effect because the wind is not actually changing direction; it's the earth that's moving below it. Thanks to the Coriolis effect all winds in the Northern Hemisphere are diverted towards the right, and in the Southern Hemisphere towards the left.

- From south to west means the air is coming from the Atlantic again. Humid air and rain.
- Strengthening wind from the west tells us of the arrival of the next frontal system.
- If during prolonged periods of rain the wind suddenly increases, the weather is just about to improve.

Note: All these rules are for Alpine pilots. There is a good chance that something similar is observable at your home sites, all you need to do is to pay attention, take notes and maybe discuss things with more experienced colleagues.

When the situation is normal, the high winds in the Alps are turned 30-40 degrees to the right by the combination of Coriolis effect and ground drag. However, if we observe a greater diversion than these 30-40 degrees it is a sign that there is an influx of warmer air up high, which will cause the thermal activity to slow down or even stop if the thermals are weak. This can be a good thing on very unstable days where the risk of overdevelopment is great – the stabilising effect of the warm-air influx puts a lid on things and keeps the day flyable for longer.

If the high-altitude winds are diverted left instead of right it means that there is an influx of cold air up high, a so-called cold-air advection. This makes the atmosphere increasingly unstable so that the thermal activity increases; thermals get stronger and last long into the evening. Under these circumstances even a small ray of sunlight is enough to trigger a good thermal. Up to a point such cold-air advection is our friend, but if it becomes strong the conditions will quickly overdevelop and the flying will be shut down.

5.30 Cold-air advection in the Pustertal, Austria. The last rays of the day generate surprisingly usable thermals, and the visibility is spectacular.

Central European weather scenarios

Central Europe is located more or less exactly at the southern extreme of the polar air mass influence. This means that the troughs pass right through; sometimes a bit further north, sometimes a bit further south, but generally influencing the weather we get. This is the reason for

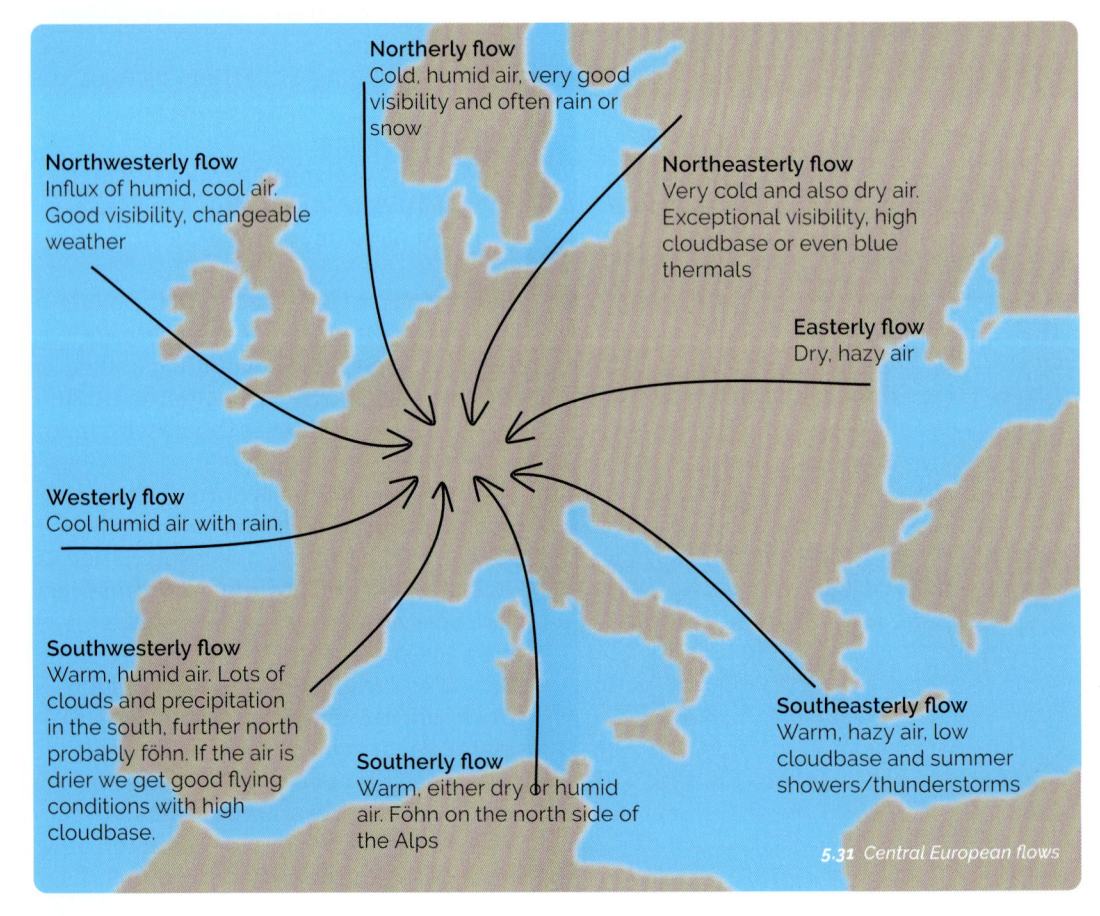

Northerly flow
Cold, humid air, very good visibility and often rain or snow

Northwesterly flow
Influx of humid, cool air. Good visibility, changeable weather

Northeasterly flow
Very cold and also dry air. Exceptional visibility, high cloudbase or even blue thermals

Easterly flow
Dry, hazy air

Westerly flow
Cool humid air with rain.

Southwesterly flow
Warm, humid air. Lots of clouds and precipitation in the south, further north probably föhn. If the air is drier we get good flying conditions with high cloudbase.

Southerly flow
Warm, either dry or humid air. Föhn on the north side of the Alps

Southeasterly flow
Warm, hazy air, low cloudbase and summer showers/thunderstorms

5.31 Central European flows

the changeable weather patterns we get. Sometimes we get polar air from the north, then a teaspoon of high pressure from the Azores. In the following illustration the different situations, and their likely consequences, are described.

Dangerous weather

If we disregard collisions due to poor visibility there are really only two weather-related dangers to paraglider and hang glider pilots:

1. Strong winds
2. Turbulence

Hang gliders can be flown faster than paragliders and therefore have an advantage. Compared to, for example, sailplanes the advantage is however quite small, so in the following we shall not discern between hang- and paragliders. Sailplanes are often able to fly around, or escape from, summer showers or cold front shower lines, whereas we really don't stand a chance.

Strong wind and turbulence may be caused by a number of factors

- **Summer- or frontal storms**, with all their associated troubles, gust fronts, extreme climb rates and strong precipitation. Beware of uncontrollable turbulence resulting from all this.
- **Cold front passages**, with high winds and strong turbulence.
- **All downdraughts as they occur in the Alps: föhn, bise, mistral and bora.** All are characterised by high wind speeds and the turbulence that follows. Simply put, strong winds mean strong turbulence. Every area has its own protected enclaves and the experienced pilot knows where to go and when to find flyable conditions in spite of a generally unflyable forecast. Note that this is a risky game as all downdraughts may suddenly break into a normally protected valley.
- **Stronger winds higher up.** In the glider forecasts they speak of 'turbulence at peak altitude'. This is not to be taken lightly.
- **Turbulence caused by thermals.** These may become very strong at times and beginners disregard this at their own peril. Hang gliders don't normally collapse but the bar may be torn out of the pilot's hands in extreme cases, or the wing may tuck. Collapses as such are not dangerous on paragliders but in extreme turbulence they may soon become dangerous.
- **Wind sheer** is generally not as turbulent as strong thermals. When two strong winds meet, and mix with some thermal turbulence, it may nonetheless become too much for us.
- **Compression.** Strongish but flyable winds may double when blowing through passes or restrictions. A

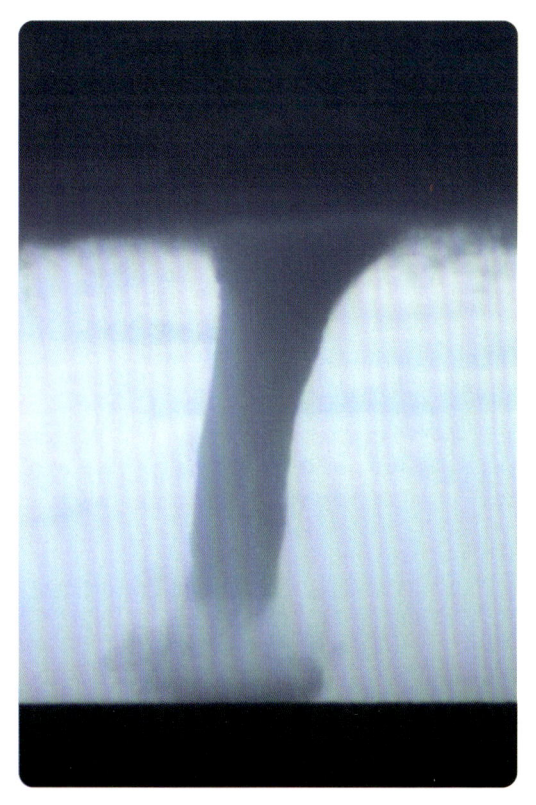

5.32 *This photo was taken from the beach in Sardinia, Italy, off the coast of Alghero. The power of such weather phenomena should not be taken lightly.*

5.33 *The clouds clearly indicate a strong wind from the left.*

strong but flyable wind may rapidly become anything but flyable when this happens, so we need to avoid venturis
- **Flying in the lee** is always riskier than remaining on the windward side of obstacles. Depending on the conditions, lee turbulence may rapidly become unmanageable, see illustrations 3.22 and 3.23, page 89-90.

Strong wind = Strong turbulence

5.34 *Trees and leaves also reveal the strength of the wind.*

5.35 *Playing with the wind in a Sirocco wind, when a southerly wind carries dust across the Mediterranean Sea from the Sahara desert to the French Alps. A relatively rare occurrence caused by southerly storms. Photo: Pierre Augier*

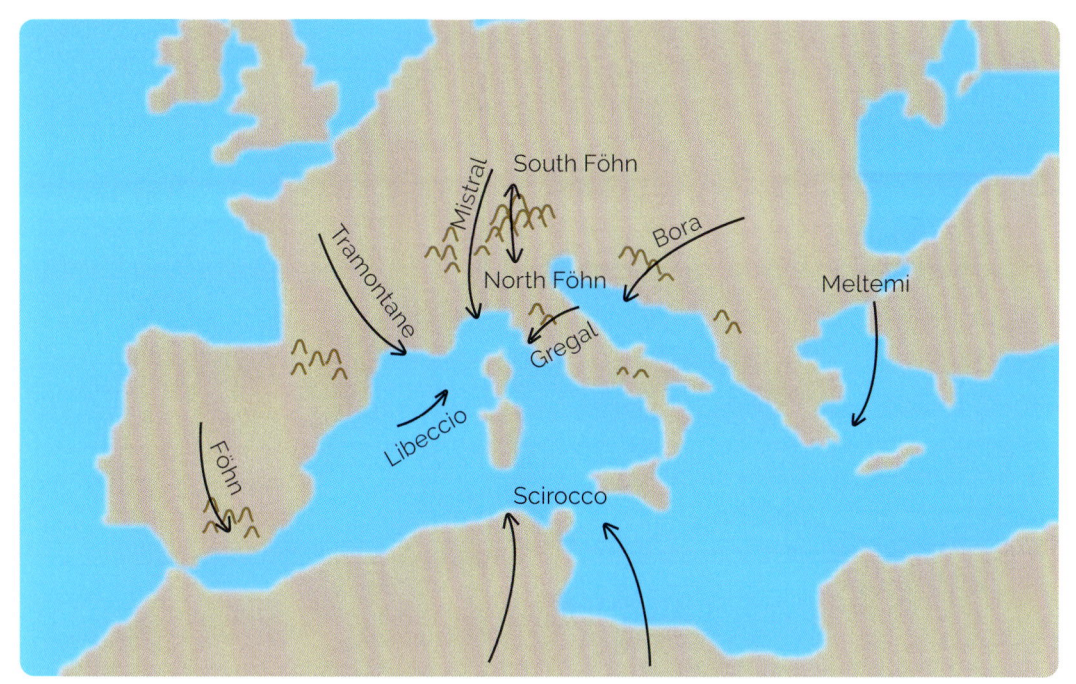

5.36 Well-known winds in Europe and around the Mediterranean Sea. The most universally known downdraught is the föhn but all strong winds cause dangerous turbulence in the lee of mountains. There will always be protected valleys or areas but there are no guarantees – if the wind speed increases it may also break into areas previously thought to be sheltered. The glider forecasts speak of 'peak level turbulence' and mean it!

Picture 5.37 *Soaring on the island of Madeira. When flying near the sea we can easily follow the wind strength development by looking at the surface. If the surface is calm we continue to fly. Once the first whitecaps appear the wind has increased to about 20km/h (11kn), and when the whitecaps become abundant it is time to land! The clever pilot does not concentrate only on the water near their landing but looks far out to sea in order to get a longer warning of things to come. Photo: Skywalk*

6 Thermal centring techniques

Gaggle flying at the Paragliding World Cup, Bassano, Italy

Chapter 6
Thermal centring techniques

We've all heard some hotshot telling stories of how he cored the thermal and spiralled up inside the narrow core. Let it be said right away, this is a bit of an exaggeration; it does however capture the feeling one gets while doing it rather well.

When thermalling in large even lift we try to circle as flat as we can to minimise the descent (all wings descend more in a turn than when going straight), whilst in strong, narrow lift we need to remain inside the core and our own descending becomes less relevant, so the bank angle is increased.

However, at all times it pays to fly with the least possible descent rate to optimise the climbing. On modern paragliders minimum sink is at trim speed. We then increase the brake input somewhat on the inner side while weightshifting into the turn as well – flat, efficient turns should be the result.

The weightshifting causes the wing to distort along the centre cell – we get the well-known little 'step' in the top surface. The step causes a skewing of the total lift vector over to the weightshifted side, and it is this skewing that makes the wing turn.

Thermals are rarely totally smooth. But sometimes we do come across homogenous, strong cores – bubbles with 6 to 8m/s (1,200 to 1,600ft/min) climb rates have been centred this way in a really smooth manner. Too bad that such situations are the exception.

> The general rule of thumb is:
> Strong thermals = strong turbulence

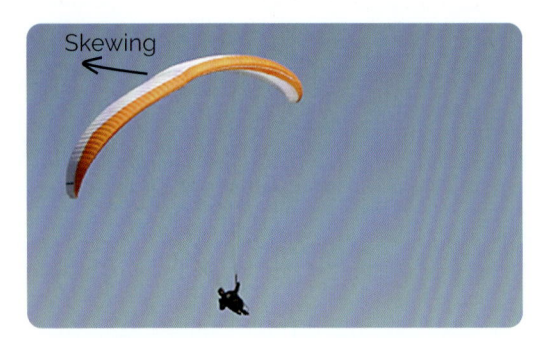

6.2 *Coring together in harmony – at 180 degrees to each other, turning flat and efficiently and approaching cloudbase with a friend.*

6.1 *Weightshift causes the wing to distort along the centre cell. This in turn causes a skewing of the total lift vector over to the weightshifted side, and it is this skewing that makes the wing turn.*

6.3 *If everybody makes room for everybody else and flies with them instead of against them, then stress in the air can be avoided. You can often observe this in competitions where up to 100 pilots share the same thermal and fly large radius turns. From below it looks chaotic, but it is often more relaxing than flying an overcrowded site such as Kössen or Andelsbuch, where you're never sure how well the hobby pilots are watching.*

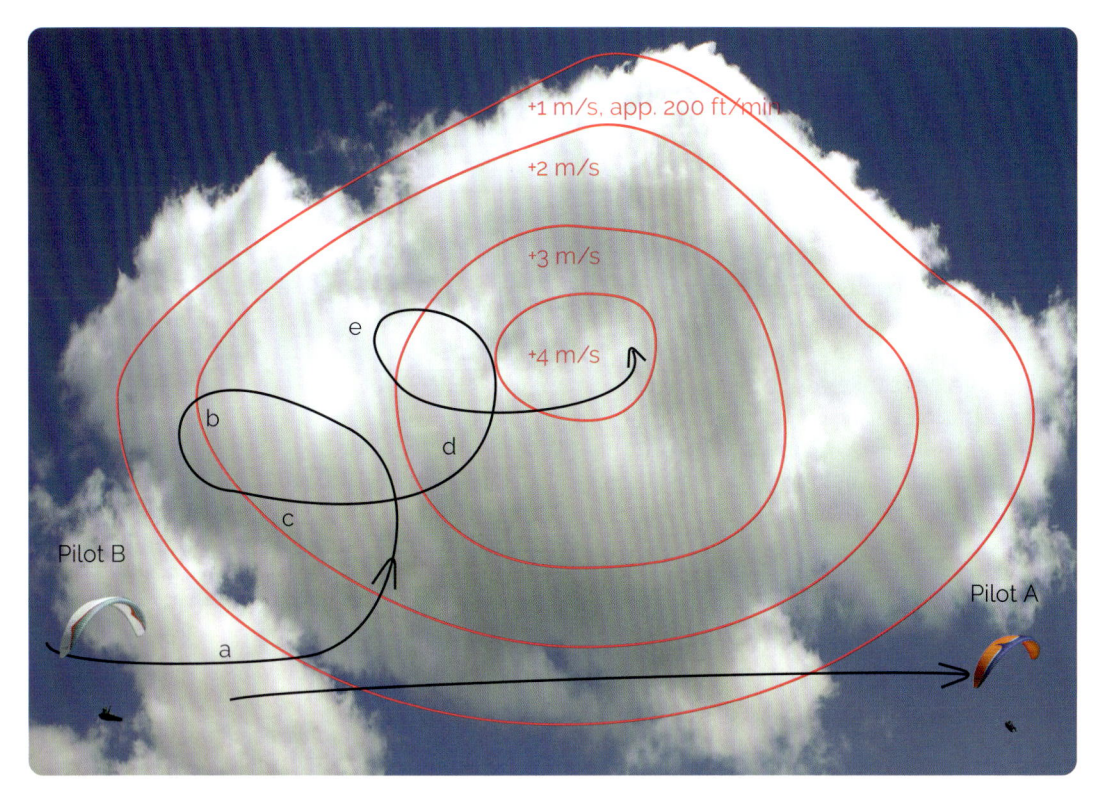

6.4 Efficient coring made easy. If the climb rate decreases, turn tighter (back to where you came from). If the climb rate increases, open up the turn. If the climb rate is constant, maintain the curve – unless someone else is climbing better nearby!

How to find the best lift

In illustration 6.4 the core of the thermal has climb rates of about 4m/s and is situated approximately in the middle of the thermal column, with the climb rates progressively decreasing towards the edges. If a pilot enters the lift zone without turning, eventually he will exit again – just as is the case for pilot A in the illustration. While crossing the thermal pilot A will have felt one side of his wing lifting more than the other, because this side was in the better lift – he will have been sitting somewhat askew in his harness.

To efficiently use the thermal, the pilot must turn towards the side that produces more lift – just as pilot B does at a. After a short while pilot B, with the help of his vario, feels that the lift is getting weaker so he is about to leave the better part of the thermal (at b) and he immediately turns hard to get back into the good lift (c). By now the vario will be getting progressively louder and pilot B opens up his turn somewhat (at d) in order to explore the size of this better climb. He just misses the best core, flies out of the good stuff at e, and turns sharply to get back in – and in

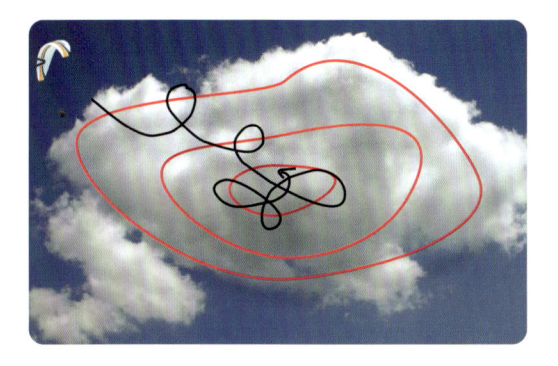

6.5 The method described here always works, even when we have initially turned the wrong way. In this illustration the pilot has missed the good core three times but still finds it eventually, simply by using the technique described above.

171

this attempt hits the 4m/s core! Now he knows how much to expect and can turn as sharply as is needed to remain in the core.

There is a reason why the big raptors always circle in thermals; it is the most efficient way. Never attempt to fly figure-eights, always make your course adjustments carefully, without too much impulse, fly the circles cleanly without sharp edges, because edges mean increased descending. Never brake too much – the wing climbs best when flown at minimum sink, which with most modern paragliders means at trim speed.

Summary – finding the best lift
Climb rate decreasing > turn tighter
Climb rate increasing > open up the turn
Climb rate remains constant > circle radius should also remain constant

HINT When I encounter lift while flying straight I always keep flying straight until the lift begins to decrease again, then I turn into the wind for my first circle.

Upwind and downwind sides of the thermal

On no-wind days there is no lee and no upwind side to a thermal. But as soon as we get any wind, the best climbs are usually to be found upwind, nearer the windward side of the thermal. Besides, falling out of a thermal on the upwind side is far preferable to falling out the downwind – simply turn back and fly with a tailwind into the thermal again.

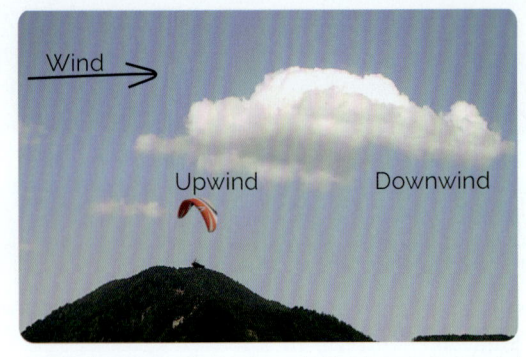

6.6 Climb rates are almost always better closer to the upwind side of a thermal.

Total Energy Compensation

Most modern varios have a Total Energy Compensation (TEC) setting where we can filter out the 'lift' caused only by changes in our velocity. If we fly fast and then brake hard, some of the excess energy is converted into altitude and we might think that we have encountered a great thermal. Setting the TEC of the vario correctly can filter out such 'fake thermals'.

*6.7 A high-end modern vario with TEC options built in
Photo: Marcus King*

HINT If I am flying with a tailwind and encounter lift I will normally start my first circle quite soon after entering the lift, to stay in the better, upwind part of the thermal. On the other hand, when entering lift while flying with a headwind I keep going straight for longer in the hope that I go all the way into the juicy upwind section of the thermal.

In front of steep faces you need less wind to successfully soar. Gréolières, France. Photo: Charlie King

Important thermalling insights

Do not change turn direction

Every time we turn we must re-centre, and all the changing of bank angles confuses the vario so that it may beep where there's no lift and give sink alarm where there's no increased sink – only when the circles are smooth once more, can the vario be relied upon again.

Hang gliders flying with both a speed probe and a TEC vario are better able to filter all this noise, whereas on paragliders the speed sensor gets too much pendulum effect to be reliable during changes of turn direction.

HINT Sometimes you end up battling to get in to a thermal against its 'internal' wind – compare with picture 1.31 on page 43, pilot B. You see that you are climbing, but don't feel you've made it to the core. If you start a turn, then you fall out of the thermal immediately. When this happens, you should continue to fly straight on for much longer than usual before beginning to turn, on your next attempt to core the thermal.

Circle radius changes should be undertaken really smoothly

Let's take an example: the pilot has done a full circle, but half the circle was flown in 2m/s lift and the other half had 3m/s. The next circle he will attempt to move a little further in the direction of the stronger lift, *without* big control inputs. Perhaps he is now able to do three-quarters of a circle in 3m/s – so the next circle is again moved a bit off to the side where the stronger lift is.

If this does not improve the situation, the thermal is too narrow for a full circle at the present turning radius, and it probably pays to tighten up the circle somewhat. Note: 1 m/s is approx. 200 ft/min (see conversion table in the front)

When to turn tight and when to turn flat?

When thermalling, the objective for most pilots is getting up as fast and efficiently as possible. To do this we fly with as little descent as we can, however at min. descent we can't tighten the turn very much. We often encounter stronger cores that are too small to remain in if we keep turning as flat as we can. In these cases it may be worthwhile to increase bank and accept

6.8 If the thermal core is very narrow the pilot must fly tight circles with plenty of bank angle. This is often the case down low, whilst higher up the thermal will generally expand and thus become easier to centre. The photo shows the good flying site Werfenweng/Bischling, Austria.

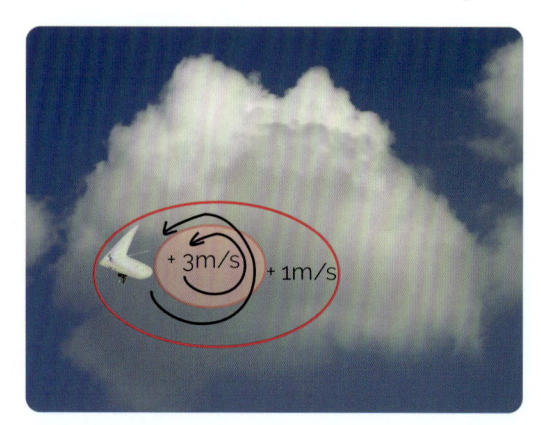

6.9 If the thermal core is small and strong we can optimise our climbing by sacrificing some of our descent rate in order to remain in the stronger core. This is done by increasing the bank angle and turning tighter. Mostly it is better to turn tight. 'Tight' means making a full 360-degree-turn in 15-18 seconds.

the higher descent rate involved, simply to stay in the stronger core. The higher bank angle also loads up the wing more and makes it more resistant to collapses, and finally remaining in a homogenous air mass is usually more comfortable than flying in and out of strong lift all the time.

Having said that, some cores simply are too small to do a full circle in them regardless of the bank angle. To optimise our climb under these circumstances we may be forced to fly in and out of the cores – we then try to get as much as possible of our circle inside the strong core. A further advantage to turning tight in stronger lift is that it is easier to orient oneself when not losing the core all the time.

In the beginning it is difficult to know exactly when it pays to increase the bank and decrease the turning radius. The vario and experience help a lot! If you have the opportunity you can easily practise using a different turn radius for different thermal strengths – the vario beeps will tell you which angle is the most efficient for your thermal.

What to do when you keep falling out of the side of a thermal?

The first thing to reflect upon is whether you fell out on the lee side or on the windward side. In both cases you need to turn around quickly, but if you fell out on the lee side the next turn should be a big, open, searching one, whereas if you fell out on the windward side it is usually enough to get back in and immediately bank up sharp again.

If finding the thermal again is proving difficult, try to be alert to even the slightest variations in sink rate. If your sink rate is decreasing, expand the circle in that direction; if your sink rate is increasing, then turn around and search in the opposite direction.

If you fall out on the lee side in strong winds it may not be worthwhile searching for too long against the wind, as there will surely be increased sink right next to the thermal and it can be quite hard to get through this and back into the thermal.

If you were going with the wind anyway, and there seem to be other options near by, you may want to consider just heading for them instead. Especially downwind it can be quicker.

> **EXPERIENCE** I like to core very tightly. Mostly I climb better this way. I only turn large flat circles in big weak thermals.

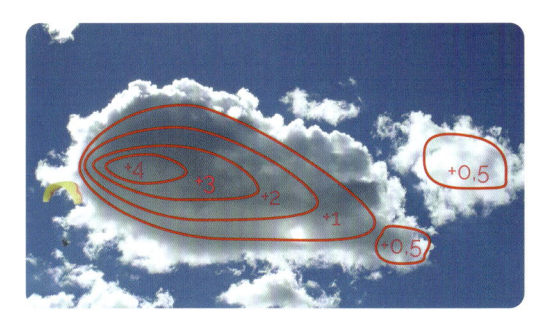

6.10 The core of the thermal is almost always closer to the upwind side. If we're coming from the leeward side we continue to fly straight until the lift decreases – this will take a while, as we're both travelling against the wind and have to fly further. When coming from the windward side (the yellow glider) we start turning almost immediately after hitting lift. If the lift is looking like this thermal we can expect to work hard to remain in the core.

6.11 Having some flying mates around makes thermalling much easier, especially on blue days. When someone loses the thermal he can quickly relocate it simply by joining the others! This photo shows a blue day in Quixadá, Brazil; climbing in the house thermal near take-off.

Flatland thermalling

Generally the tactics for flatland thermalling are not that different to mountain thermalling. Differences occur due to wind drift. If you circle continuously without re-centring then you will fall out of the lee of the thermal; if you straighten your upwind leg too much, then you'll fall out of the front.

It's important not to lose a thermal. This prompts the question: What should I do if I lose a thermal?

The answer: Search for it again, find it and centre it properly!

Never fly on further when you're low – flatland pilots have fewer chances of getting a low save than mountain flyers. Observe the wind currents particularly carefully – is one wingtip being lifted more than the other? Are you getting pulled to the centre? Follow drifts and currents immediately.

HINT Flatland flying appeals more and more to me. It's different, trigger points are not as easy to identify, coring a thermal is more difficult, you bomb out a lot, but with perseverance you learn what to do and then it begins to become real fun!

EXPERIENCE During flatland flying in Turkey I often fell out of the lee of thermals. By consequently flying against the wind (often for long periods) I managed to find the thermals again. On occasion I was flying in winds of over 40km/h. Thermal drift was so extreme at the bottom, I could hardly believe it. In a weak thermal I covered 30km just trying to centre properly!

6.12 Flying coach and SIV instructor Jocky Sanderson compares thermals to a rising tablecloth in his excellent film Performance Flying (available to watch in chapters on YouTube – search "Jocky Sanderson" to find his channel).

If you fly directly towards the centre, then you first note an increase in speed as you are sucked in. Flying alongside, you feel a side pull to the centre. If you follow this pull, and turn to go with it, then you'll usually find the thermal core. Initially a thermal has often a strong drift component, which only reduces higher up, when climb rates increase.

Mountain thermals also pull to their cores, but due to the relief the large drift component at the bottom is often less.

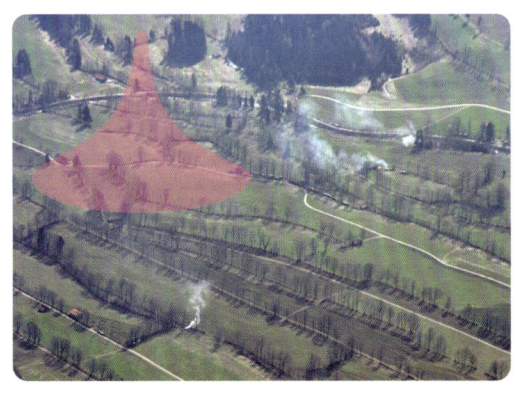

6.13 Converging smoke trails demonstrate the tablecloth thermal model. In this picture note that all the smoke trails are flowing up to the left corner of the picture – this is where I managed to core the thermal and climb out.

HINT In my book Cross Country Flying I have written a detailed chapter on flatland flying.

Flatland flying in Andalucia, Spain. Photo: Jérôme Mapoint

Cores of different strengths next to each other

If a long ridgeline is facing into the sun, the entire slope may produce lift as one very large lifting area with many different embedded cores. The cores will often have different climb rates, depending on the area that feeds them.

Let us take a hypothetical example. Two thermals form close to each other, one has three degrees excess temperature compared to the surrounding air, the other only two. The former will obviously rise faster, and if

> **HINT** When flying XC you need to have a good understanding of the maximum available altitude on the day, regardless of it being a blue or a cloudy one. This knowledge will help you to decide if it pays to spend time searching for that thermal you just lost, or you should rather be heading along. If you lose it close to the max. altitude and you're not just about to go on a big transition, by all means just continue instead of wasting any more time searching.

> **HINT** If a pilot nearby is riding the express elevator we must join them as soon as possible. When flying with other pilots I often wonder why so few join me when I locate something good.

we're on the slower one it pays to mover over to the faster rising thermal – provided we know of it, which we can only do if someone else nearby is climbing faster than we are.

If the better thermal is further away it may not pay to move to it – not only do we lose time and altitude on the way there, we also lose time locating the best core in the new one. However, if the better thermal is on our intended course line I have actually often been lucky while gliding from one core to another one, by finding an even better one on the way there!

But assuming there wasn't such a new bonanza thermal on the way, the whole process of changing thermals will usually cost more than it gains in terms of rapid height gain. Besides, thermal cores often tend to join into one big core higher up – if that is the case then it is often possible to expand the search radius within the thermal in order to join the better core.

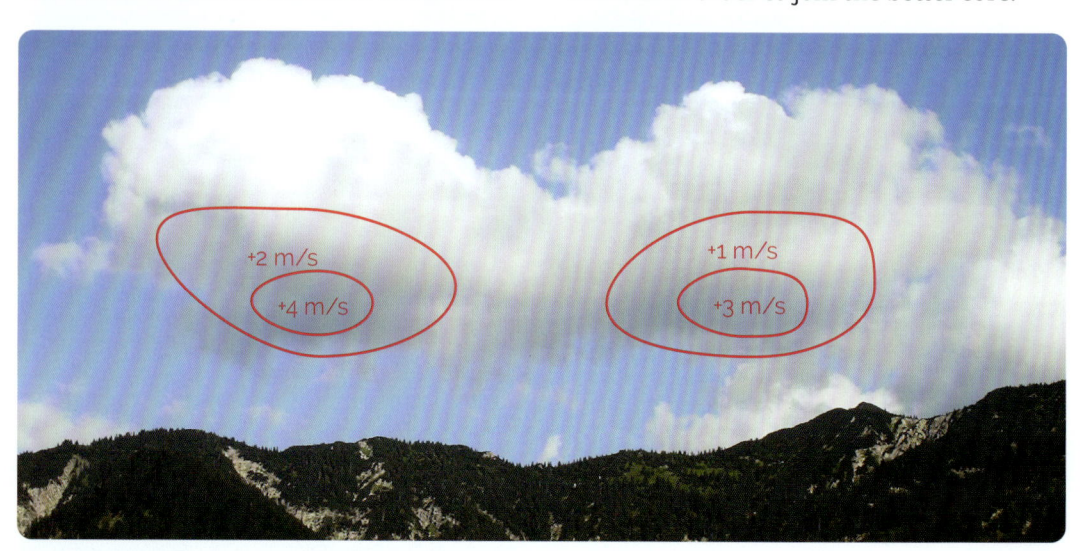

6.14 When thermals of varying strength are located close to each other it pays to move from a weaker to a stronger one. If however the distance between them is greater than a short glide it will often be better to stay in the one you have – mostly the climb rates start to equalise higher anyway.

Brief Summary
If everybody is in comparable lift, some slightly stronger, some weaker, changing core is not worth it. But if the invisible hand suddenly plucks someone close by up, move there immediately!

EXPERIENCE Once while thermalling in front of the notorious Wank in Garmisch-Partenkirchen (Germany) I finally found a good core which gave me 5m/s integrated climbing. I stayed with it until about 300m beneath cloudbase where I headed out – or so I thought. Instead I flew right into the proper core, which was no less than 10m/s! If only someone had been in it I could have seen it a lot earlier.

HINT When circling in a weak thermal I am very aware of everything in the surrounding air that may point to a better climb. This can be other pilots, birds, leaves, dust, spiderwebs, anything really. As soon as something is going up faster than me, I go there. In strong thermals my strategy is different – there I simply concentrate on optimising my climb.

6.15 If a pilot is climbing faster than another in the same thermal it may be due to the vortex effect described in picture 1.17. In any case one of the pilots must now reverse his turn direction, and in this case where the lower pilot came last he should do it. Photo: Peter Rummel

Reversing the turn direction in a thermal

This is something that should generally be avoided as we always join an already existing gaggle by turning in the same direction, however there are situations where reversing is inevitable. Let´s say two cores join, each with their gaggle of pilots in them turning opposite ways, or a gaggle dissolves, then joins forces again albeit turning the opposite way this time.

These are just examples of situations where there's no avoiding a turn direction reversal.

The clever reversal method

Thermals drift with the wind, and in narrow thermals it can be tricky to do a direction reversal without falling out of the side. The trick is to move to the upwind side, where falling out of the side is less critical.

Falling out of the downwind side is only critical in strong winds and strong thermals, as can be seen from the track C in illustration 6.16 on the next page.

EXPERIENCE Once in a comp I got it just right and could use the vortex ring to catch up to a gaggle above me very fast. Unfortunately I had to reverse my turn direction and, during the reversal I fell out of the lee side of the thermal. I quickly lost 500m and felt very frustrated. Nowadays I always take care to position myself right before doing something like this.

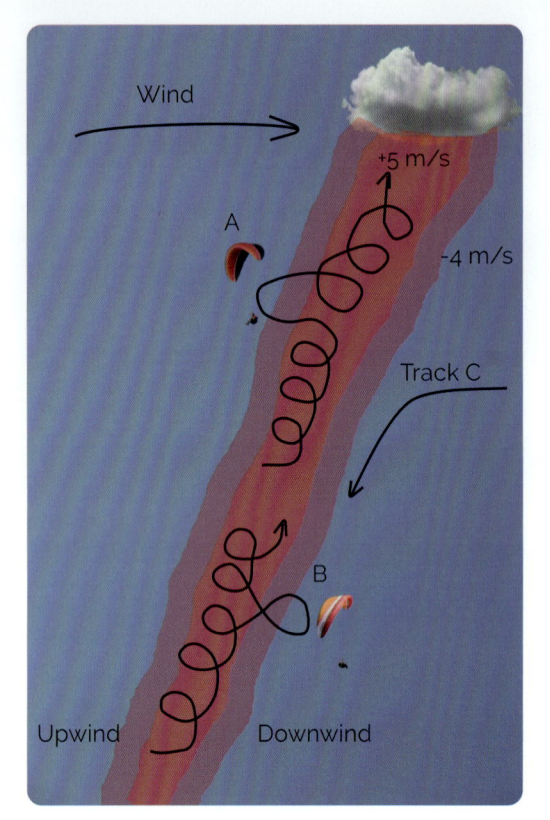

6.16 *Cross section of a windblown thermal. Pilot A is turning left then flies out the upwind side to reverse his turn direction. From there he flies with a tailwind back into the thermal, with minimal altitude loss.*

Pilot B does her reversal on the lee side and must battle a headwind to get back into the thermal. If the wind and thermal are strong however, this might not be possible. Instead the pilot will find themselves flying the track as in C. This is pushing against the wind to re-join the thermal but being flushed in the sink just downwind of it. Turn and run!

If there's no wind there's also no upwind and downwind, so a turn-reversal may be done anywhere.

Bouncing off the side of a thermal

If we approach a strong thermal head on our wing gets pitched back, sometimes very much so. Hang gliders pull in to accelerate whilst paragliders release the brakes to counter this back-pitching motion – but hang gliders are far more efficient at this, and in extreme cases paragliders may even enter a deep stall. If this happens, the pilot must first solve the deep stall (see page 21), then decide the next course of action. There are several possibilities:

1. To fly somewhere else – this thermal is too strong to be fun anyway. Beginners should always choose this option.
2. Try to enter again, this time flying at higher speed - ½ speed bar is usually enough. Chances are we'll get in this time, but we may suffer an asymmetrical collapse in the process.
3. Fly around the thermal and try to enter it from the other side.

Wind shear

Even good pilots struggle with wind shears. It is simply not easy to climb in conditions where there are wind shears,

6.17 *Sometimes the wing may be pitched back quite far when it meets the rising air inside the thermal. In extreme cases paragliders may enter a deep-, or even a full stall, due to this pitching motion. If this happens, first solve the problem, and then consider if this thermal is ok for you.*

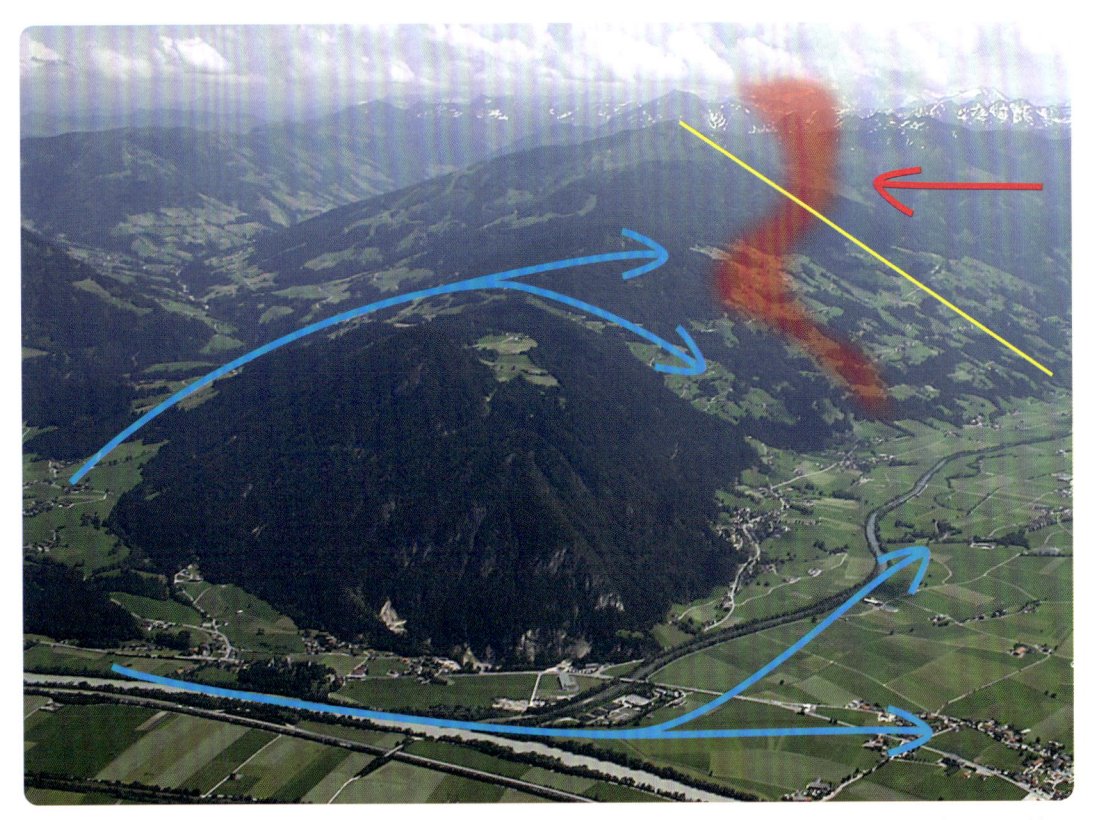

6.18 *The entrance to the Zillertal Valley, Austria. In the afternoon the valley wind flows over the low ridge in the foreground from the left (blue arrow). Thermals may still form on the lee side and get pushed towards the middle of the valley. Once they get higher they encounter the higher-altitude winds (red arrow) and are pushed in a new direction. On days when the valley wind is strong the lee side of the small mountain gets dangerous due to rotor – and the thermals are totally blown apart as well. A late XC pilot coming from the Achensee may still make the crossing provided his altitude is sufficient to arrive above the yellow line, where the mountains are high enough to be above the valley wind influence. Blue line: valley wind; red line: wind at altitude.*

the thermals get broken and are often weak. To get through, one must use all the tricks in the book, take every little puff of lift and feel one's way around the air with all senses on full alert. Once through, you are rewarded by good climb rates again.

Lets take an example: there's not much wind at any level, but around 2,500m there's a noticeable wind shear. We have already bounced off it several times, getting to the same altitude then losing the lift.

Next time we open up our search pattern somewhat in order to try and locate the thermal again, all the time looking for nature's subtle hints, like butterflies, cobwebs, leaves and birds. It is easy to think that the thermal won't go any higher, but perhaps there's cloudbase way above, giving evidence to the opposite.

If this is the case, or if there are pilots up above the difficult layer, it gets easier. Simply try to visualise which cloud belongs to which thermal and draw an imaginary line between them – that is the area where the thermal should be.

HINT If I'm all alone in the air and encounter difficult climbs like the one mentioned above, I sometimes close my eyes in order to be able to concentrate 100% on feeling the air and listening to the vario.

HINT Most pilots tend to look at the ground while thermalling, especially when they are low. This allows them to monitor the drift quite accurately – if the thermal is drifting it is easy to see on the ground. But there may be wind shears changing the drift direction, and following a thermal through these can be really hard if you're looking at the ground. Instead, I try to pretend that I'm really high and simply concentrate on feeling the thermal. This works well for me!

HINT Low down all thermals suck in air from their surroundings. The attentive pilot will notice this lateral movement of the air, both by watching their GPS and by feel. If you feel that you're being pulled in a certain direction, go with the flow and you'll find the thermal! Higher up the opposite is the case – before encountering a thermal we'll generally feel a slight headwind combined with increased descent rates – all due to the vortex ring structure of the thermal column.

HINT If we don't keep concentrating on centring the thermal we will normally fall out of the lee side. The reason for this is that the wind pushes us slightly more than it pushes the thermal, so if we just make perfectly round circles we will eventually fall outside the lifting area

Rules for sharing thermals

Thermal flying has its own etiquette that is important to know and to apply:

- The pilot who finds the thermal decides which way to turn in it

- The right-hand pilot has right of way

- The faster climbing pilot has right of way

The middle one has the interesting implication that if we join a gaggle turning left then they must give way to us! Since nobody likes to be pushed out of a thermal by a newcomer it is however much better to join in the way shown in illustration 6.19 on the right: slot in behind a pilot when you can see the back of their head.

EXPERIENCE Beginners often know no better and violate the etiquette mentioned above – make sure you are not one of them.

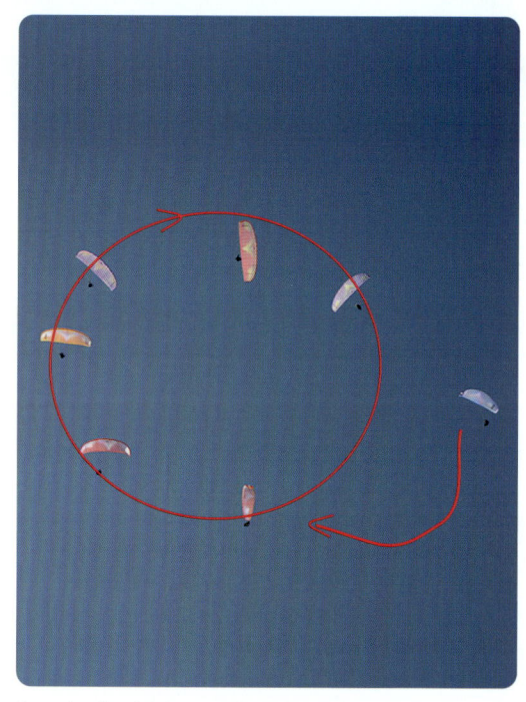

6.19 *A pilot joining a gaggle of thermalling colleagues should never insist on their right of way. It is much better to do a gentle curve that allows us to slot into the open space. Always bear in mind that if it wasn't for this gaggle we might never have found the thermal in the first place! If everybody behaved like this in thermals we could avoid many dangerous situations and bad feelings between pilots.*

Climbing well together to the wispies near Laragne in southern France. Photo: Marcus King

Paragliders can't see much behind and below themselves. They can core really tight.

Hang gliders can't see anything above themselves. They also have the ability to core tightly, however their speed in the thermals is higher.

Sailplane pilots can't see anything beneath them. They fly very fast (around 100km/h when thermalling) and can't turn so tight.

6.21 Sailplane pilots have excellent outlook forwards and upwards, but little or none downwards and towards the back. Thermal with them as you would a paraglider or hang glider..

Thermalling with different types of aircraft

It is not uncommon to be sharing a thermal with hang gliders, paragliders and sailplanes. To avoid conflict and danger, all parties involved should understand the specific limitations of each other aircraft involved.

When paraglider and hang gliders share a thermal with sailplanes it makes things easier for all if the former turn relatively tight so that the sailplane(s) may circle around them. If someone has to reverse turn direction, politeness dictates that it should be the textile pilots as sailplanes need *very* big thermals to reverse without falling out.

Due to the enormous performance advantage of sailplanes they are unlikely to share your thermal for long anyway, as they generally spot something better far away in the distance and just hightail it over there.

When thermalling together with one of 'the others' always keep his visibility

HINT The following rule of thumb is useful for ballast calculations: 5kg extra ballast gives a speed increase of 1km/h.

6.20 When sharing a thermal with more pilots it pays to adjust the angle between you so that the individual distance is maximised. If three pilots are sharing, they should be at 120 degrees to each other, if four are sharing they reduce the angle to 90 degrees etc.

6.22 If two pilots are sharing a strong, narrow core they must look out for each other all the time. The best way to manage this situation is to place oneself directly opposite the other pilot, at 180 degrees. Then keep a constant eye on each other as you turn. Also see photo 6.2 on p170.

6.23 When paragliders and hang gliders share lift it is preferable that the hang glider turns somewhat more widely than the paraglider – this way they don't change positions among themselves all the time, as would be the case if their radius was the same.

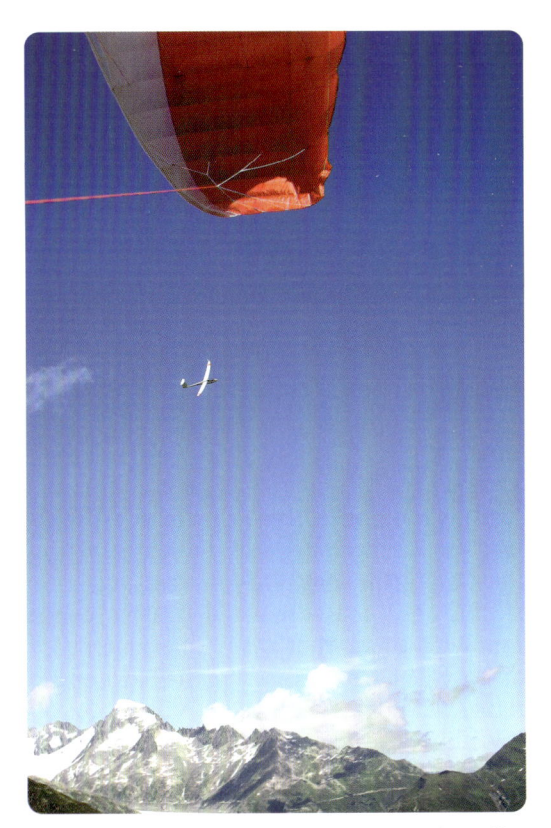

6.24 In this shot both paraglider and sailplane are thermalling in a way where they are always in each other's line of sight. This is a good way to avoid trouble. As paragliders can turn tighter, they may find a stronger core and climb faster, closing the gap between the two.

limitations in mind. Avoid placing yourself in his blind spot.

Paragliders fly somewhat slower than hang gliders, so if the hang glider makes a slightly larger circle you will both need about the same amount of time to do a complete 360. Some say that it is easier for the paraglider pilot to adjust his radius, so it follows that the responsibility to do so is mainly his. The hang glider should remain constant to help the paraglider adapt. The same can be said for sharing lift with sailplanes.

If it gets too crowded for your comfort, simply fly out and let the others climb past you for a bit then rejoin the core of the thermal below them – it is only a problem when several pilots are at the same altitude.

6.25 Paragliders and a sailplane thermalling in opposite directons. The paragliders are higher, so there is no real problem. But if they were at the same height the paragliders should change direction. Goms, Switzerland.
Photo: Advance

> **EXPERIENCE** Once on an XC flight I ran into a big gaggle of competition pilots battling it out. I flew with them for a while as our courses were the same, but whenever I could feel them getting all too aggressive I left them alone for a bit – their stress levels were surely much higher than mine, since I was only out to enjoy myself.

Flying without a vario

Good pilots can fly almost as well without a vario as with, and many make a point of turning it off once in a while to hone their feel and intuition instead of always relying 100% on technology. This is excellent training as it forces one to use all the other fantastic senses that nature has given us, and if we never do it we may feel lost or naked as soon as the vario is off.

Without the help of the vario, sensing the air must be felt with the bottom instead of heard with the ears. Feeling the changes in vertical air movement is relatively easy, but sensing the lateral pulling and pushing of thermals requires more practise and skills.

Just as when we're riding an elevator it is no problem to feel the initial acceleration but once the cruising speed has been reached we don't feel the motion any more.

This makes flying without a vario even harder, as flying from –3m/s into –1m/s can easily feel like entering a good thermal. To avoid ending up 'thermalling' in sinking air it is necessary to keep taking fixes on recognisable objects on the ground. In the mountains this is no problem as long as we're still below ridge height, but in the flats, and when above the ridges, it gets trickier. In the mountains we use a peak close by, and the view behind it to discern whether we're making any vertical progress, in the flats we need to be even smarter than that.

All the info, from the fixed-point lines to the sensations in the seat and the way the glider moves, are combined into an overall picture of climb versus sink. Finally, flying together with a group of pilots makes going without the vario much easier.

> **EXPERIENCE** Even your sense of smell may help you locate thermals. I once had a strong smell of fresh wood in my nose as I entered a good thermal – it had brought the smell up from the forest being cleared below.

Griffon Vultures are nature's soaring machines. Photo Marcus King

Sharing a thermal. The clouds indicate a meteo wind coming over the back of the hill. Note the glider the photographer is flying is called the Gracchio – named after the Alpine chough. Gracchios are some of the most skilled aviators in the sky and can often be seen to really enjoy aerobatics, loops and barrel rolls. Photo: Marcus King

7 Valley winds

Flying a valley system in the French Alps. Photo: Skywalk

Chapter 7

Valley winds, the crucial mountain wind system

Understanding valley winds is a prerequisite for safe flight planning in mountain regions. Anyone who has taken the time to get to the bottom of them, studied the theory and made their own observations is surely a much safer pilot in the air. In the following paragraphs I will outline the most important issues.

Valley winds can occur in both summer and winter, but they get much stronger in the summer. Any day in the mountains that is thermally flyable is also a valley wind day.

The formation of valley winds

Illustration 7.1 shows a cross-section of two different areas, one flat, the other mountainous. On a sunny day, both these two areas will get the same amount of energy from the sun.

In the mountains, certain areas (the slopes facing into the sun) will heat up dramatically whereas the shaded slopes won't, and the warm slopes will in their turn heat the overlying air.

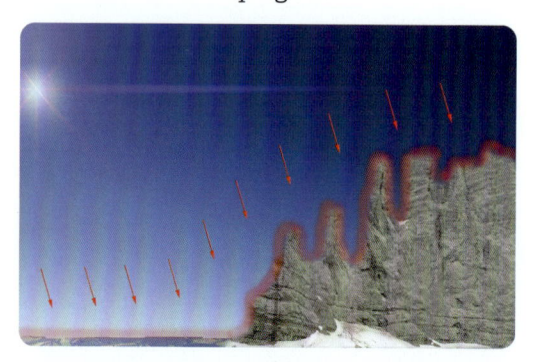

And this is where it gets interesting! Because the mountains take up so much space, there is much less air to heat in the mountainous regions. It follows that the temperature rise is far more distinctive in the mountains than in the flatlands.

Adding to the imbalance is the fact that the mountain air is also drier, and dry air heats faster than moist. Finally the mountain air is generally also cleaner which adds even further to the better heating profile.

The warmer air is lighter than the colder air in the flats, and the air pressure drops during the day in the mountains. We call it the heat low.

The Alpine heat low

In the Alpine region the heated air spreads out up high and gets cooled down, then sinks back down north and south of the actual mountains creating a circular flow around the entire mountain range. The process sets in on all sunny days, sometimes stronger, sometimes weaker. In the winter it may be really weak but still there.

For simplicity this whole process was previously often described as a case of warm air rising and sucking in air from the surrounding flatlands. This is

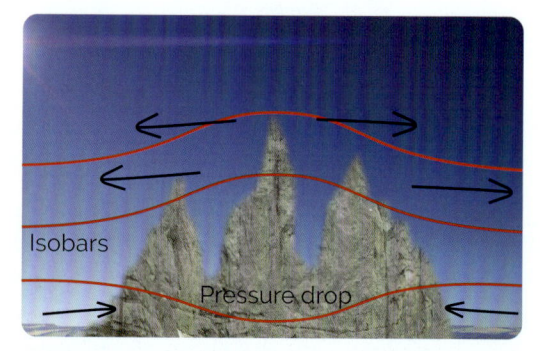

7.1 Cross-section of a flatland region meeting a mountain range. The two equally-sized regions get the same amount of energy from the sun, but since so much volume in the mountains is taken up by rock, there's much less air to heat – it follows that the heating happens faster and reaches higher temperatures than in the flatlands.

7.2 Formation of a heat low in a mountain range. The relatively warmer air in the mountains expands and the pressure in the mountains drops. Up high, the air flows laterally away to sink back down again far away, and at ground level the air flows in from the sides to fill the low pressure – and the valley wind sets in.

only partially correct since the reverse conclusion would be that there are only valley winds on days with thermals, which we know isn't the full story. One example here would be an old high-pressure with hardly any temperature gradient, no thermals worth mentioning yet the valley winds can still get surprisingly strong!

Of course the valley winds get even stronger as soon as thermals add their dynamics to the equation.

The rising thermals also suck in air from the sides. This influx of air becomes much more pronounced in true mountainous regions as opposed to hilly country.

However, the air thus circulated actually sinks again in the near vicinity and can never account for the large-scale heat low as we know it from mountain chains like the European Alps.

The heat low over the Alps is only a few hPa lower and thus doesn't show up on the isobar maps, as these have a 4-5 hPa resolution.

Valley winds may reach surprisingly high up into the mountains, sometimes flushing over ridges more than 1,000m high. The average speed in wide valleys in the Alps is around 20-30km/h but in extreme cases, like in the Himalaya and the Karakoram valley winds are known to reach 80km/h.

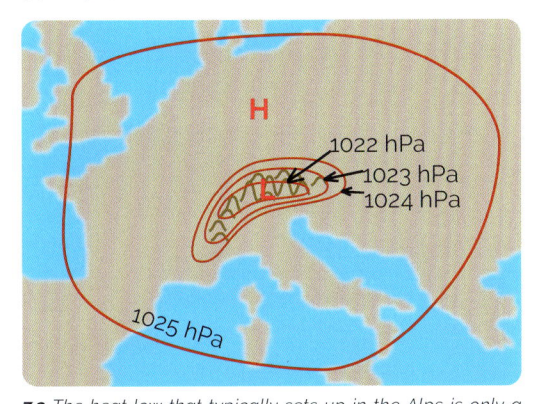

HINT *Always* hook up your speed system before you fly – even if there's only a breath of wind on launch. The valley winds may be much stronger than you anticipate, even on days with little or no thermal activity.

Valley-wind strength during the course of the day

In the low Alps we can expect the valley winds to start blowing around 9am, slightly later in spring and autumn, and slightly earlier on very good days in midsummer.

At this time it is still weak and battles the katabatic mountain winds. The further we move into the high Alps the later the valley wind arrives.

Around noon the wind is strong enough to overflow minor ridges, at 2pm it is nearing its peak, and at 4pm we can expect it to begin abating again – all times based on midsummer conditions.

Around 6pm it should be noticeably weaker again, but it will often continue to blow, albeit weak, right until sunset, when the katabatic flow takes over again. The mountain wind begins slowly and builds up during the night, only to be replaced by the valley winds again the following day.

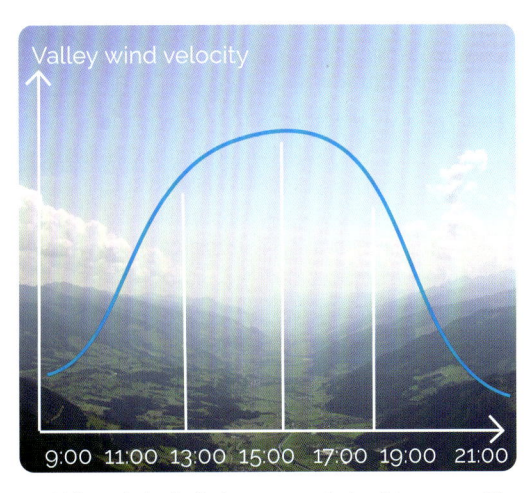

7.3 The heat low that typically sets up in the Alps is only a few hPa (hectopascals) lower than the surrounding air mass. Since standard meteorological isobar maps don't have such a high resolution (they tend to work in 4 or 5 hPa steps) the Alpine heat low doesn't actually show up on them.

7.4 Valley wind velocity in summer, during the course of the day. Peak strength is between 1pm to 5pm.

191

HINT Knowing your local area helps you predict when it pays to start heading for launch. I know my home mountain Brauneck (Germany) rather well. For example the important times to know in the summer are as follows: katabatic flow/mountain wind on the landing till approximately 9:30am, same on launch till 10:30am. Beginner-friendly winds on the landing till 1pm.

7.5 Even when there's no wind on launch the wind beneath the inversion may be very strong. If the inversion lifts the valley winds become weaker. Always hook up your speed system, even if you think you won't need it!

The Bavarian wind

The so-called Bavarian wind influences the entire northern section of the Alps. This wind is caused by the heat low and may get very strong, often overflowing mountains up to 2,000m and reaching all the way to the main dividing range. Such local phenomena may be observed at many places around the planet and are important to know both for safety reasons and for planning XC flights efficiently.

Valley wind strengths during the year
Spring: Medium strong – up to 10-20km/h
Summer: Strong – up to 40km/h
Autumn: Medium strong – up to 10-20km/h
Winter: Weak – 0-10km/h

Valley wind strength depends on the following factors

- **Valley length** – long valleys give faster stronger winds
- **Venturi effects** – narrow sections accelerate the wind
- **Macro-meteorological wind direction and strength** – if it is blowing the same way as the valley wind they tend to strengthen each other, whereas opposite directions have the opposite effect. Some places are known for inversed valley winds caused by other winds overruling the logical flow.
- **Temperature gradient** – a good temperature gradient accentuates the valley wind formation
- **Thermal strength** – see above
- **Inversion altitude** – if there's an inversion at ridge height the valley winds may get accelerated by the venturi effect beneath it. See illustration 3.66, page 113.

Glacier wind

The air overlying a glacier will get cooled by the ice, get heavier and flow down. Once this downdraught reaches the valley floor it meets with the valley wind and causes turbulence. If it meets a ridge oriented perpendicularly to the flow it may make the ridge soarable, or it may converge with other winds to cause a convergence to set up, see illustration 3.35b, page 96.

7.6 The glacier cools the air, and the colder, heavier air flows down into the valley where it meets the valley wind and causes turbulence and unpredictable direction changes

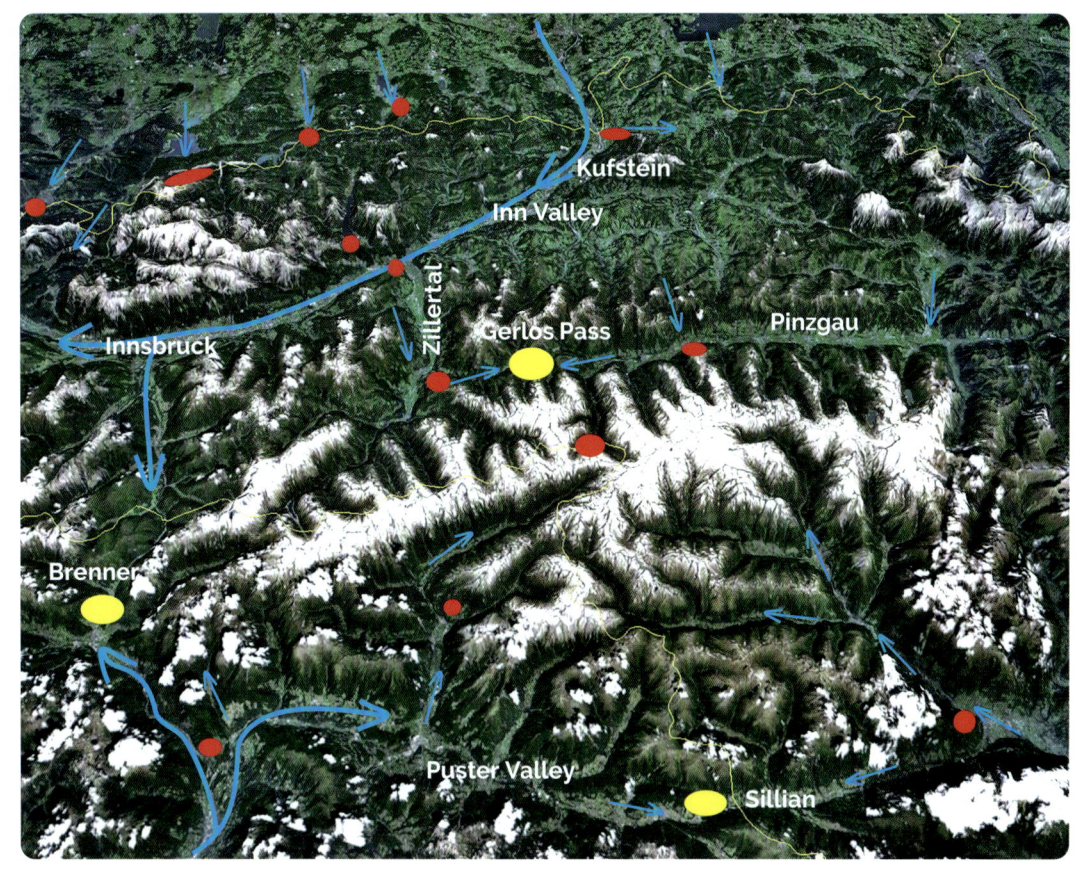

7.7 *An aerial view of the Austrian Alps with valley-wind directions drawn in blue, convergences in yellow and valley-wind soaring ridges marked in red. Notice how the winds split when valleys split. Image: World Wind / Nasa.*

Valley wind courses

To understand valley wind systems it makes sense to take a look at an image like the one in 7.7. In this case (the Alps) the general orientation of the chain is E-W, and the main influx of air due to the heat low thus comes from N and S. But once within the Alpine region, the winds do not remain north or south – rather, they follow up the valleys towards the centre of the heat low, located around the main dividing range (the glaciers in the image).

Notice that the north wind around Kufstein turns and becomes east at least until the mouth of the Zillertal, where the main body continues west towards Innsbruck, but a significant part flows up the Zillertal as north wind again. Further up the Zillertal the wind branches again, with one part blowing up towards the Gerlos Pass, now a west wind!

If the valley wind is strong it is important to avoid ridges that are being flushed by it (like the previously mentioned low Steinerhof rigde at the mouth of the Zillertal, above the word Zillertal in illustration 7.7). Such lees are turbulent and produce no useable lift, see illustration 7.9, next page.

Another good example is the Thurn Pass (blue arrow east of the Gerlos Pass) where the north wind (Bavarian wind) breaks into the Pinzgau Valley and overrules the local valley wind coming from the east. The XC pilot wishing to get past here in the afternoon does so by switching from the north side of the Pinzgau to the south side. At Hollersbach, opposite the Thurn Pass, it is possible to soar back up from

7.8 The Bavarian wind overflows the Thurn Pass and hits the Hollersbach ridge across the valley. Here, the wind is diverted straight up, which makes the ridge soarable from very low. Image: World Wind/Nasa

HINT A good rule of thumb says that the valley wind will flow against the flow of any rivers following the valley bottom. Imagine water sloshing in the bathtub – this is a good way to think of how valley winds behave in valleys. The water/wind will behave differently depending on whether the terrain is shallow or steep. As with most rules of thumb there are local exceptions and it always pays to get local advice before launching into an unknown flying arena.

surprisingly low in the Bavarian wind overflowing the pass (see illustration 7.8).

I have already mentioned the low Steinerhof ridge at the mouth of the Zillertal, where the valley wind blowing from the east will often overflow in the afternoon. There's even a launch on the lee side of this little ridge – no points for guessing where the wind is coming from there in the afternoon. Also check illustration 6.18, page 181.

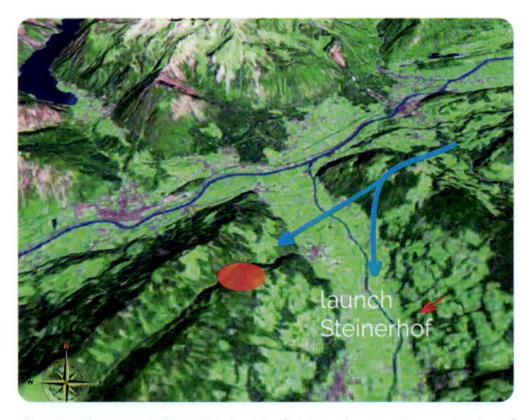

HINT If the main valley has little side valleys branching off (like the Thurn Pass in Pinzgau) the prevailing wind direction in the main valley may be overruled by winds coming from the side valleys. On the opposite side of such a side valley junction the winds may blow in both directions. At Hollersbach in Pinzgau there is east wind east of the valley wind influx (against the main valley wind direction) and west of the influx the extra wind from the Thurn Pass serves to strengthen the normal valley wind.

Illustration 7.9 The Steinerhof launch at the mouth of the Zillertal (red arrow). In the afternoon the valley wind blows over the ridge and causes tailwind on launch. Opposite the Steinerhof ridge there is a soarable section where one can soar the valley wind till sunset. Image: World Wind/Nasa

7.10 Another local exception to the general rules takes place above Innsbruck in Austria. If the macro-meteorological wind is from the south if flows over the Brenner Pass south of Innsbruck and hits the Karwendel chain north of town. Right on the Hafelekar launch above Innsbruck this wind splits so that one part flows east, the other west, along the Karwendel. This photo was taken from the Hafelekar launch viewing south.

7.11: *Valley winds can be visualised by observing how fog flows into the valleys. Valley winds follow valleys!*

7.11a: *The famous flying site of Zillertal, Austria. Looking to the east we see the Pinzgau Valley. Photo: UP / wolfgang-ehn.de*

Soarable ridges and valley-wind lee sides

Before launching we should always consider the following:

- Where can we expect the valley wind to blow from?
- Where is there a chance of soaring the valley wind in case thermals pause?
- Where will leeside conditions appear?

If a site is new to you it can definitely help to speak to a local pilot and ask about the valley winds. They will have different effects at different times of day, and will affect your route choice.

Sometimes during a cross-country flight we may encounter weakening conditions for a while, often caused by thin layers of high cloud. When this happens, a ridge facing into the valley-wind flow may save us from an early landing before allowing us to climb out again when conditions allow. Sometimes we may even make good distance using only soaring. We explore such things further in the next chapter.

HINT If you find yourself descending down into the valley wind long before the day is over, you must check your options carefully. Often more than one soarable place presents itself and it is important to choose the right one. Look for a ridge with a good connection to a mountain behind it, as these will be much easier to get away from again.

It is not uncommon to find a small ridge where one can soar until sundown yet never climb out from, and finding oneself there early in the day is almost worse than landing prematurely. The best possibilities are found on ridges tall enough to rise above the valley wind, as a strong valley wind effectively disrupts any thermal development (see picture 7.14).

7.12 Soaring a relatively wide ridge oriented perpendicular to the valley wind. If the ridge is low, hooking a thermal from it may be tricky.

7.13 Route planning when taking valley winds into account. The direct route to the bowl (red arrow) is good if we have plenty of altitude. However, if our altitude is so low that we're likely to pass over the flatter A section at minimum altitude it is better to take a detour (yellow arrow).

7.14 This is the illustration to the hint on this page. The small hill in the foreground is perfectly oriented into the valley wind flow, and can have us soaring there until sunset. But climbing out from it will be hard, so we opt for the less-than-perfect soaring face in the background, where the going will be harder but the climb-out possibilities are better.

Visualise how the air flows around the landscape to work out where to climb and where to avoid. Photo: Charlie King

The Venturi effect

In chapter 3 we briefly touched upon the usefulness of water to visualise the flow around obstacles. But water can be used for more than visualising turbulence. In fact it is an excellent means for learning about all the attributes of flowing liquids or gases, like the Venturi effect.

Whenever a flow is forced through a constriction we can observe Venturi effects. The flow speed in the constriction increases, and the pressure drops.

7.17 A gap in an otherwise closed chain – all wind coming from either side must pass through here. No wonder the winds must increase a lot here. Note that side rotors will also form, see illustration 3.12, page 84.

7.15 A classical Venturi, albeit with water. The valley narrows and the flow speed increases dramatically. If the wind was already strong before the constriction we can safely assume that we'll be going backwards in the constriction.

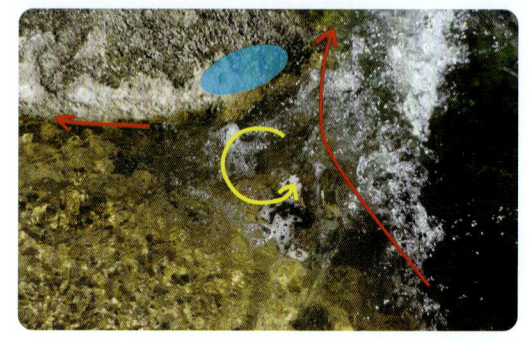

7.18 An interesting look at the flow around a rounded hill. Here, the hill is a rock in a creek and again the water acts as our visualisation guide. It flows fast against the hill and even forms a rotor (left, yellow). Further downstream (downwind) the flow is laminar once again. On the right it hits the hill and a soarable liftband forms where the flow is upward (blue). Further right the flow is parallel to the hill, and soaring is not possible.

7.16 The narrow gorge just west of launch at the famous flying site of Bassano, Italy. Time and again this gorge eats pilots who underestimate the Venturi effect and blunder too far in, only to find that they cannot get back out against the wind. There are some small landing options in there but it is far from ideal.

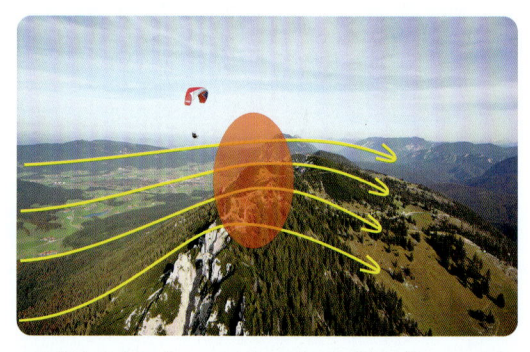

7.19 If winds from the general weather pattern hit a mountain, then at this point much higher wind speeds will be measured than in the surrounding air. Even if wind speeds of 40km/h are measured here (shaded area), it still may be possible to fly in the surrounding air. The only problem is getting up. Site: Rauschberg, Ruhpolding (Germany).

HINT In order to jump from one soarable ridge protruding into the valley wind flow to the next against the valley wind, it pays to fly a large curve around the area of sink and the lee right in between the two ridges. This is especially the case when the thermal lift doesn't reach high enough to break out of the valley wind flow.

Competitions are excellent occasions to observe which of the route choices are the most efficient, as there will be several pilots trying out all the different options. The longer, curved route avoids the worst of the sink and pilots choosing that one over the direct route generally arrive slightly later but considerably higher than their more impatient adversaries, see picture 7.13.

Knowing the wind direction and velocity at ground level

Working out exactly what the wind is doing at different altitudes isn't always straightforward, but at least at ground level we have several good indicators to help us out. If the day is thermally active there should be valley wind, and if we need to land we'll generally be facing down the valley.

HINT In a valley bend the wind strength is greater on the outside of the curve than on the inside!

When appraising the wind on the valley floor take account of:
- Macro-meteorological wind direction. If the valley wind is in the opposite direction, the valley wind may be inverted.
- Any other valleys nearby that could influence the wind direction.
- Any glaciers reaching all the way down near the valley floor. The cold glacial air may influence winds locally.

Hints for assessing wind direction at ground level

7.19 The large house and the little island cause small, local lees where the water is smooth – the wind is coming from the right.

7.20 The upwind end of the pond has a smoother surface, something that is visible from quite high. Lakes situated high in the mountains are good for judging wind direction out of the valleys – in this case the wind is coming from the right. This is a good tip for those who want to fly vol-bivouac.

7.21 The anchor is always fastened at the bow, and the mast is closer to the bow than to the stern. Since the boat will always align itself with the wind, boats at sway are excellent wind direction markers. In this photo the wind is quite weak, or the water would be more disturbed.

7.22 Hot-air balloons are great for showing the winds up higher. When they land the ground level winds are also easily visible. Photos: Nina Brümmer

7.25 Most deciduous trees have leaves with lighter-coloured bottom surfaces. When a stronger wind hits these trees the bottom surfaces of the leaves becomes visible and tell us where the wind is coming from. These 'white trees' are also excellent thermal markers up wooded slopes!

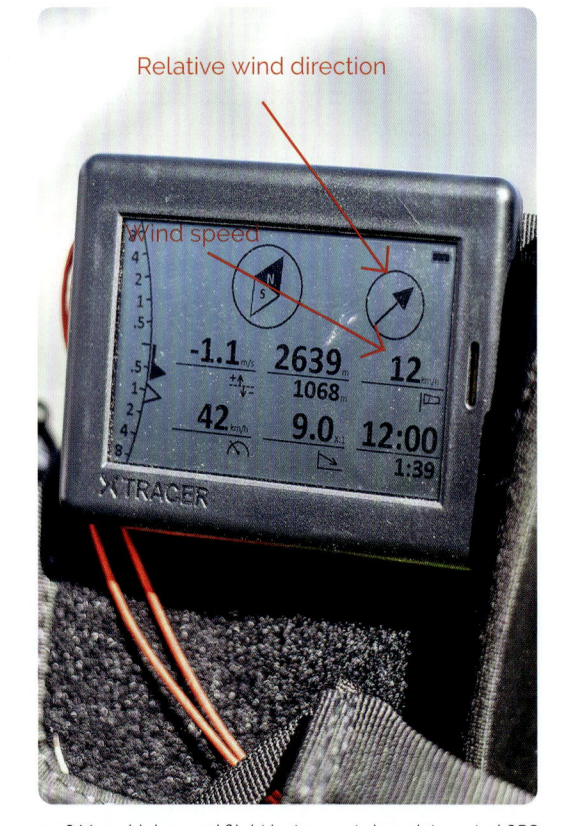

7.23 Windsocks indicate different wind directions. A quick trip to the peak reveals which one is in the lee.

7.24 Windsocks are easy to see even from up high, but they only do their job when placed correctly. They should be out in the open flow, on peaks or shoulders, with no obstacles around. If not they only serve to confuse us.

7.26 Many higher-end flight instruments have integrated GPS and a wind-speed and wind-direction indicator. In this case the instrument indicates a wind speed of 12 km/h and a wind direction coming from off to the pilot's right (NNE).

200

A typical Venturi situation – strong winds are to be expected in the canyon. Moustiers, France. Photo: Advance

Crossing a valley while calculating the wind

If it looks like you're going to sink into the valley wind on a crossing, then it's always best to head upwind while you're still up high and in the weaker winds at altitude. See photo 7.27.

7.28 The famous Grimsel Snake in Goms, Wallis, Switzerland. Valley winds in the Haslital are stronger than those in the Goms Valley. The later it gets in the day, the stronger the Haslital wind and the more it breaks over the Grimsel Pass, sinking and accelerating into the Goms Valley. 30-40km/h and -10m/s sink are what you can expect here (own experience!). As air in the Haslital often contains more moisture than that in Goms, a condensation cloud often forms over the Grimsel pass indicating the wind – even if you think you can't see it.

In Goms the wind turns to the west and forces the normal valley wind back. Where the two valley winds meet, you can often find useful convergences at altitude; down low it makes for nasty turbulence. If this happens down at Fiesch, then it is safer to fly up to Goms, and land in an easterly there, or down to Brig in a westerly. XC pilots fly to one ridge before the Grimsel Pass – see the picture 7.35 on p204. The Grimsel Snake is enhanced with northerly winds, and may disappear completely in southerlies. If you want to cross the Grimsel Pass, you need to get there early, or get up very high.

7.27a The plan is to fly from A to B. Cloudbase is not sufficient to arrive above the valley wind, so pilots should bear left and follow the green route. When the pilot sinks into the valley wind this will drift him to point B. Failing to keep left at the beginning would result in the pilot following the red route – this means a lot more flying against the valley wind and arriving much lower (if at all) at point B.

7.27b Crossing the valley to the Lüsen you need to hold course to the right to compensate for the valley wind.

7.29 Two hours later the Grimsel Snake was much higher, wider and stronger. At this time the wind was already blowing over the Sidelhorn, the last peak before the pass.

7.30 Dedicated anemometers are even more sensitive than wind socks. Furthermore they are generally placed on high points and thus give a more correct reading – but they are small and can only be seen from close up. Wind streamers also need less wind than true windsocks.

7.32 Smoke, dust or even pollen can be great for marking the air movement on the ground as well as in the air.

7.33 Irrigation systems are visible from far away and are good wind markers.

7.31 Landing gliders are good for wind direction appraisement. Beware though: if the pilot doesn't flare and brake, the wing may overshoot and land on its leading edge, causing us to believe he landed with a tailwind. This is Cerro Arco, Mendoza, Argentina.

7.34 Attention! If the dust plume is caused by a moving vehicle the wind direction is not entirely aligned with the plume. In this case the wind direction is indicated with an arrow, and the deviation between the plume and the actual wind direction depends on the vehicle speed.

7.35 *The Grimsel Pass in Goms, Wallis, Switzerland, between the lakes and the glacier. At this altitude you've got a good chance of getting to the other side without feeling the (invisible) Grimsel wind. Compare with picture 7.29.*

Another reason for inverted valley winds

On days where the entire mountain chain is experiencing uniformly sunny weather the centre of the heat low will be located around the main dividing range. But if parts of the mountain chain have very different weather, like in the picture above where the southern Alps are covered in clouds, the centre of the heat low moves correspondingly. If, for example, France and Switzerland are covered in clouds, the heat low will move east, causing confusing valley wind patterns in certain areas.

One such area is the westernmost part of Austria, close to the Swiss border. The normal valley wind blows from the east, up towards the border. On days where the centre of the heat low is displaced towards the east due to cloud cover in Switzerland, this valley wind may invert and blow from the west.

Pilots flying in the region may not be able to see the cloud cover on the other side of the border, and can be surprised by the confusing valley wind direction upon landing.

The sea breeze

The sea breeze is very similar to a valley wind: the land heats better than the sea, and causes a regional heat low to form. The heat low sucks in air from the

7.36 *The obvious big bend in the Inn river identifies this valley as the flying arena around Landeck, Austria. If the western Alps are covered in clouds, the centre of the heat low will be displaced towards the east and the valley winds here may be inverted.*

HINT Pilots should always seek out the latest weather forecast before going to launch. This will tell if adjacent regions have substantially different weather patterns that may influence valley winds. Thus, unusual situations are less surprising.

surroundings, in this case the sea.

Sea breezes may travel far inland and mix with valley wind systems, influencing both strength and direction far from the sea. The sea breeze is also both stable and humid so thermal development is generally adversely affected if an area is under the influence of a sea breeze.

Sea breezes are great for soaring dunes or cliffs on the coast. France's Dune du Pilat is such a sea-breeze dune-soaring spot. The time of year should be taken into account when considering a trip to a soaring spot – late autumn is rarely a good time for sea breezes to form.

When the sea breeze begins to blow it pushes cold air inland. This cold air often triggers a line of thermals topped by large cumulus clouds, often somewhat lower than the cloudbase further inland. We call this line of big clouds the sea-breeze front. Seaward of this line no thermal

7.37 Panoramic flight over Eze, near Monaco in the south of France. Once the sea breeze sets in such flights become possible for most, making the amazing scenery available for everybody to see.

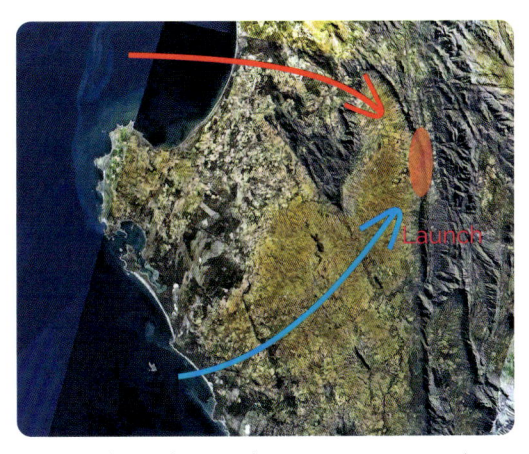

7.38 An interesting sea-breeze convergence sets up sometimes in Porterville, South Africa. Lots of flying goes on here between November and February. The peninsula extending into the Atlantic gets sea breezes from both sides.

First you fly from the launch north on early thermals, mostly with a tailwind into the Citrusdal (red shaded zone). At some point you find yourself flying against the wind, and you can usually gain a lot of height as the sea breeze pushes under the warm air. Turning round you get a 30km/h wind from the south, the blue sea-breeze convergence.

Again, fly high where it's nice and cool – ground temperatures of over 40°C are not unusual! Both sea breezes create a big convergence, but usually mean the end of cross-country flying. Image: World Wind/Nasa

Flying the sea breeze in Pipa, Brazil. Photo: Nina Brümmer

EXPERIENCE Volker Schwaniz has noted that the macro-meteorological wind may overrule sea breezes if it is strong enough.

HINT Large islands also experience sea breezes. Often these will blow onshore everywhere so that any cliff or dune all the way around the island is soarable.

On the Canary Islands the trade winds rule the show, blowing from the northeast. The mountains on Lanzarote are low and flying is only done on the northeast side of the island, where the coastline faces into the trade winds.

But on Tenerife Mount Teide, the highest mountain in Spain at 3,715m, effectively blocks the trade winds so that a microsystem can set up on the south side of the island. The south side is flyable, with good thermal development, even on days when the trade winds hammer the north side. Flying in a big lee like that is not for everybody, and newcomers are advised to join local pilots for their first exploits.

7.40 In Tenerife, Spain, Mount Teide (3,715m) blocks the strong NE'ly trade winds and allows pilots to fly on the south side, in the lee of the mountain.

development should be expected. As the day progresses the sea breeze front pushes progressively further inland, and any pilot lucky enough to reach the line can fly good distances parallel to the coast.

7.39 The sea-breeze front, clearly visible through the large and heavy cumulus clouds. Further inland the cloud development was more modest. The photo is from Monaco, taken from above the launch and looking north.

Understanding how valley winds work will allow you to fly big mountain terrain like this in Chamonix, France. Photo: Ozone

8 Soaring

Soaring Sossusvlei, Namibia. Photo: Nina Brümmer

Chapter 8

Soaring

Soaring means flying in a lift band caused by the wind meeting an obstacle. As Alpine pilots we're used to the obstacle being a mountain, but in reality it can be anything, and people have soared buildings, forest edges, stacks of baled straw and probably many more things that I haven't heard of.

Soaring is more predictable than thermalling: as long as the wind hits the obstacle at a reasonably perpendicular angle there will be lift in front of the obstacle.

Most XC flights involve at least some soaring along the way, and good soaring ridges are a fast means of travel when we're heading far away.

How to soar slopes, ridges and mountains using dynamic lift

When soaring in dynamic lift we simply fly back and forth in front of the hill, taking care not to let the drift push us too far back and always turning away from the hill when we reverse direction. The track viewed from above should look like an elongated 8.

On big, lifty slopes the lift band may get wide enough to allow 360s but great care should be taken as the downwind drift is great and especially inexperienced pilots will often be surprised by the sudden increase in groundspeed when we go from headwind to tailwind. Hitting a slope downwind *always* hurts, regardless of the geology.

The pilot should try to remain in the best lift. This depends on slope inclination and wind strength, but a rule of thumb in mountains could be between 20 and 80 metres from the slope. If the soaring slope in fact is a vertical wall and the wind is weak, the lift will be considerably closer to the ridge than that. The stronger the wind becomes, the further away from the slope we fly.

The pilot must always keep a safe distance to the soaring slope. There are no hard and fast rules, but if you can look yourself in the eyes and honestly say that you can cope with a collapse at the current distance then you are probably OK.

Hang gliders need to keep a greater safety distance than paragliders, as they take longer to correct if the outer wing gets lifted. They must first build up some speed flying along the new heading before they can steer back out, whereas paragliders are quicker to get onto a new heading even following disturbances. It goes for both aircraft that if the soaring is rough and turbulent you'd better find somewhere else to soar.

If the wind hitting the soaring slope is laminar the flying generally becomes stress-free and extremely pleasant. Dune soaring is great fun and probably the least stressful form of flying.

Influence of topography on the lift band

The ideal soaring mountain is broad, free of obstacles and high, just like the one in the photo on the previous page. The best lift occurs when the wind is perpendicular to the mountain orientation. If the wind

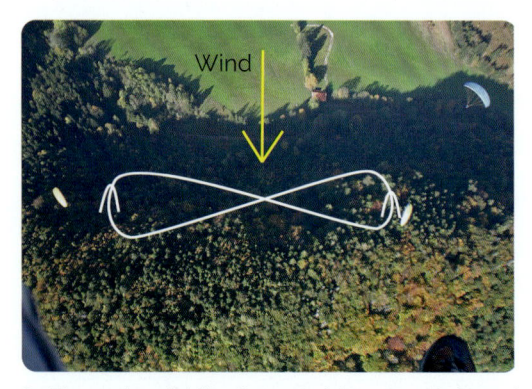

8.1 *The soaring pilot flies figure-of-eight patterns in front of the slope, taking care to fly every turn away from the hill. If several pilots share the same lift band they must keep all other pilots at their own level in sight.*

8.2 When soaring ridges with a non-uniform slope, like the one pictured, it is noticeable that some areas will offer better lift than others. In the picture the wind is coming from the right, and the left side of the shallow gully is more into wind than the right side, resulting in better lift on the left.

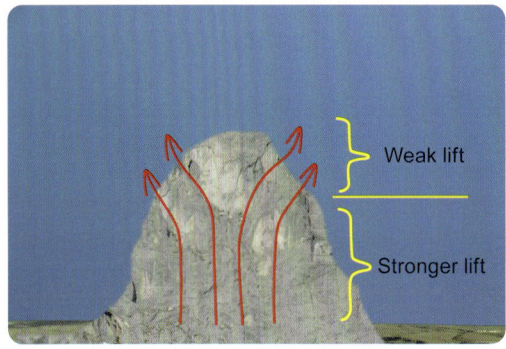

8.3 When soaring rounded hills it quickly becomes apparent that the top section isn't a very good lift generator as all the wind flows around the hill instead of over it. In this example the wind is coming from the direction of the observer and flowing onto, and around, the rocky hill.

is angled from either side the pilot flies faster on the slightly downwind legs of the figure-of-eight, slower on the upwind legs. This may lead to the false notion that the upwind leg lifts better, but in reality the real reason is that one flies through the good bits faster on the downwind leg.

Rounded hills are only soarable low down, up high the wind flows around them rather than over, see the water flow in illustration 3.13, page 85.

Mountain slopes are almost always criss-crossed by secondary spurs, landslides and gullies etc that are oriented differently to the wind compared to the main ridge. Along these the lift will be different, something that the good pilot notices and takes advantage of.

Most pilots aim to soar to the greatest possible altitude. But many mountains are irregularly formed and have flat sections interspersed with the more vertical parts. It is often possible to soar up past such plateaus but care must be taken to avoid landing up there. The vertical motion of the air around the edge of the plateau will often suck in air from the plateau as well, leading to turbulence and tailwind behind the edge.

The best way to climb past such plateaus is to use a thermal embedded in the dynamic lift to get high, then allow oneself to drift back to the main ridge again. You should aim to arrive high so that the next thermal you catch is more usable and can take you even higher still. Another option is to look further along the ridge; maybe there's a place where the plateau is narrow enough to allow the switch back to the main ridge without risking a high landing.

8.4 A tricky plateau (marked in red) west of the south launch in Bassano, Italy. In front of the plateau edge the ridge is often soarable in the afternoon, but when thermals flow up the face they suck in air from the plateau and cause increased descent. Many pilots have had to top-land there.

HINT Anyone wishing to top-land on a rounded hill should be aware that on the top there is hardly any lift but plenty of wind. We may find ourselves descending faster than we expected.

211

Collision avoidance when soaring

The pilot flying with the ridge to his right has the right of way. But practically all soaring pilots should always keep an eye out for anyone soaring at the same altitude. Before turning, pilots should look over their shoulder to make sure no one is endangered by the turn, and furthermore we should always avoid trapping anyone between ourselves and the ridge, or another pilot.

If several pilots are soaring together it makes sense that everybody maintains the same distance to the ridge. When meeting someone head on, the pilot with the ridge on the left flies a curve out from the ridge and lets the oncoming pilot pass between him and the ridge. The reason for this rule is that we always evade by flying right, however the pilot having the ridge to his right cannot do this without crashing into the mountain!

There's a further advantage if everybody maintains a similar distance to the slope; everyone can turn when it suits him without risking a collision with someone flying slightly behind yet further out from the ridge.

> **HINT** The wingtip vortices cause our wing to shudder when we fly through the wake behind another glider. The closer we get the more dramatic the shuddering becomes. Tandem gliders carrying more weight trail stronger vortices.

8.6 Soaring the Marriott Hotel on the coast in Lima, Peru. This pilot would have the right of way if another pilot was meeting him head on, as evading to the right would lead to a collision with the hotel!

8.5 When soaring pilots must keep a good look out to avoid colliding with each other. The rules of the air help us do that. One of them says the pilot who has the slope on their right has right of way. Another says that pilots taking off must give way to pilots already in the air. Developing good airmanship is part of becoming a good pilot. Point Cartwright, Australia. Photo: Tex Beck

You can risk flying in close to the hillside when soaring early or late in the day when there isn't much turbulence.
Photo: Charlie King

8.7 Overtaking is done to the right, and if that isn't possible we don't do it! Red must overtake yellow on the right. In the UK the rules are different and allow a pilot to overtake on either side, so long as they don't block another pilot's exit. In the photo, overtaking on the right means flying out of the main lift band and over the surfzone. Overtaking on the left would mean squeezing through the gap between pilot and cliff. Turning early and flying back, therefore not overtaking, is also an option. Photo: Werner Luidolt

EXPERIENCE If the situation described in picture 8.8 takes place on a shallow hill in the flatlands it is necessary to crab around in the weak lift generated by steeper sections of the hill, moving from one to the next up along the slope. Once higher the chances of connecting with a proper thermal are much better.

8.8 The ridge in the picture is soarable in the yellow zone, and thermals may come through in the red zone. Compare to the situation in Illustration 8.15, page 219. If there are no thermals we soar the yellow area, but once thermals are added in to the equation we may attempt to connect with one in the red zone. We would then climb out while drifting back.

8.9 Soaring south of Iquique, Chile. Flying is possible here all day in the sea breeze from the Pacific. Photo: Nina Brümmer

214

Above*: The steeper the hillside, the less wind required to ridge soar. On gently-sloping dunes you need a good deal of wind. If the wind comes at an angle, then even more is needed, but then it usually takes you up nice and high. Dunes at Torra Bay, Namibia*
Below*: Smaller sites need more wind or a steeper angle. When soaring cliffs like these in Normandy, northern France, you should aim always to stay above the height of the cliff – once you drop below the lift can disappear quickly. Photo: Jérôme Maupoint*

Vector analysis of soaring winds

Lift as a function of wind strength and slope inclination may be analysed using vectors, as wind is a force with a direction just like anything else we analyse with vectors. The lifting component is what keeps us airborne, and the horizontal component is our headwind when soaring.

Let us take an example: In the illustration below (picture 8.10) we have a wind speed of 25km/h down near the foot of the ridge, increasing to 40km/h at crest level. Through vector analysis we may deduce that we get a headwind component of 20km/h and a lifting component of 15km/h down low, whereas at crest level there'll be 30km/h headwind and 26km/h lifting component.

The 30km/h headwind component at ridge height, but in front of the ridge, is still just flyable if we assume that the paraglider has a trim speed of app. 35-36km/h. But right behind the crest line (point A in the illustration), where there is no vertical component to the wind, the headwind is suddenly 40km/h – too much for comfortable flying.

> **EXPERIENCE** I once flew the site shown in picture 8.10. It was an amazing experience to soar along this forested dune stretching for several kilometres. I climbed to the top following the topography, then edged forward a bit to continue climbing. As I got higher the wind increased gradually so that I had to keep pushing out over the sea to remain safe. Eventually I reached a maximum altitude of 600m ASL, 400m out over the sea.

This is the actual wind strength when there's no splitting it up into vertical and horizontal components. It follows that launching on top would be all but impossible while the flying in front of the ridge is still entirely possible.

The vector analysis makes it abundantly clear that soaring should take place in front of the ridge, not over it. If you find yourself getting pushed back over the ridge, and even worse behind it you'll find only wind and no more lift, and if this headwind exceeds your own airspeed you could quickly find yourself going down through the rotor behind the ridge.

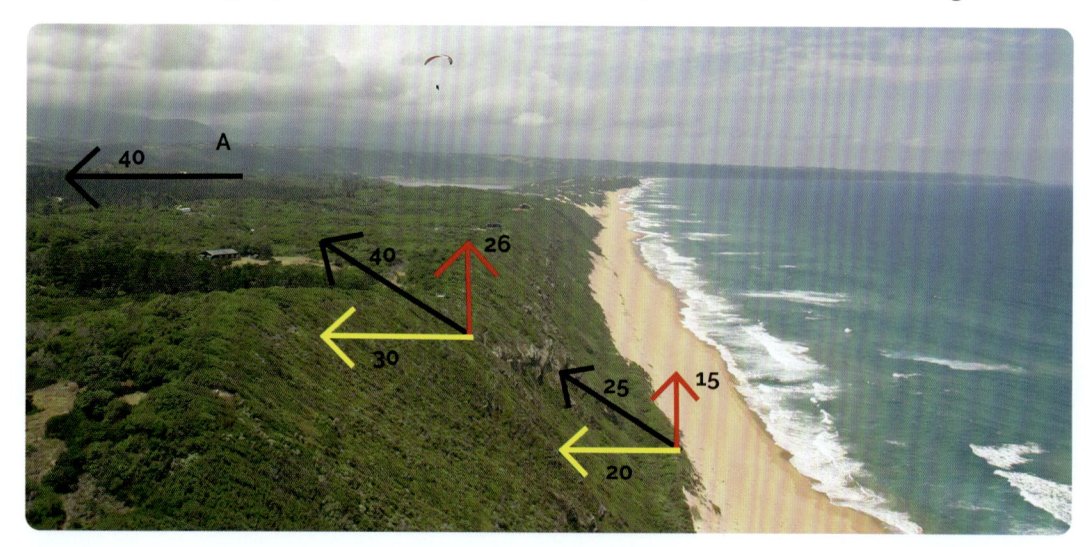

8.10 Vector analysis of the headwind and lift components when soaring in dynamic lift (in km/h). The black arrow is the wind speed, yellow is the perceived headwind and red is the lift. Right above the ridge the wind speed equals the perceived headwind, whereas there is no more lift to be found. Just to spice things up further the ridge even acts as a Venturi, accelerating the wind additionally. The picture shows Paradise Ridge in South Africa. Photo: Nina Brümmer.

8.11 *The closer pilot is doing it right by staying well out in front of the ridge. The pilot behind is pushing the limit and in this case actually struggled to get back out on the upwind side of the ridge. Laragne, France.*

Hang gliders have a considerably larger safety margin in terms of speed, and cannot be blown back under normal, flyable conditions, but paragliders are always at risk when soaring near their maximum speed limit. Going down through a rotor close to the deck in strong winds is a serious matter and should not be taken lightly.

HINT If there's a cloud layer above the ridge the Venturi effect may be accentuated. The clouds act like a lid, funnelling the wind.

EXPERIENCE I had a close call while soaring back in the very early days of my flying career. I was climbing up the upwind side of a rock face in southern France and chose to do full circles as soon as I cleared the peak. However, the lift I had wasn't thermic but purely dynamic, and as soon as I had done the first full circle I was hopelessly pinned behind the crest, going backwards even on speed bar. So I chose to try to run away with a tailwind and overfly the rotor, except my altitude was insufficient for such a manoeuvre.

It turned into a full-blown SIV course going down through the rotor, and if the mountain hadn't been as steep on the downwind side as it was upwind I would surely have crashed. As it turned out I found calmer air again down near the valley floor and could even continue my flight, albeit with a big adrenaline overload.

Since then I have approached soaring with increased diligence, and I hope my experience will also help you to avoid similar situations. I know that humans learn best the hard way, but this was a learning experience you could live without – trust me.

8.12 *This illustration shows the path of the best lift. As you can see (red arrow) the best lift moves upwind from around the crest level – it goes up and out, sometimes surprisingly far. On coastal sites, for example, when the wind is strong, you will often observe the seagulls flying high and far out from the obvious lift band. It seems impossible to reach them, but working the lift higher and then pushing further out will allow you to do so. The picture shows the top-landing site in Meduno, Italy.*

8.13 If the wind is weak, and the drift and the turbulence thus equally negligible, it is possible to soar very close to vertical rocks. This pilot is clearly comfortable getting extremely close – he probably knows the site and conditions well.

Safe distance when soaring

There are a number of factors influencing the recommendable safety distance both laterally and vertically when soaring. None of these are hard and fast rules, and nothing beats sound judgement, but having a few simple hints in mind will help you remain safe.

The stronger the wind becomes, the greater the safety distance should be. There are two reasons for this, namely turbulence and drift.

Turbulence first: this is exponentially related to wind strength. If the wind increases from 15 to 30km/h, the turbulent area behind an obstacle grows to four times its previous expanse. It follows that a ridge that is pleasant and smooth to soar in 15km/h wind may be all but unflyable at 30km/h – and our safety distance must reflect this.

The next thing to consider is the drift, also increasing with wind strength. If we encounter bad air, and our aircraft takes a hit, we need to make sure that we have sufficient open air to operate in whilst we correct the situation. Soaring a paraglider close to a vertical cliff in strong wind and suffering a collapse could have us hanging from a rocky outcrop in no time, counting our broken bones.

Finding and using embedded thermals when soaring

We generally don't get much higher than the highest peak along the ridge using solely dynamic lift. To get higher than that we need to find an embedded thermal rising well clear of the topography – but how do we locate it? This is one of the big questions new pilots always ask, and there is a lot to learn.

We start by soaring as high as we can get. Then we start to explore the horizontal expanse of the lift band – how far out in front does the lift go? Once we know this our chances of identifying a

8.14 A good ridge for soaring. The clouds indicate that there are thermals embedded in the dynamic lift. To find it the pilot searches for areas where the lift band is wider, and the lift thus expands out further from the slope.

HINT Sensitive pilots can often feel the temperature difference when encountering an embedded thermal in dynamic lift.

HINT Once above the hill the thermals should be centred in the usual manner. Note that strong thermals drift less with the wind than their weaker counterparts! In strong wind it makes sense to wait for a strong thermal before leaving the comfort of the dynamic lift, as the chances of not making it and simply getting blown back are greater in moderate winds.

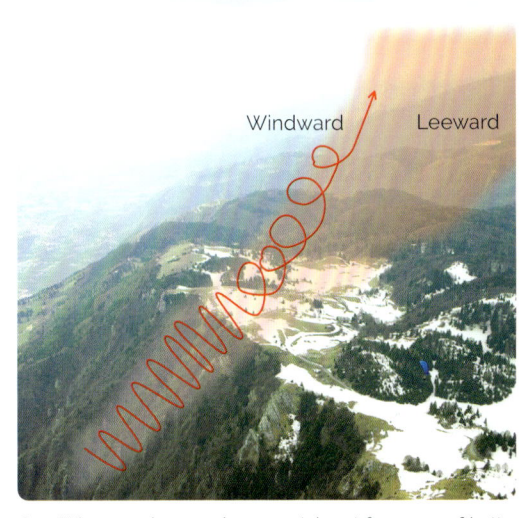

EXPERIENCE In weak soaring conditions I may opt to do full circles in the embedded thermals even low down. If the thermal is just 70m across or more I find that I can climb better by doing 360s than by flying figure-of-eights. Hang gliders will need somewhat more than that. If the wind is strong I soar normally – strong wind and steep slopes mean good climb rates anyway and you will quickly climb up.

8.15 When soaring we always watch out for areas of better lift. If we meet such an area we do a turn away from the hill in order to verify if it is a thermal or not – if the lift remains strong even further out from the slope it is probably a thermal. If the wind is not too strong we may decide to centre it right away, and circle next to the slope. This however doesn't work in a strong wind, where we'll surely be pushed against the slope on the downwind leg – in such cases figure-of-eights is the way to go. Once above ridge height the first circle should always be away from the ridge, so that if we fall out we're not in danger of dropping behind the ridge. A few turns later we can relax and concentrate on the thermal without paying so much attention to the terrain anymore. The picture shows Monte Grappa in Bassano, Italy.

passing thermal are far greater, since the thermals will usually expand the width of the lift band considerably.

The first sign of the embedded thermal remains the increased climb rate. Once we have located such an area, we turn away from the hill and head out perpendicularly to it. If the lift doesn't decrease at the distance we discovered above, we have got ourselves a thermal.

The safest procedure now will be to fly in small figure-of-eights in the thermal until ridge level. Circling down close to the slope is risky because the drift on the downwind leg may push us against the mountain.

To centre the thermal we continue in figure-of-eights until well clear of the top, then push out upwind until almost at the edge of the thermal. Now we may initiate our first full 360. We continue like this, with somewhat longer upwind legs than downwind, until well clear of the top – then we can allow ourselves to drift a bit with the thermal.

The advantage of this method is that we always remain inside the upwind part of the thermal, and will almost surely fall out the upwind side if we get a circle wrong. This is far better than dropping out the back, where we have both strong descent and a headwind to battle in order to join the thermal again.

If the wind is close to the limit I advise against doing 360s even above the ridge. The risk of getting blown back into the rotor is simply too high.

How much wind do we need to soar?

There's a launch in the Valle de Abdalajis in southern Spain where the cliff in front is about 250m high and virtually vertical all the way. Newcomers often don't even bother to launch in light winds, thinking they'll just glide down to land, but the pro's know better: with just 5km/h wind and a vertical face it is actually possible to soar!

The shallower the slope the more wind we need to soar.

EXPERIENCE My home mountain, the Brauneck in Germany, has launches facing south and north. The south launch is rather shallow and requires about 25km/h wind to be soarable, whereas the north launch is steep and works with only 15km/h. Taking off is easier in 15km/h than in 25, so I prefer soaring the north side.

8.16 It takes just 5km/h wind to soar a vertical cliff of a certain height – the shallower the slope, the more wind we need. The photo shows a slope in Gourdon, France, with what feels like enough wind to fly using only a jacket...

8.17 Another example of a steep slope producing soarable conditions with very light winds. This is in the high Alps, in the region around the Matterhorn, Switzerland. Photo: Ozone

When soaring a slope in light conditions small cliffs can increase the lift enough to allow you to climb. They are also classic thermal triggers. Photo: Charlie King

XC soaring

Soaring can help us make good distance on our XC flights. There are two possible scenarios.

The first method takes advantage of secondary ridges pointing into a main valley. We may use the valley wind to soar these and fly XC. We soar up each ridge to the maximum altitude, then fly a large curve out into the main valley to avoid the lee behind the little ridges. On the next ridge we repeat this process, see illustration 8.20. The track in illustration 8.22 shows it clearly. Note that this only works in strong wind, where the rotor behind the ridges is best avoided.

The second method is more straight forward and involves blasting down long uninterrupted ridges facing into wind – in this manner the XC pilot may really get some kilometres under his belt. This is also the reason why the FAI, World Air Sports Federation, does not accept flights done solely in dynamic lift for badges or records.

8.19 This sand dune rises to 120m high near Sandwich Harbour, Namibia. We soared along it for miles, flying XC on the coast with no turbulence, no valley crossings and plenty of landing space.

8.18 Cloudbase is often very high in the Pustertal, Austria. Should the thermals become unreliable we often prolong our flight with dynamic soaring – this has saved many XC pilots from landing during brief overcast periods. As soon as the clouds are gone, the thermals start kicking off again.

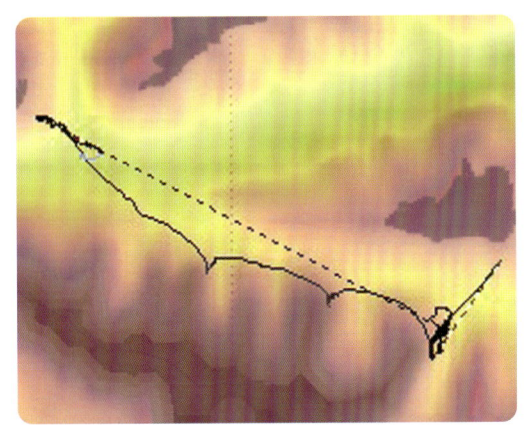

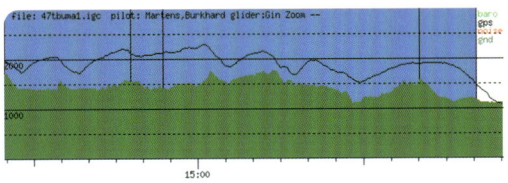

8.20 XC-soaring in Sillian, Austria. The wind is from the east and blows at approximately 25km/h. Note the big curves out into the main valley each time the pilot leaves his soaring ridge to fly to the next one to avoid the turbulence behind the ridges.

8.21 Iquique, Chile. The sea breeze allows for XC soaring all along the coastline. Pilots have flown 300km here using a mix of thermals and dynamic soaring.
Photo: Nina Brümmer

8.22 When soaring the secondary ridges in a large primary valley, make sure you avoid the lee behind the ridges by flying a large curve out into the main valley every time you leave a ridge. Begin by building height at A, fly a curve to B, then to C etcetera. The photo was taken in Sillian, Austria.

Soaring sand dunes

Soaring sand dunes is the same as on other hillsides. You can save yourself some energy by kiting: climbing diagonally up the dune with canopy assistance.

To do this, inflate your glider and steer it to hang over to one side (wingtip almost touching the sand) and pull you up the dune. Once you're at the top, straighten up and fly!

You can do this to the left or the right. If the wind is a little off, then assisted climbing works much better in the direction where you're running against the wind. See the following picture.

If the wind is strong enough, and the ground firm enough, then you can let your feet slide. To practise, gently sloping dunes or flat sandy areas are best. Loose sand is softer than other ground, this makes things less painful if you get it wrong and get towed!

EXPERIENCE I had some of the best coastal soaring flights of my life on the dunes in Namibia. After 20 years of flying, I learnt assisted dune climbing here, and I am very impressed with it. It's one of the most important things the commercial operators teach you in Namibia, and without learning this we would probably never have got airborne on the steep dunes in Sandwich harbour and Sossusvlei.

Another couple of words on Namibia. Sea breezes begin around 11am when they are strong enough to soar. By 1pm they are sometimes too strong. The dunes at Swakopmund are somewhat turbulent from embedded thermals. The very impressive dune at Sandwich Harbour runs directly down to the water's edge – here soaring is as smooth as in a valley wind.

The sea breeze at Sossusvlei (see the title picture of this chapter) comes through very strongly between noon and 1pm. From 6pm onwards, flying is more pleasant.

8.23 The dunes between Swakopmund and Walvis Bay in Namibia are perfect for training
Photo: Nina Brümmer

8.24 If the dunes are very steep as in this photo, or the sand very soft, then it's very exhausting climbing up them to launch. Use your glider to assist you! Photo: Nina Brümmer

8.25 Sandwich Harbour, one of the finest dunes to soar. You need to use the assisted climbing technique to get airborne. Even if it looks easy it's important to remember that accidents can happen in strong winds and in the lee of the dunes

8.26 Sossusvlei in the Namib Desert. Over the years this amazing area has become more popular with travellers as well as pilots. Even if it looks remote and wild, we must always be aware that it is a privilege to fly these special places and act accordingly

Cloud soaring

Big cumulus clouds actually also work as obstacles obstructing the wind. By climbing up in the upwind side of the thermal, where the lift is usually best anyway, the pilot may manage to connect with the dynamic lift on the side of the cloud and thus climb to well above the cloudbase without ever losing visual reference. Once you have tried this you won't forget it again – very spectacular.

In controlled airspace there are rules about how far from clouds one must stay, but in free airspace the rule is simple – we must remain free of cloud.

EXPERIENCE Once in a competition in Alsace in France we encountered a big, 1.000m-high cumulus cloud en route to the next turnpoint. Some pilots managed to soar up the side of it and fly around it whereas others had to pull big ears to glide under. The former group arrived at the turnpoint 1,000m higher than the latter! Aside from the joy of having made such a move, just having flown alongside such a cloud made the whole trip extra worthwhile.

8.27 Prerequisites for cloud soaring are as follows: The wind must increase around cloudbase level and the air mass must be unstable, compare with illustration 1.39. This cloud was really very big and would surely have worked, however, since cloudbase was already high nobody attempted it.

8.28 In order to soar a cumulus cloud we first climb as high as possible in the upwind side of the thermal, then move to the side of the cloud.

8.29 Flying in cloud is forbidden. If a pilot gets sucked in, then their flight planning was not good. After a few minutes water begins to run down your lines, or freezes as ice on the lines. After five minutes water your gloves are soaked, and after 10 your whole harness is wet. Photo: Mads Syndergaard

8.30 In Teba, Spain, a castle ruin adorns the soaring ridge. The best altitude is always reached right in front of the old tower

8.31 Soaring in the valley wind over 'little Lanzarote' at the foot of the Brauneck over Wegscheid. Compare this photo with page 92

Soaring Palo Buque, a fantastic soaring site, Iquique, Chile.

Fly all day at Canoa Quebrada, northeast Brazil.

Dune 7, near Walvis Bay, Namibia

Dune 45, Sossusvlei, Namibia

The smoother the soaring hill, the closer you can get to it – dragging your feet through the sand is fun at Sossusvlei!

227

9 The temperature gradient

Mount Fuji in Japan, flying from Asagiri. Photo: Jérôme Maupoint

Chapter 9
The temperature gradient

The temperature gradient (also lapse rate) tells us how much colder the air gets as we travel vertically up through the atmosphere. It is normally drawn as a graph in a coordinate system, where Y is the altitude (or pressure) and X is the temperature. Vertical resolution is often set to 100m.

The faster the temperature decreases with altitude, the higher the instability of the atmosphere – and that is what makes the lapse rate so interesting to us, as we generally want to have an unstable atmosphere so that thermals may form.

If the temperature decreases slowly with altitude, or even briefly increases, the atmosphere is stable. The more stable it becomes, the unlikelier it is to have good thermal development.

The temperature gradient is a great tool for predicting a number of things about the flying conditions of any given day.

If we have the temperature gradient, the humidity at ground level and the predicted maximum temperature of the day we may already deduce the following values:
- Cloudbase altitude,
- Trigger temperature (the temperature that air pockets must reach in order to be released as thermals),
- The likelihood of thunderstorms, the amount of cloud coverage and the expected day quality in terms of thermal strength.

Admitted, this all sounds rather complex. However by using a number of easily understood examples in the following pages I will slowly guide you through until you have a far greater understanding of this magnificent tool for pilots.

The temperature as function of altitude is physically acquired by releasing weather balloons (called radiosondes) sending their measurements (soundings) back to earth via radio.

9.1 This radiosonde was found in the Isartal. The instruments are attached to the lower end and transmit the soundings back down to earth via radio

The actual coordinate system, with its complex combination of isotherms, saturated and dry adiabats and the mixing ratio, will not be described in detail – my aim is to point to the general

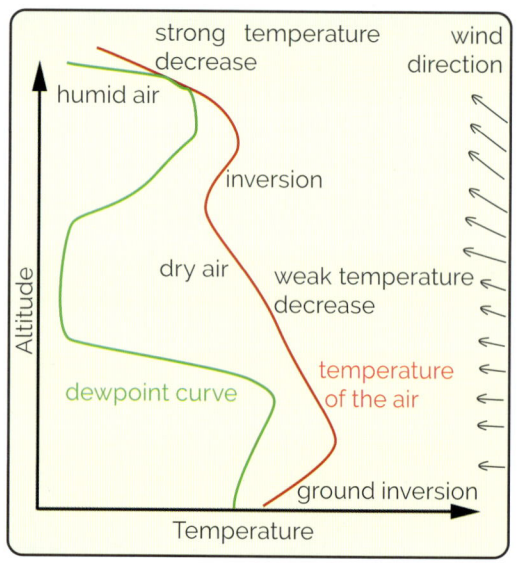

9.2 By reading the temperature we can learn a lot about the prevailing flying conditions. The red line shows the temperature as a function of altitude/pressure; the green line is the dewpoint curve. If they are far apart the atmospheric situation is dry; where the two lines meet the relative humidity is 100% (which means the radiosonde has gone through a cloud). The harder the red curve leans left, the greater the instability. If the red line takes a turn to the right it means that the temperature is increasing at that level, so there's an inversion there.

usefulness of the temperature gradient for pilots.

Radiosonde or weather balloon

A radiosonde is just a balloon with a bunch of instruments attached. It helps the meteorologist by collecting data that would otherwise be out of reach. The soundings contain information about temperature, humidity, pressure and in recent years also position and wind speed etc. The soundings are transmitted by radio to the ground crew.

There are plenty of temperature gradients to look at on the internet, try searching for 'emagram', 'tephigram', 'Stüve diagram' or 'Skew-T log-P diagram', all different ways of depicting the same thing. Illustration 9.2 shows a real life temperature gradient or lapse rate.

The radiosondes all over the world are all deployed at the same time, namely at midnight and noon UTC. They rise to about 30,000m before the balloons burst, and transmit data all the way up. By releasing them all at the same time, meteorologists acquire something akin to an atmospherical snapshot of the global weather twice every day.

As pilots we must know which soundings to base our observations on. In the central Alps there are three different launch sites: Innsbruck, Munich or Stuttgart. If the general flow is from the south I go with the Innsbruck one, if the flow is north the Munich one is more suitable. By westerlies the Stuttgart soundings are also interesting.

The temperature gradient in illustration 9.2 is an example only. As there are at least four different standards for making these diagrams (see above), they will look somewhat different almost every time you cross a border. The important thing to work out with each new diagram is which of the lines indicates the dry adiabatic temperature decrease in the ideal atmosphere, and compare that to the actual curve. In some, the dry adiabat is

> **The dry adiabatic temperature decrease with altitude is -1°C/100m.**
> Once the rising air mass condenses as a cumulus cloud the temperature continues to decrease, but along a saturated adiabatic line. This line isn't constant but is normally given as -0.6°C/100m.

shown as a vertical line in the diagram, but most have them tilted somewhat to the left. Where the day curve follows the dry adiabats the atmosphere is indifferent, where it is leaning more to the left the atmosphere is unstable, and less means a stable atmosphere.

On the right-hand side of the temperature gradient diagram we usually get the wind direction and strength, shown with arrows. In illustration 9.2 the wind increases somewhat with altitude, and turns from east to southeast.

In the so-called standard (but non-existing) atmosphere the temperature decreases 0.65°C/100m upwards through the atmosphere on average.

The saturated adiabatic cooling is slower because the condensation process releases energy stored through evaporation. The energy is released as heat and slows the cooling down. The colder the air mass is, the faster the saturated adiabatic cooling happens. This is due to the fact that cold air can hold less moisture, and the influence of the condensation process on the air mass temperature is thus lower. In very cold air the saturated adiabat and the dry adiabat are almost identical.

How to roughly estimate the temperature gradient through the data you have to hand

If no real temperature diagram is available we may almost make one ourselves with the help of a detailed weather forecast, like the glider forecasts issued by many national weather services. This gives you data as in table 9.3 above.

Table 9.3 Temperature in the atmosphere

Altitude	Temp.	Wind direction	Wind speed
metres	°C	°	km/h
1,000	25	210	5
2,000	18	220	10
3,000	10	240	10
5,000	2	230	20

Altitude	1,000 to 2,000m	2,000 to 3,000m	3,000 to 5,000m
Temp °C/100m	-0.7	-0.8	-0.4

Table 9.3 In the table you can see that there's a temperature difference between 1,000 and 2,000m of 7°C (25°C minus 18°C) which gives us -0.7°C/100m. This is a remarkably good day, with an unstable atmosphere low down and a strong inversion between 3,000 and 5,000m to stop the clouds from going ballistic.

If we can get hold of the values mentioned in the table above it is actually possible to build a rough impression of the day in our minds. The example shows a particularly good XC day, where the atmosphere up to around 3,000m is very unstable. We see this from the fact that the temperature drops fast with altitude, and the thermal quality is accordingly good. Of almost greater importance is the fact that somewhere between 3,000 and 5,000m the temperature decrease with altitude becomes far less conspicuous, indicating the presence of a strong inversion somewhere in this layer – very convenient, as this puts an effective lid on the cloud development and stops the cumuli from growing into Cb's or filling the skies with flat, inactive clouds stopping the sun from reaching the ground. On this day the shower probability is very low!

Had the opposite been the case, with a temperature at 5,000m of, say, -8°C, the temperature gradient in this layer would have been -0.9°C/100m and we would have known for sure that no inversion was stopping the cloud development. On such a day the likelihood of overdevelopment is high, and we would most likely have to terminate our XC attempts some time into the early afternoon.

Rules of thumb for applied use of the temperature gradient

- If the temperature gradient (all given in °C/100m) is positive it means we have an inversion. This stops thermal development at the affected altitude.
- From 0 to -0.2 the air is stable and the thermal development extremely poor.
- If we find values between -0.2 and 0.4 we can assume weak inversions

9.4 If the clouds continue growing long into the evening the atmosphere is probably unstable. On this day the values were between -0.7 and -1.0°C/100m all the way up.

and poor thermal development in the layer. If these values are found up high (at cloudbase or above) it is good, lower down they adversely affect our climb rates.
- Between -0.5 and -0.6 the thermals are still weak but perfect for learning thermal flying. The air isn't too turbulent, but at the same time there aren't any big distances possible in this sort of air mass. At these temperatures it takes a long time before a thermal bubble releases from the ground, and once it does it climbs slowly. Such thermals are easy to centre and pleasant to fly, but they only release with long intervals.
- Once the temperature gradient shows values of -0.6 to -0.8 the thermal quality becomes good. The thermals are strong, and so is the associated turbulence. Such values indicate excellent XC weather.
- Values above -0.8 indicate extreme thermal development and very high descent rates between them. On such days thermal bubbles release from the ground as soon as there is the slightest temperature difference, and rise as small fast bullets causing rough air with difficult thermalling. These days aren't particularly well suited for XC flying.
- If there is no inversion to stop the cloud development, chances are that the day will either overdevelop or the clouds will soon shut out all sunshine so that no more thermals may develop.

The ideal temperature

The perfect day with strong, enjoyable climbs without too much turbulence has a gradient of somewhere around -0.5 to -0.6 at lower levels, increasing to -0.8 to -0.9 up higher. Around cloudbase the gradient should decrease again, to around -0.4. This will slow the thermals down gradually and decrease the boundary turbulence.

Still higher we would prefer a weakish inversion and some dry air, to stop overdevelopment and excessive cloud development.

Such a day is a pilot's dream – plenty of strong, smooth thermals, moderate turbulence and a high cloud base virtually guarantee successful flying endeavours.

For beginners a slightly less pronounced temperature gradient is better, ideally around -0.5 to -0.6 at all levels up to cloudbase. This causes the thermals to be wide and inviting, and the turbulence to remain controllable even by inexperienced pilots. The better we become the more aggressive a temperature gradient we can tolerate.

9.5 Large, well-defined thermals and a distinct vertical limit to the cloud development. On this day there was an inversion between 2,000 and 3,000m and temperature gradient at this level was −0.3˚C/100m.

9.6 A good day for thermalling beginners. Large, gentle thermals with an inversion just above cloudbase to stop the clouds from growing too big. The gradient at lower altitudes was around −0.55 and the inversion at 3,000m.

There's a neat way to acquire the data needed without having access to full-blown diagrams, namely by finding the temperatures at the top of ski lifts. The altitudes of these is always known and the temperatures often published either through radio or internet. Once we have these we may calculate our own gradients for the relevant altitudes.

Glider pilots have used this trick for years and found that the difference between these two top stations should be around 6°C to 9°C, giving a gradient of -0.58 to -0.84°/100m for the day to be good.

If the gradient is lower than this the thermals will be weak, a higher gradient may cause the day to overdevelop either vertically or horizontally, both to the detriment of the day's quality.

EXAMPLE The Säntis in Switzerland is a mountain peak at 2,500m and the temperature on the summit is 12°C. The Jungfraujoch, also in Switzerland, is at 3,500m, the temperature there is 5°C.
The height difference between the two is 1,000m (3,500m − 2,500m).
The temperature difference between the two summits is 7°C (12°C − 5°C)
We can say the temperature changes 7°C in 1,000m. Therefore the temperature gradient is calculated to be −0.7°C/100m.

9.8 The Rosengarten, Dolomites, Italy, towards the evening. The temperature gradient shows a moderate inversion at higher levels, leading us to assume that the weather will remain nice for the next few days at least.

Determining cloudbase and height

The tempature gradient diagram is useful for more than just learning about thermal quality. It can also be used to determine cloudbase altitude and how high the clouds will grow.

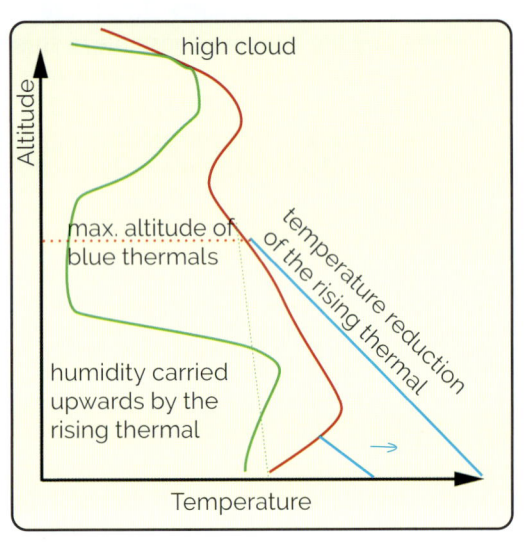

9.7 In the day's temperature gradient diagram, draw a line from the expected day temperature on the X-axis and corresponding to a dry adiabatic temperature decrease of -1.0°C/100m (blue in the illustration). Where the blue line meets the graph we can read the altitude where the thermals stop on the Y-axis (provided they remain blue, and the air cooling thus remains dry-adiabatic).

But will the thermals remain blue? In the above example the answer is yes, for the following reason. The dotted green line goes from the dewpoint at ground level (the bottom of the left curve) to the temperature graph for the day, and indicates where the cloudbase will be in case there are clouds. If this altitude is above the maximum thermal altitude, the day will remain blue. Note that to be able to determine the altitudes accurately we need a Stüve-diagram paper.

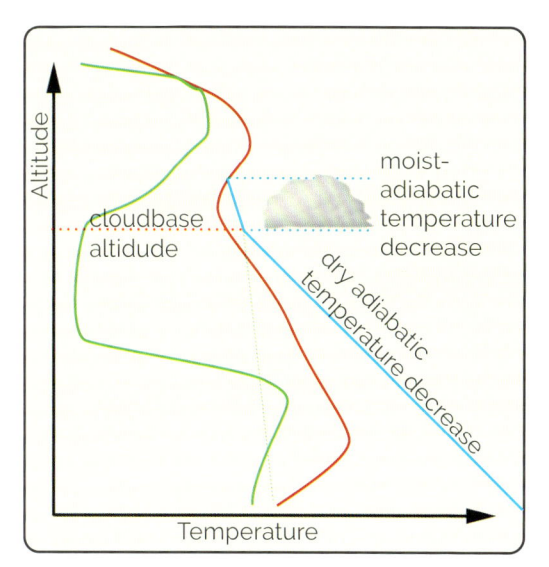

9.9 The same air mass as in illustration 9.7, however the day temperature continues to rise. The blue line now begins further right and consequently meets the dotted green line indicating the humidity in the air mass before meeting the temperature curve. From this point the temperature decrease is moist adiabatic due to the condensation taking place (-0.65°C/100m), and the difference between the altitude where the thermal begins to condense and the altitude where the blue line meets the temperature curve indicates how high the clouds may grow.

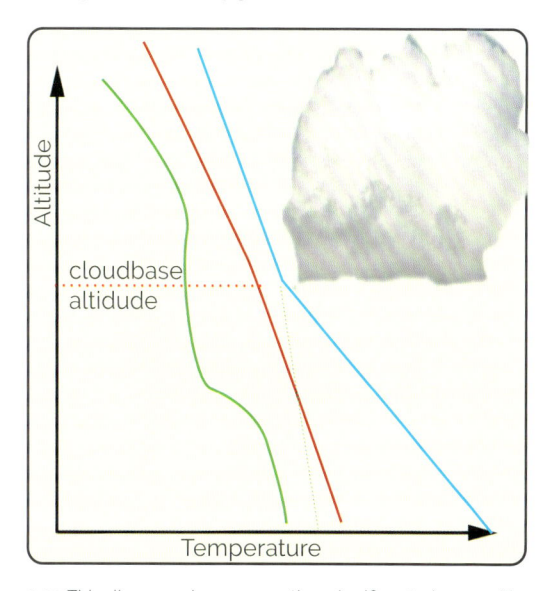

Identifying a subsidence inversion from a temperature-gradient diagram

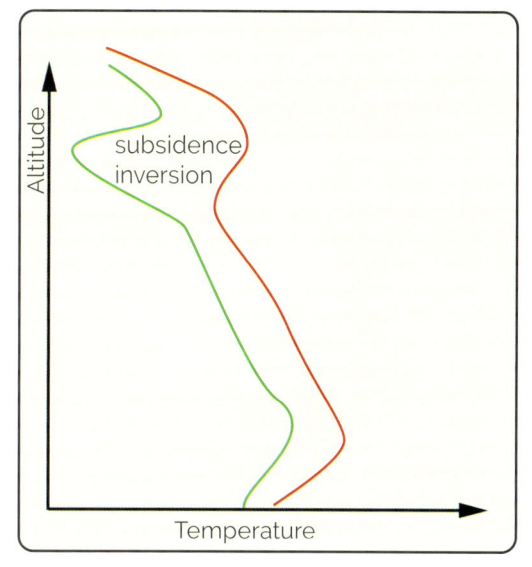

9.11 This diagram shows a typical subsidence inversion as briefly described in Chapter 3. The subsidence inversion determines if the day is good for flying or not: if it is high we have plenty of spread available for thermal development; if it is low the thermals cannot rise and the day becomes poor.

Notice that around the level of the subsidence inversion the temperature increases with altitude, and simultaneously the dewpoint line takes a sharp turn to the left, indicating drier air. This is the exact image indicating a subsidence inversion.

9.10 This diagram shows a weather significant air mass (the two curves are closer to each other), and furthermore the red curve has no inversion built in anywhere. Finally the blue line never meets the red curve so there's no lid on the thermal development – the thunderstorm is brewing.

None of the clouds are tall – this is the subsidence inversion in action. A good sign. Flying the flatlands in Quixadá, Brazil

235

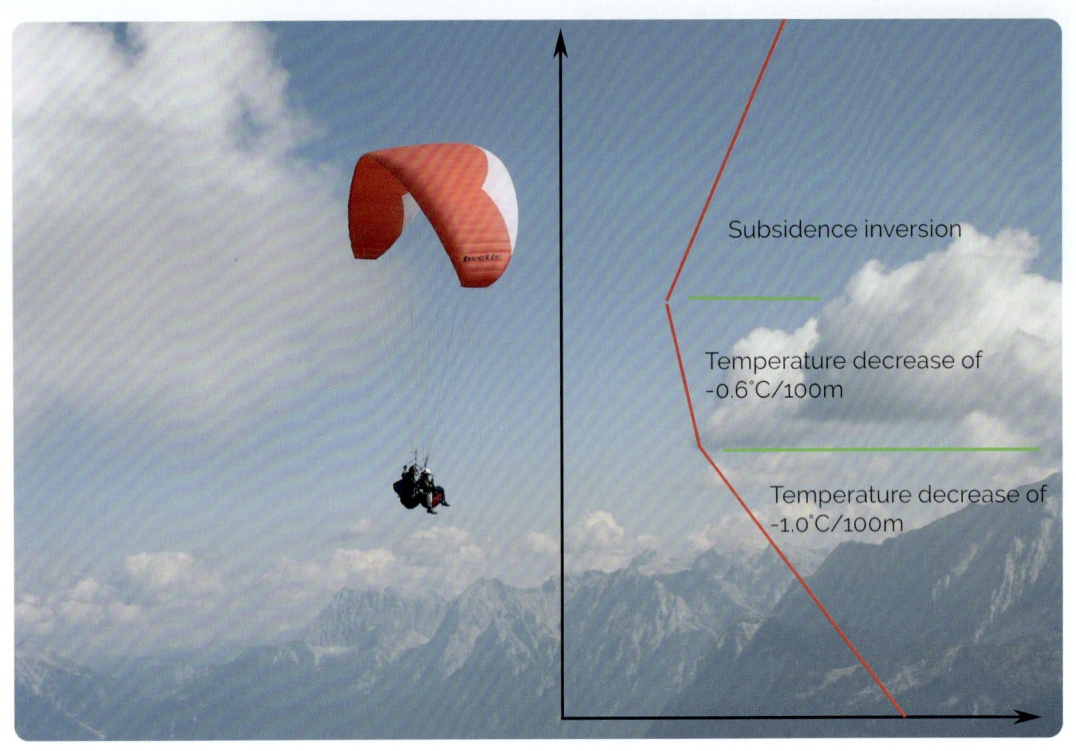

9.12 In this photograph I added the adiabatic temperature gradient, dry lower down then moist from cloudbase up. Notice how the cloud has a distinct upper ceiling caused by the subsidence inversion. The photo shows the Garmisch-Partenkirchen flight arena in Germany.

9.13 The stuff of dreams. High cloudbase, high subsidence inversion stopping any overdevelopment. Perfect. The picture shows the Pustertal (Italy/Austria), with the Grossvenediger (left) and the Grossglockner (right).

Picture 9.14 *When the air is very dry the cloudbase becomes correspondingly high. On this day near Lienz (Austria) we had a cloudbase around and slightly above 4,000m, but in the Ötztal the air was even drier and pilots were getting to 5,000m (approx. 16,500 ft)!*

9.15 *It is actually far easier to determine cloudbase using the relative humidity than using the Stüve diagram or the emagram, as we did in illustration. 9.9.*

Determining cloudbase altitude through humidity

There's another way to roughly determine cloudbase, namely by using the air humidity at ground level. That is the moisture which will be carried upwards by the thermal and which will eventually condense and form the clouds. It is actually rather self-evident; the drier the air mass, the higher the cloudbase. In the following table the approximate values are given – the humidity is measured with a simple hygrometer.

Table 9.16
Relative humidity versus cloudbase
Measured in metres over the point where the humidity was measured

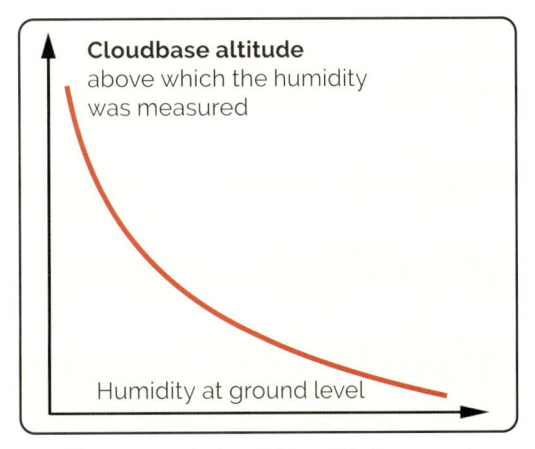

Rel humidity (%)	Cloudbase (m)
20	3,400
30	2,600
40	2,000
50	1,500
60	1,100
70	800
80	500

9.17 *The same content as table 9.16 but expressed as a curve. Cloudbase climbs as the air dries out – once the air becomes very dry cloudbase rises very fast.*

Cloudbase development during the day

It is common knowledge that cloudbase rises during the day. Here is the explanation why.

As the day wears on, the humidity at ground level decreases as humidity is continuously transported up by the rising thermals.

Secondly, the higher the temperature at ground level, the further the two curves in the thermodynamic diagram are apart – we say that the spread is high (the term 'spread' refers to the distance between the temperature curve and the dewpoint curve in a thermodynamic diagram). When the ground-level temperature increases by 1°C cloudbase climbs approximately 125m!

On a normal thermally active day the cloud base may climb 500-1,000m during the day. In extreme cases cloudbase may climb far more.

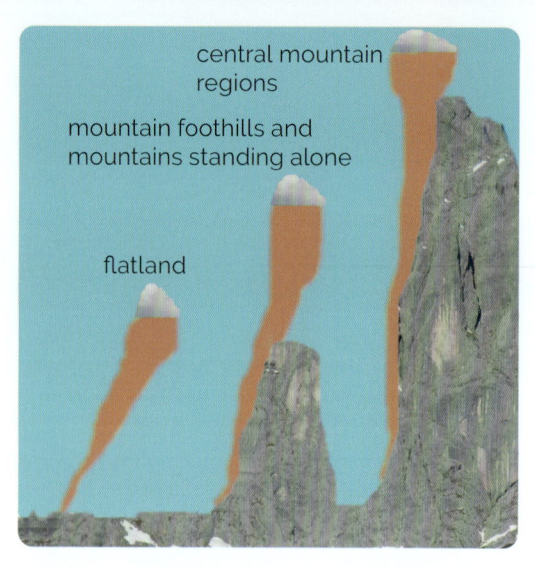

9.18 The condensation level and thus cloudbase level depends on a number of factors, with the most important one being the available humidity in the air and the temperature gradient. As a general rule, cloudbase will be lower in flatland regions than in adjacent mountain foothills, and the difference to central mountain regions is still greater. On days where the flats have a cloudbase of 1,500MSL, the foothills may often get 2,300MSL and the Alpine dividing range even 4,000MSL! Sailplanes can go far under a 1,500MSL ceiling but paragliders and hang gliders prefer a little more working space.

9.17 Cloudbase rises during the day, sometimes by more than 1,000m. During this process we may observe the clouds going from small in the morning to large around the best thermal time, and back to small again towards evening. That is the way a good day should look! The photo shows the Bavarian foothills in Germany.

238

Gliding forecast

Some national meteorological services issue gliding forecasts during the gliding season. As thermal flyers these forecasts are of great value for our flight planning. A glider forecast usually contains the following information:

- Wind speed and direction at various altitudes. If the wind speed increases dramatically at a certain height we know that we should expect turbulence at this level. Once we know the wind directions we can also determine which mountain ranges are in the lee and which may be soarable.

- Condensation level/cloudbase. Or it may simply state that the day will remain blue.

- Thermal trigger-temperature. The temperature that an air mass must reach in order to rise all the way to condensation level. Anyone flying before this temperature has been reached will find only calm air.

- Thermal life cycle and duration.

- Particular dangers. If it says: "No particular dangers" then the day is perfect as there are no storms expected, no strong winds at ridge level with associated turbulence, no föhn and no new frontal systems expected. Note that such a statement pertains to the general meteorology, not the involved pilot skills!! Avoiding lee is still the pilot's responsibility.

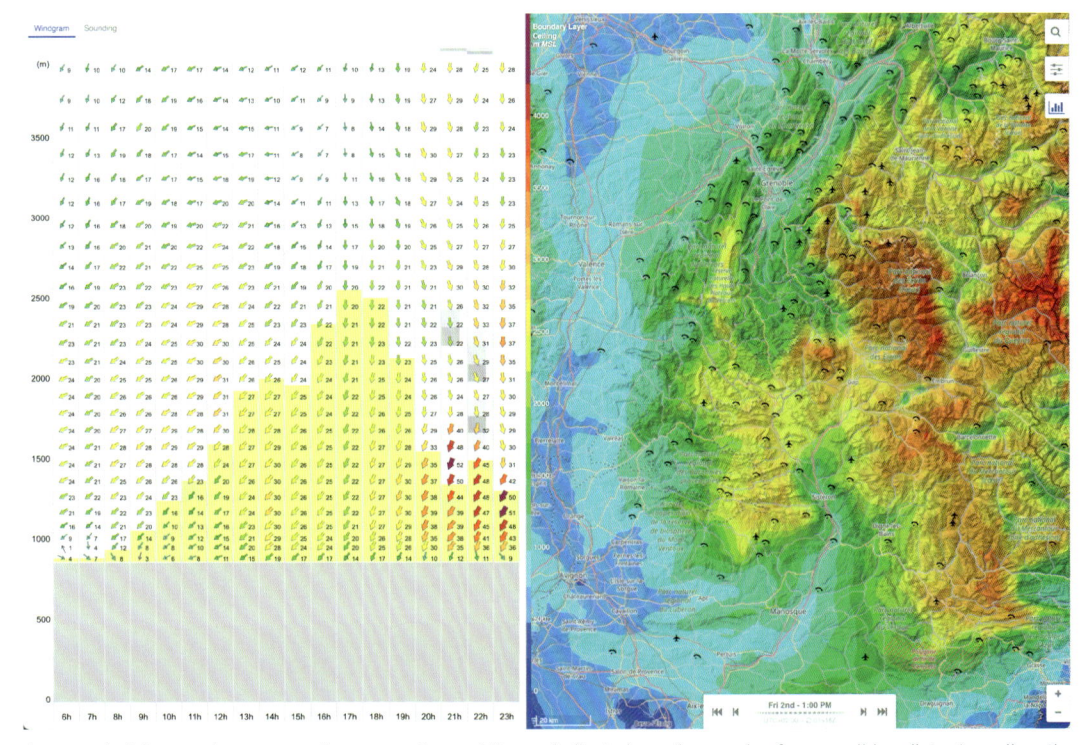

*A screenshot from **meteo-parapente.com**, a site providing a dedicated weather service for paraglider pilots. As well as the windgram shown the site can show the nearest sounding data. There is a whole raft of data that can be displayed on the map including predicted thermal strength and cloudbase height.*

World weather forecasting

By Ed Ewing

Understanding how a weather forecast is made can help you understand how accurate it might be, and how much trust you can put in it. Today, weather forecasters use some of the biggest supercomputers in the world to predict the weather worldwide up to 14 days in advance. International, national and regional forecasting all has a part to play.

Meteorological information is collected by satellites, ground observation stations, aircraft, ships, marine buoys, weather balloons and automatic and manned stations. The information is interpreted by meteorologists for specific tasks: for example a three-day forecast for the general public; a mountain forecast for the ski industry; storm or hurricane forecasts for the emergency services; or a rain forecast for local authority flood response.

In free flight, we look for a soaring forecast. These are often provided on a regional and local scale and are often created from freely-available data by pilots who are also amateur meteorologists. You will find links to your local or regional soaring forecasts on flying, gliding and paragliding club websites.

Forecast models

There are two main types of forecast models. Global ones cover the entire planet, while local ones cover specific areas such as continents, countries or mountain ranges etc. Both types of forecasts work to a certain resolution. If you imagine the world divided into grid squares, this is what is meant by resolution. The sharper the resolution, the harder it is to get the forecast right and the more computing power is needed.

Where the terrain is flat and uniform, for example deserts or oceans, a bigger resolution of 10km to 50km is used. In mountain ranges or densely populated areas a much finer resolution is used: typically 5km. Resolving weather

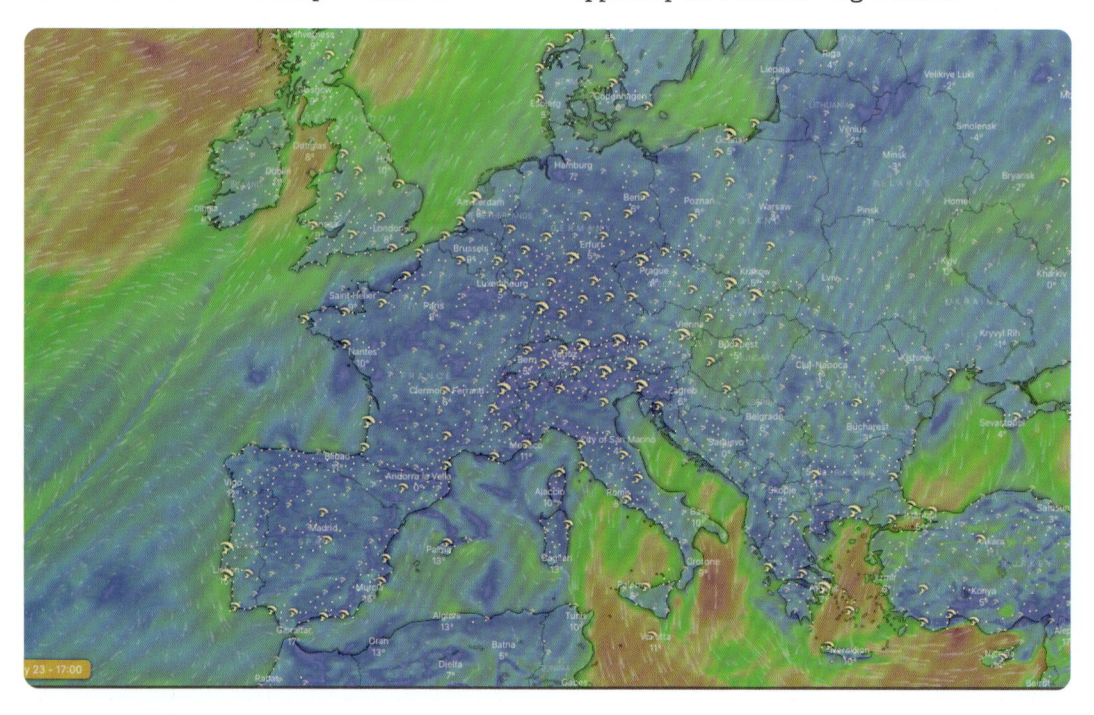

Windy.com combines data from several global weather models and paragliding sites to give very good forecasts

forecasts down to 1km squares is extremely hard, which is why you will often hear meteorologists say they are happy to predict "Showers in the afternoon" but not exactly where those showers will fall.

As pilots we need to take account of local and often hyper-local weather phenomena, for example slope winds, gusts, dust devils and thermals. At this level of resolution it becomes up to us to interpret the weather and to explain and predict what is about to happen. This is why we need to stay alert and learn to read the weather 'naturally', without constant reference to apps or weather data. Of course, we also need to understand and learn to read the apps and weather websites too. We need to be able to do both.

There are a handful of global weather forecast models. Some of the most important ones are described here:

ECMWF - European Centre for Medium-Range Weather Forecasting
Resolution: Down to 5km
Forecast depth: Up to 10 days
Updated: Twice a day
Widely regarded as the best and most reliable model in existence today. Famously, it was the only model to correctly predict the track of Hurricane Sandy in 2012, a hurricane that caused $70bn damage across eight countries from the Caribbean to Canada.
Website: ecmwf.int

GFS - Global Forecast System
Resolution: 27km
Forecast depth: 10 days
Updated: Four times a day
Updated every six hours by the American meteorological service it has a reputation as being good for oceans, but doesn't take topography into account so well. It is made up of four models which work together: atmospheric, ocean, land and sea-ice models.
Website: bit.ly/3vR2ipi

ICON - Global German Standard
Resolution: Up to 7km
Forecast depth: 5 days
Updated: Four times a day
Created by the German Meteorological Service ICON is considered to be even more accurate than the ECMWF because it has better resolution, especially in Europe.

UM - United Kingdom Met Office
Resolution: 1.5km (UK), 10km (global)
Forecast depth: Three days
Updated: Twice a day
The Unified Model, also known as the UKMO, is the most reliable model for the UK due to its very good resolution. It is considered reliable and has formed the basis for some regional small-scale models like New Zealand and Australia.
Website: Metoffice.gov.uk

CFS - Climate Forecast System
Resolution: 108km
Forecast depth: 30 days
Updated: Four times a day
A global numerical model produced by NOAA (USA) the model is based on historical weather observations. It aims to predict a general forecast for each calendar day. It has a poor prediction value but is useful for long-term planning – for example if you are planning a trip and want to find the best time of year for certain weather.
Website: bit.ly/3lGMscl

Windy.com

Windy.com uses data from at least six global models and many regional models to create its 'live' forecasts of wind around the globe. It has numerous layers, including a database of paragliding and hang-gliding sites, and kite-surfing locations. It predicts the weather up to 10 days ahead. It is an excellent place for pilots to start their journey into becoming a weather forecaster and local expert.

10 Need-to-know

It doesn't get much better than this! Photo: Adi Geisegger

Chapter 10

Need-to-know

This chapter contains miscellaneous nuggets of insight that didn't fit in any of the other chapters but couldn't be left out due to their importance.

The polar curve

The polar curve of a gliding aircraft is simply a graph showing the relationship between speed and sink rate in a coordinate system.

To construct a usable polar curve for a paraglider or a hang glider is not necessarily an easy task. The first prerequisite is absolutely calm air – not a common occurrence anywhere. Second is a good memory, or simply a voice recorder or camera, a vario and a speed probe. Early mornings offer the best chances of recording an accurate polar curve. I won't even begin to list all the possible errors that may adversely influence the final result.

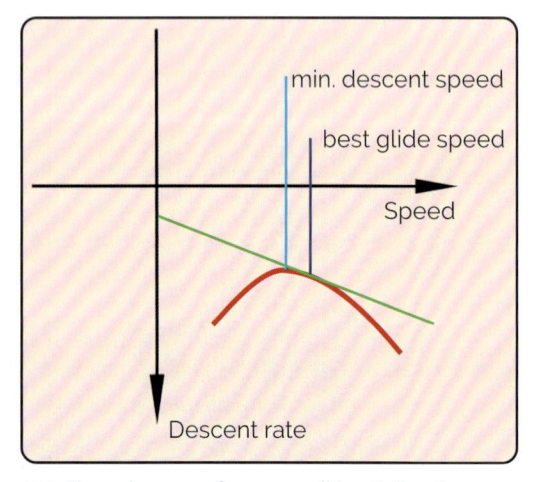

10.1 *The polar curve for a paraglider. Notice the green tangent line through the coordinate system origin; where the line touches the curve we may read the speed for best glide on the X-axis. The highest point on the curve indicates the minimum sink of the wing, to be seen on the Y-axis.*

It is important to know how the polar curve looks in principle. That is useful for optimising our gliding in different situations – it doesn't matter so much if the actual polar is accurate or not.

How a polar curve is acquired

In order to get a sufficient number of coordinates in our coordinate system to draw the polar we simply fly at all the speeds our wing is capable of (for example in 2km/h increments), all the time recording the sink rate corresponding to the different speeds.

Once we have all the values (speed/sink rate) we plot them into the coordinate system. Table 10.2 shows a table with the values for a modern sports-class wing. Notice that both axes are in m/s, so we'll have to convert our speed measurements into m/s before entering them into the table. With these numbers we can also calculate our L/D ratio, often referred to as our glide ratio, by dividing A (speed) with B (descent rate).

Table 10.2
Polar data of a 'good' paraglider
The measured airspeed is converted into m/s then divided by the descent rate and we already have the glide ratio (L/D). Flying altitude 2,000m, temp 4°C, humidity 65%.

Speed km/h (meas.)	Speed (A) m/s (calc.)	Sink (B) m/s (meas.)	L/D = A/B (calc.)
25	6.9	1.6	4.31
30	8.3	1.3	6.41
34	9.4	1.15	8.21
38	10.6	1.1	9.60
41	11.4	1.2	9.49
45	12.5	1.5	8.33
50	13.9	2.0	6.94
55	15.3	2.3	6.64

How to glide the furthest?

This question is of elementary importance to the XC pilot, particularly when crossing difficult areas. If we're crossing a wide valley we normally want to arrive at the other side as high as possible so that we increase our chances of locating lift and continuing the flight.

The wing in the example above has an approximate trim speed of 40km/h, at least with the wing loading used for the polar measurements. The best glide ratio is calculated to be 9.6 in the table. If there's absolutely no wind then this is the best speed to glide for long transitions.

Note that most paragliders are designed to have their best glide in calm air with the brakes untouched and no speed bar applied.

Optimising the climb using the polar curve

It doesn't take a degree in maths to work out that the best speed for thermalling is as close to the minimum sink speed as possible. If we return to the example from the previous page it is easy to see that for this particular wing the minimum sink is around the 38km/h mark, in fact not very far from the speed for best glide.

It always surprises me when I meet or overhear people saying something along the lines of: "There I was with the brakes buried almost to my hips and the others were still climbing better!" One glance at the table is enough to tell us that we get absolutely nothing out of flying too slowly.

How to glide with a headwind

If we look at a headwind situation from a polar curve view, we simply change the origin of the tangent line on the x-axis corresponding to the wind speed. The tangent touches the curve further down the slope, indicating that the optimal speed for gliding against the wind is higher than when we wish to go far in calm air.

HINT If in doubt it is always better to glide a little too fast than a little too slow.

10.3 Minimum descent rates, an aerodynamic body position and the use of significant weightshifting are vital parts of thermal flying.

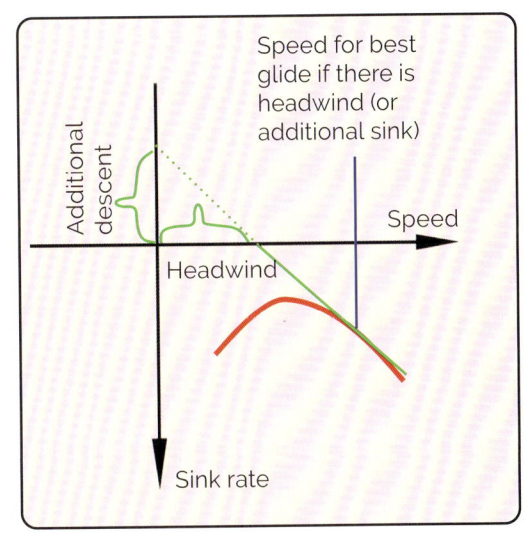

10.4 When flying with a headwind the speed for best glide is shifted right, or further down the slope of the polar curve. In order to go the furthest with a headwind we must thus increase our speed to beyond the trim speed.

> **How to fly with a headwind**
> If there is up to 10km/h headwind we use only a little speed to 1/3 bar. Around 20km/h it pays to speed up to around 2/3 of the full range of the speed system, and only when the headwind reaches 30km/h is it worth going at full speed.

> **How to fly in sinking air**
> If the surrounding air is sinking 1m/s, the vario is showing approx. −2.1m/s and glide ratio is reduced to nearly half. We should accelerate 1/2 to 2/3. Once the needle hits 3m/s, corresponding to a surrounding air mass sinking with 2m/s, we must go very fast to escape.

NOTE: It is good to be aware of the fact that the glide angle is severely affected by a headwind. If the wing in the example above flies into a 20km/h headwind the glide angle becomes much steeper and the glide ratio is only half of what we would get in calm air. This translates into the understanding that even small valley crossings are all but out of the question if there's a strong headwind.

In real-life flying it is rare to be going at full speed on a paraglider. It is only necessary if there's a Venturi effect stopping us from getting over or around a spur or similar – or on final glides in competitions.

> **HINT** When flying with a crosswind we must go slightly sideways (called crabbing) in order to counter the drift. Note that the headwind rules apply – we must speed up to reach best glide. The more crosswind, the faster we must fly to optimise our glide angle.

How to fly in descending air

We can also use the polar curve coordinate system to work out how to fly through sinking air. To do this we must move the origin of the tangent up the Y-axis corresponding to the descent rate we meet. Again it is clear to see that the tangent touches the graph further right, indicative of the need to speed up in sinking air. See illustration 10.4.

NOTE: When flying through an air mass sinking 2m/s our glide ratio is reduced to around 3.4, almost regardless of whether we're going 40 or 50km/h! This means that getting out of the sinking air mass is top priority, either by speeding up or by changing heading. Aside from that we can only hope that we can get through it before we run out of air to fly through.

> **HINT** If we find ourselves low and desperate it pays to search downwind, ie with a tailwind even if it means flying back the way we came from for a while, as this allows us to explore a far greater area than if we keep insisting on going against the wind. It is better to fly a long detour than to be sitting on the ground!

How to deal with a tailwind

Gliding with a tailwind is great; it gives the impression that one can go on forever. If we look at the coordinate system again we can see that the origin of the tangent line is shifted left, which means that the tangent touches the speed polar curve further left as well. Further left is closer to the speed for min sink so it follows that it pays to slow down a little in a tailwind.

Notice that the gap between speed for best glide and speed for minimum sink is narrow on modern wings so don't overdo the braking part – on the wing used in the examples above we should never slow down to an airspeed of less than 38km/h as this just makes the sink rate increase again!

Active piloting

This enchanted concept keeps turning up wherever two or more paraglider pilots are gathered. I'm going to put it as straight as I can: if you fly a lot you learn a lot! This also translates into the important insight that if you're a novice you do yourself a favour by not flying during the most thermally active times of the day. The more turbulence you encounter, the greater the chances that you'll hit that bit of air just beyond your own capabilities. Far better to approach turbulence in a gradual manner and learn active piloting step by step.

Many paragliding schools offer safety and performance training courses. If you haven't yet attended such a clinic I would recommend that you do so, as this is really the best way to prepare oneself for learning active piloting. In the following I will however explain the concept in more detail – note that all this doesn't in any way replace good safety training but it could make your learning curve steeper.

Active piloting is the name we have chosen for the art of always keeping the glider vertically above the pilot and travelling at the same heading as the pilot. It sounds simple, but it takes a lot of practice to get it right.

In order to pilot actively the pilot needs to know the brake pressure of his wing – sensing the changes in the brake pressure is the first prerequisite for getting the timing right.

Novices generally react too late to the changes in brake pressure – and please don't interpret this as some sort of reproach, all comes to him who practises!

How to react when the glider pitches back

When we meet a lifting air mass, like a strong thermal, the glider pitches back to a greater or lesser extent. Sitting in the harness it feels not unlike the sensation when we tilt a chair backwards. Note that the brake pressure increases whilst the wing is getting pitched back.

To counter the movement the pilot releases the brakes precisely enough to maintain the brake pressure at the level where it was before the wing started to fall behind. If he gets the timing right the pitching will be greatly reduced. As soon as the wing has stopped pitching back the pilot should begin to dampen the surge by reapplying brakes, taking care to only brake enough to stop the wing right above his head.

10.5 *The glider suffered a side-collapse, immediately followed by a counter-collapse on the opposite side. Both collapses would have been avoidable for the skilled pilot, but the glider is a forgiving model and has hardly changed its heading.*

10.6 *When entering a strong thermal the glider can pitch back quite strongly.*

The whole sequence happens very fast, and the pilot should instinctively do the following:
- Release the brakes as the wing begins to pitch back. Failing to do so will make it fall even further behind.
- Begin to catch the surge as soon as the wing reaches the most extreme point in the back-pitching movement.
- Be back to the normal brake position once the wing is back over your head – braking more will just replay the sequence.

How to react when the glider shoots forward

If we drop out the side of a strong thermal, or otherwise hit sinking air, the glider shoots forward. If it surges too far the leading edge will collapse, so we always aim to control all the surges to avoid collapses. A surge is easy to identify through the brakes because the brake pressure decreases, and extreme surges may have us almost facing the ground, feeling like we have been tipped out of a chair.

As long as the surge is happening we must apply more brake. In extreme cases it may be necessary to brake up to 100%.

As soon as the forward pitching moment ceases we must begin to release the brakes

10.7 *When the glider surges we must try to stop it by applying brake. The most common mistake here is to brake too little and too late – and this is what allows the wing to collapse. Very skilled pilots can prevent practically all collapses, especially on wings with good feedback through the brakes and risers.*

> **HINT** Practise active piloting whenever you fly by always attempting to keep the wing right above your head. Consciously note the relations between brake pressure, harness movement and glider position in relation to yourself. Good exercises for increasing spatial awareness in the sky are deliberate pitching movements (dolphin flying) and wingovers. Be sure to approach all of these gradually and with caution, and only with sufficient altitude.
>
> Once you get it right the movements are very rhythmic, but note that wingovers going higher than 45° are best learnt over water and with competent guidance.
>
> Pilots who are consistently able to fly long series of high, rhythmic wingovers are almost guaranteed to be skilled at active piloting as well!

again – once the wing is above our head again the brakes should be back to the initial position.

If we get the timing wrong and release the brakes too late the glider will pitch back and we'll find ourselves in a pilot induced oscillation. If our timing remains off it is possible to increase the oscillations until the wing either stalls or collapses over the leading edge.

Side (asymmetric) collapses

Before the wing collapses above you it talks to you, warning you of what is about to happen. The brake pressure decreases on the affected side, and the lines all go slightly slack. We notice the latter because we tip to the affected side in the harness.

If we're quick we may respond by applying more brake on the affected side, enough to keep it from surging forward but not so much that we risk spinning or even pitching the affected side back. Once we get this right collapses will be a thing of the past.

Getting the amount of brake input right when one side of the wing wants to collapse is not always easy. Note that it may be necessary to briefly apply up to 100%, to avoid the wing collapsing.

If we get the timing wrong and the collapse gets us anyway we should stabilise our heading by applying opposite brake. To do this, brake the open side and weight-shift to the open side, but only so much as you need to maintain the heading. In order to know our heading it is better to look forward than up! Beware, it is easy to accidentally apply too much brake on the open side and inadvertently stall it – if this happens we call it a cascade incident, and such things are beyond the scope of this book.

One of the things you learn when you do a safety course is how surprisingly little steering input is normally needed to stabilise the heading with one side collapsed. Inexperienced pilots generally pull too much and get into trouble for it – see the words about cascade incidents above.

Once we have stabilised our heading the collapse will most likely be sorted out all by itself. If there is still some canopy folded under, pump it out with one or two deep, powerful but short pumps on the collapsed side – little dabs on the brake have no effect, but take care not to stall the collapsed side!

Do yourself the favour of practising all these things under qualified supervision and preferably over water – they are your life insurance, but can get you into a lot of trouble if you get some of it wrong.

Training programme

Anyone wishing to excel in any given activity must train to improve. This is pretty clear, but we can add that a person training in a goal-oriented manner, all the time focusing on learning from mistakes and applying theoretical knowledge to the practical situations, will improve much faster than someone who just goes flying and doesn't think much about it either before or after.

Flying a lot is good, but not the whole story, which is one of the reasons I came up with a training programme for you to refine your basic skills, integrating theoretical knowledge and practical skills.

Start by practising the exercises at your home site, and then take them with you to new flying sites so that you may build up your experience bank fast.

Exercise 1

10.8 An induced collapse as you would do on an SIV course. Docile wings forgive most of our mistakes while higher-level wings may show more dynamic reactions.

10.9 Climb to cloudbase, then leave the thermal and lose 300m of altitude fast. Rejoin the thermal and climb back up as fast as you can. Repeat, but lose 500, then 750m etc. The goal is to practise the centring technique and learn about the structure of thermals.

Exercise 2

10.10 Switch back and forth between two reliable thermals. Climb up to cloudbase in one, glide over to the other, repeat there but leave 200m beneath cloudbase to return to the first thermal. Once there, climb again but only till 400m beneath the cloud, then switch to thermal 2 again. Continue until you are almost on the deck. The goal is to learn how to find the thermals at any altitude and to improve our skills at low scratching.

Exercise 3

10.11 Learn about the expansion of the thermal. Once you have located a thermal try to widen your circles for every full 360°. Sooner or later you will find the boundaries of the thermal. Then re-centre and note which turn radius gives you the best climb rate. Goals: learning about the ideal turn radius for a given thermal. Learning about the size and shape of thermals.

Exercise 4

10.12 When soaring on thermally active slopes practise exploring the expanse of the lift band, particularly away from the slope. Fly away from the slope until there's no more lift, then return and do the same further down the ridge. If you happen upon an embedded thermal try to bite into it and take it as high as you dare without risking being blown back over the top. Goal: to learn to discern between dynamic and thermal lift and to exploit thermal lift in combination with dynamic lift. Photo: Sospel, France, near Monaco.

Exercise 5

10.13 Practise thermalling to the opposite side of what you normally prefer. Goal: to become proficient at thermalling both ways. Having this skill sorted makes quick centring much easier as we rarely hit thermals right in the middle and it is almost always best to turn one way or the other right from the start. High above Mittenwald, Germany.

Exercise 6

10.14 Try to change directions in the thermal. Try it both on the upwind and on the downwind side. Goal: you may need to be able to do this soon enough, and having practised it beforehand is always good. It also builds your awareness of upwind and downwind in the thermals.

Exercise 7

10.15 Switch off your vario for a while and practise flying, and thermalling with no external aid. Goal: to hone your sensitivity towards the subtle messages the air is transmitting through your eyes, ears, buttocks and hands. Beware of subtle changes in speed when you fly in and out of thermals – feel it on your face and listen for it in how your glider reacts. Also note the changes in brake-line pressure – it increases when you fly into a thermal and decreases when you hit turbulence or fall out of the thermals. Try to notice if the air is being sucked in towards the thermal or pushed away.

Use fixed points to register climbing and sinking. This is easy beneath ridge height but gets more complicated above the terrain. Use two peaks that are aligned and notice if the one further away is becoming more or less visible with time. If you see more of it you are either gliding towards it or climbing! Photo: climbing out from the Rauschberg with no vario! Germany.

Exercise 8

10.16 Fly between two known thermals, once in a wide left arc, once right. Notice which of the routes was best. Repeat to see if the result is also repeatable. Goal: to learn that the best route isn't always a straight line. Detours may often be better in the long run. Photo: the Drautal near Greifenburg in Austria.

You don't need a vario to fly the socks off any paraglider pilot out there. Griffon vulture. Photo: Marcus King.

251

Exercise 9

10.17 Attempt to fly to a thermal marked by circling gliders. Climb to cloudbase in the new thermal. Goal: to improve your distance-judging. Other gliders are generally much closer than we think, mostly a lot closer! Manilla, Australia.
Photo: Martin Scheel / azoom.ch

Exercise 10

10.18 On a day with abundant cumulus development, practise discerning the ones that are forming from the ones that are decaying. Always attempt to approach only forming clouds and avoid the decaying ones. Try to judge the life cycle of the clouds around you in minutes. Goal: to learn about cloud life-cycles. Karakoram.
Photo: Ozone / Philippe Nodet

Exercise 11

10.19 Practise your groundhandling skills and your reverse launches. All you need is an open field and a bit of wind. Groundhandling is the best thing aside from flying that you can do for your glider-handling skills. You can even practise collapses by pulling in an A-riser while the wing is inflated above you – try to keep it flying without letting it touch the ground. If you're there with a friend, make a small battle where you attempt to get in the way of your buddy – whoever has his wing touch the ground first has lost! Such games are great fun and will make you a better pilot too. Remember to wear your helmet and gloves! Photo: Nina Brümmer

10.20 Playing in the valley wind. Whoever has his wing touching the ground first has lost! In this case we had to declare a draw after 15 very sweaty minutes.
Photo: Nina Brümmer

10.21 Playing with our favourite toy. If you're not wearing your harness, steering with the A's and D's is the easiest way. With the harness the D-risers are still useful for steering but remember to wear gloves when you grab paraglider lines – they make painful burns. If the wind gets stronger you should always wear a helmet.

10.22 If the launch is shrouded in fog but the wind is blowing just get your wing out anyway and start playing. The photo shows the Krippenstein launch in Austria.

10.24 Hay bales, benches, rocks, logs or garbage containers; anything goes if the objective is to climb obstacles while balancing your wing above your head. Photo: Mike Küng

Top-landing

Top-landing hasn't really got anything to do with thermal flying, it is however an important skill to have and can save car retrieve hassles, give you an opportunity to warm up before a second flight, enjoy the solitude of the mountains in tranquillity, *and* it can save you from having to land in a valley bottom where the valley winds have become too strong or too turbulent for comfort. Here are a few hints for safe top-landings.

Top-landing is generally both more demanding and more dangerous than just floating down to the official landing site at the valley bottom. However there are exceptions, like when the main landing field has come under the influence of a sudden strong valley wind, a valley wind convergence or something similar.

As an example, in Fiesch in Switzerland the local pilots tend to avoid the main landing when the Grimsel-wind breaks into the valley as this causes the conditions to become turbulent there.

Some of the things that need to be considered when setting up for a top-landing are wind strength and direction, likelihood of rotor formation over the chosen landing spot, likelihood of sudden thermal activity that may change the wind direction completely etc. Never force it, always keep your calm and rather make 10 or 20 failed approaches than stalling in

10.26 At the Monte Avena the pilots approach from behind, just like a normal landing in the valley floor. The landing field slopes gently towards the edge, leaving no space for rotors to form.

10.25 One of the greatest top-landing areas I know is Monte Avena above Feltre in Italy. The best way here is to fly back over the top of the mountain where there is no lift, lose the height there and come in towards point A against the wind from behind. On thermally-active days there is usually enough wind to almost park above A, and wait until low enough to glide forward to right next to the parking. Remember to keep pointing into wind! This method only works in places where there is no lee behind the edge; look for a place with a gentle slope rather than an abrupt change in landscape.

from too high, or going in with a tailwind. If the wind is too strong and/or the lift too abundant simply abort the attempt and leave it for another day.

Note that most top slopes are far less suited for the purpose than the one in these photos – in Europe, other well-known easy top-landings include the Castelluccio in Italy, Aspres sur Büech in France or even the Dune du Pilat, also in France. All of these are great places for practising your top-landing skills before graduating to more demanding sites.

A good top-landing site has a gentle transition from steep slope to level top with no sharp edges (see 3.9 and 3.10, page 83). It is also comforting if there is no steep opposite slope behind the top where you could get blown to in case the wind is stronger than expected, and grassy fields are much preferable to rocky expanses – the latter tend to be dotted with prickly brush anyway.

If the wind is not straight onto the slope you must beware of this and always point your wing into the wind anyway – failing to do so will almost surely give you an involuntary dragging experience.

If the lift in front of the slope is strong, as in the picture 10.25, it pays to move to the point A and simply 'park' there until you are low enough to glide forward to the landing. This works because there is no lift at A, only wind, compare also to picture 8.10 on page 216.

If we have chosen a dome-shaped hill for our top-landing attempt it is important to know that any dynamic lift from further down the slopes is simply blown around the top at peak level, so there may be less lift and more wind than expected close to the top. It may suddenly sink quite fast!

If there is a healthy breeze blowing it is important to not flare hard upon landing, as this will just see you getting dragged backwards off your feet. Brake gently to make the touchdown soft, then balance the glider above you until you have turned to face it – only then should you kill it either via the brakes or, in very strong winds, via the C-risers.

The reason for turning around first is that you may then run with it instead of being pulled backwards. Practise this manoeuvre at the landing field before you need it in earnest.

Slope-landing

Paragliders land across the slope whereas hang gliders land against it, 'fly on the wall' style. Don't try this on a paraglider, it will hurt.

When slope-landing on a paraglider, first you need to work out if there's any headwind component to help you make your landing soft. The wind is rarely straight onto a slope so there will often be one way where you fly slower than the other.

10.27 *Paragliders slope-landing. If the wind is strong, simply 'park' and wait until you are low enough to glide forward and land. If the wind is light, flare normally. If it is strong, don't flare. Instead, keep the glider above your head, turn, and collapse it.*

Cross-country flight planning for new XC pilots

I've written an entire book about cross-country flying and the best cross-country sites in the Alps, but nevertheless I'd like to present a short summary on planning and preparation here.

1. Basics

Pilots who want to go cross-country must be able to thermal correctly, and not just in big smooth thermals, but also small rough ones triggering from close to the ground.

It is important than no-one is afraid of landing out. This can be practised. Choose yourself a different field to land in, and land there. With a paraglider this is really not much of a problem. Hang glider pilots have told me how they drove their planned cross-country route before flying it, just to check out the landing possibilities.

Never worry about getting home again – somehow and sometime you'll get there.

2. The three most important rules

- The secret to success is to fly high, higher and higher still. Take every climb you can get, rather than flying low and fast.
- Always fly at best glide. See p 244 onwards on polars.
- If you find a thermal, use it and don't give up on it.

EXPERIENCE In Greifenburg Gerhard flew into the well-known lee behind the Anna-Schutz House and landed out. Barbara found this most amusing, and asked him why he hadn't looked in Burki's book to check things out here. After an evening's reading Gerhard made it to Sillian the next day. He was most pleased, but still somewhat annoyed at his mistake the day before.

3. Preparation

To fly in areas you don't know, you need to make some careful preparations beforehand. Not doing so can leave you standing on the ground on a great day, while others sail happily over your head.

Take a good look at the flights of other pilots before going to a new area. Beginners can build themselves routes via turnpoints (TP on the map below) from thermal to thermal, more experienced pilots check where to cross large valleys, and save these points in their GPS.

The regions where several pilots have thermalled should be noted – here are

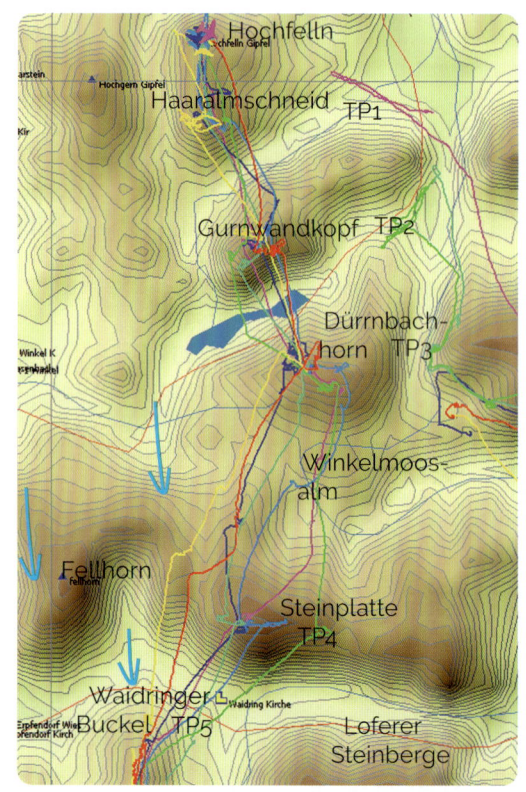

The first few kilometres from Hochfelln, my home site in Germany, are almost always flown via the same route. Flights can be downloaded as IGC files from online servers such as xcontest.org and xc.dhv.de. It is somewhat tiresome to add lots of turnpoints to your GPS manually, and much simpler with software. I use the SeeYou software from naviter.com which also has a super FAI triangle planner.

reliable thermal triggers. If you look for these points and enter them into your GPS, then try following this route when you go flying. Set up your GPS to automatically jump to the next point once you have passed the current one.

Work out ahead of the flight what your options will be, especially if there are several thermal sources, or only one. For example, at TP5 it would seem that there is only one good spot. Good planning should always be flexible, and have an alternative prepared, should the first choice not work.

It's evident that thermals don't remain at the same position all the time. Depending on wind and the time of day, thermals will wander, so it makes little sense to put all thermal sources in your GPS. However, on the standard routes, arrival times at particular points will usually be similar, so you can expect to find the thermals you have identified before.

EXPERIENCE The first time Nina flew from Hochfelln she had saved the turnpoints above in her GPS. She flew with four others to TP2, where she was then left alone as the others took a shortcut to Pinzgau. Thinking, "Drat, where are they all going?" she followed her GPS, and made it without any great difficulty into Pinzgau. In the evening she learnt that the 'shortcut' used by the others didn't work out – two bombed out and the other two arrived in Pinzgau much later.

A good place to start to look at other pilots' tracklogs and flights is XContest.org or your national XC league website. You can also ask other pilots – they are usually happy to talk about their flights.

When strong westerlies are blowing, the Hochfelln is not usually used for cross-country flights.

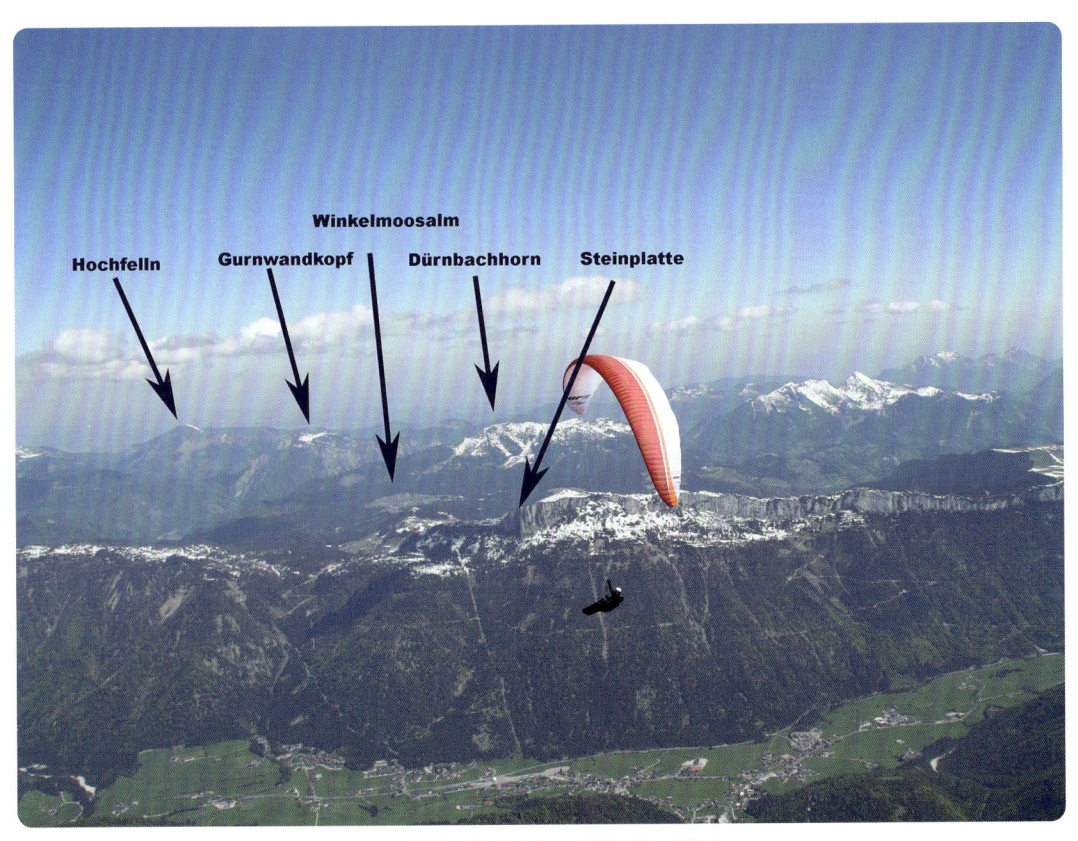

Looking back over the first kilometres from Hochfelln. Photo taken at Waidring (TP5).

11 Hints and tricks with Bruce Goldsmith

Thermal flying at Bruce's home site in France. Photo: Marcus King

Chapter 11

Hints and Tricks

By Bruce Goldsmith

The mental model

When you fly XC in any type of terrain you are searching for areas of lift to climb in and other zones to glide through with the objective of covering distance over the ground. In order to achieve this, you should try to build up a mental model in your mind of how the air is moving in the sky in 3D. What forms this mental model and how to update it and the ability to change this model as fast as possible are what makes a really successful XC pilot.

Things that influence the mental model can be weather systems, fronts, sea breezes etcetera, or valley winds or local effects, topography, sun and shadow patterns. I am always trying to link ground sources with the thermals I can see as well as the clouds. The timing of cycles is also an effect that is difficult to predict and looking for visible indicators is the only true clue to this.

You should constantly be updating your mental model all the time and be aware of other possible models also. A good pilot is one that is able to change his mental model quickly using only a small amount of information. This information can come from any of your senses.

Sometimes when I am gliding, attempting to find information, I try to make myself as sensitive as possible. I try to go in a kind of super receptive state, when I make myself extra sensitive to anything around. I feel for movements in the wing, I try to open my eyes extra wide and adjust the focus in and out to scan for objects in the air. Objects in the air can very often tell you a lot about what the air is doing. You could see another glider or bird. Sometimes I have seen some grass flying up through the air caught in a rising thermal, or even a plastic bag.

Smell can even tell you some information, you can often smell where a thermal started from the scent in it, though I must say that smell has not really helped me to find lift.

Flatland flying

Flatland flying has many similarilties to mountain flying. In mountain flying the

11.1 Clouds tell you immediately what is going on with the air. Photo: Marcus King

11.2 In mountain flying the biggest terrain throws off the biggest thermals

biggest cliff or mountain throws off the biggest thermals. In flatland flying the most important features also produce the biggest thermals, but the trick is to identify the most important features.

In the mountains the most important features are completely obvious, it is the biggest mountains and especially the ones that face the wind and the sun. In the flatlands there are no mountains so you need to be aware of more subtle features.

However there are often just as many thermals as in the mountains so you need to understand which features are most important in the prediction of thermals.

It is best to separate your decision-making into three different categories.

Clouds. When you are flying high, clouds are the most important signal of what is going on in the air.

At any height, other flying objects. At all levels other flying things can give you a sure image of where to find thermals. There is no guessing needed if you see a glider or a bird thermalling and climbing you know for sure that there is lift there.

Ground sources. This is maybe the most difficult item to identify but particularly when linked with the first two items, it gives the location for the birth of thermals. When you are high you should use the clouds as the main source of influence on your decision making. When you are low you should use ground sources. At all levels other climbing objects can be used and take preference over both ground sources and clouds. There are of course all the shades of grey in between.

Sometimes it is good enough so that you can link ground sources to clouds. I remember one particular occasion that I experienced on an XC when I was getting low in the flatlands and I could clearly see the source of a cloud street was a small rise in a field with a tiny building in it. The field was dark earth and had recently been ploughed and so was absorbing more heat than the surrounding grasslands.

The small house was acting as a thermal trigger breaking the thermal away from

11.3 Manilla, Australia during the FAI Paragliding World Championships. Photo: Bruce Goldsmith

the ground. Then directly downwind from the field I could see an active cloud and it was the first cloud in a cloud street heading directly downwind. I arrived above the house with just 30m and found the climb I had been hoping for: 3m/s all the way to cloudbase. It was remarkable to see such a clear thermal source even though the feature was very small.

Thermal rumours and legends

When flying in flatlands the smallest things can set off thermals or become thermal triggers. You might well hear some of these stories from pilots who have been there and got the T-shirt in flatland flying:

A pilot landing. There can be no thermals around and a pilot goes down to land. The tip vortex of the pilot landing can be enough to break the bubble of superheated air close to the ground and start the release of a thermal.

Sheep running. I have heard of cases in Australia where hang glider pilots get low and line up their approach to a landing paddock full of sheep. The act of the glider flying low over the field causes the sheep to run about and this can be enough to trigger the thermal. Some hang glider pilots actually search out the sheep and shout at them when low to get the sheep to run around!

Power lines. I have found many times that power lines are good thermal triggers. The reason for this is not clear. Some say that the power lines themselves do not cause the thermals but it is the area cleared of forest and bushes below the line that causes the thermal. Another explanation is that it is the surface of high tension power lines that is hot and maybe this causes a constant flow of hot air over the wires that causes the thermals to trigger. Whatever the reason power lines can make good thermal triggers, and have helped me several times when low.

The horse-race thermalling concept

On any XC flight it is important to climb as quickly and efficiently as possible in each thermal. In competition approximately half the time is spent climbing in thermals and so often you can get more of a lead from outclimbing pilots than you can by gliding faster or better than them.

So to climb fast in a thermal you need to be in the best lift and climbing in the most efficient way. Observation is important and you should be carefully looking at any other gliders or birds around you and if anyone is climbing better than you, you need to change your thermalling pattern to take the same lift as them.

You should never be outclimbed by someone. So climbing in a thermal is a vertical race to climb the fastest. Never be content to simply circle in the same lift, you should always be modifying your circle to climb better and centre on the best area of lift during each turn.

You can compare climbing in a thermal to a horse race. However it is more sophisticated than a horse race because it

11.4 A pylon on a mountain pass – a perfect trigger!

11.5 Livestock in a field can trigger thermals in the flats

is not just about choosing the best thermal and climbing the fastest. You should be constantly looking for stronger lift and better cores and changing from one area of lift to another.

So if you compare this to our horse race, it means that you have to choose the horse which takes an early lead in the race, then when another horse starts to race through the pack you should jump onto that new horse, then as he tires out you should jump on another. You should be constantly choosing the very best horse to win the thermalling race.

Thermalling hints

Finding the core is very important. The core of a thermal is the place where the thermal is lifting the strongest, If there is wind then most often the core is to be found upwind. This is because weaker thermals are more offset by the wind than stronger ones.

So if you are already in a weak thermal then as part of your 360 you should straighten out as you turn into wind and start to search upwind to try to check if there is stronger lift upwind. Try to continue to check upwind until you find that the lift strength decreases, then just go back to the strongest lift you found and use that.

You can see from this example that you may have to fly through weaker lift or even sink before you find the stronger core, though this is often not the case. The lift often just gets stronger and stronger as you search upwind and fly into the stronger core.

You can also see that the stronger thermals cut better through the wind. To start with, a thermal is a mass of air attched to the ground. This mass of air can weigh hundreds of tonnes. It is attached to the ground like a bubble and is not drifting with the wind.

As it breaks away from the ground the thermal then starts to get accelerated by the wind. Smaller thermals will get accelerated faster by the wind than bigger ones. This is both because of their size as well as the fact that the stronger thermal is moving faster vertically.

This explains why stronger thermals are to be found upwind, but it also gives another very important characteristic that the paraglider can use to his advantage. If you want to fly upwind then it is even more important to find the strong cores.

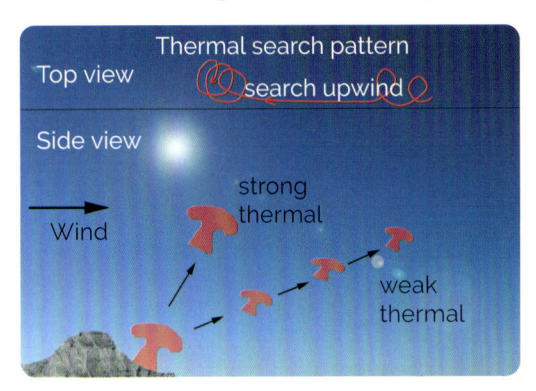

11.6 Top and side view of strong and weak thermals

11.7 Piltriquitron, El Bolson, Patagonia, Argentina

The hexagon theory

In the 1960s a group of university meteorologists visited the Sahara desert to study cloud formations over a perfectly uniform desert. The sand stretched for hundreds of kilometres in every direction and the idea was that the clouds would form in a way that was not influenced by the thermal sources but simply by the natural circulation of the air.

The result of this study was the amazing hexagon theory of cloud formation. This really is one to know about.

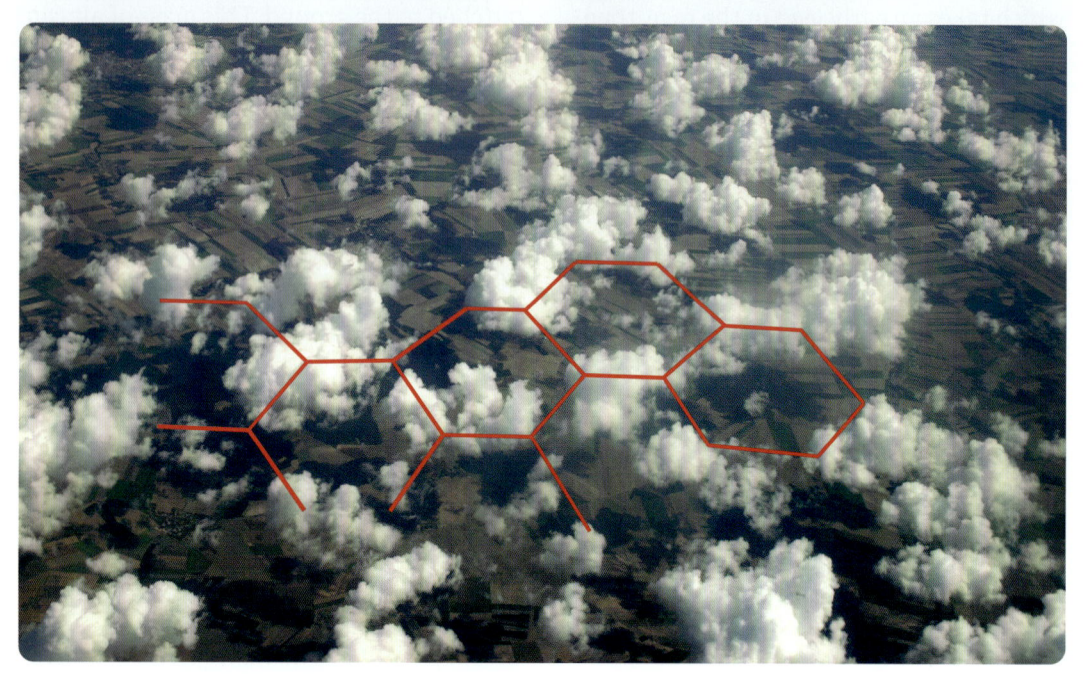

11.8 Hexagon clouds. The hexagon theory states that over flat and uniform terrain clouds will form in a hexagonal pattern with the sides of the hexagon each being 6km. In nil-wind conditions the sides of the hexagons will all be the same length, but as the wind picks up, one side of the hexagon will be aligned with the wind direction and will become longer. The stronger the wind the longer that side will become. Hexagon cloud formations can be found mostly in the flats.
Photos: Bruce Goldsmith

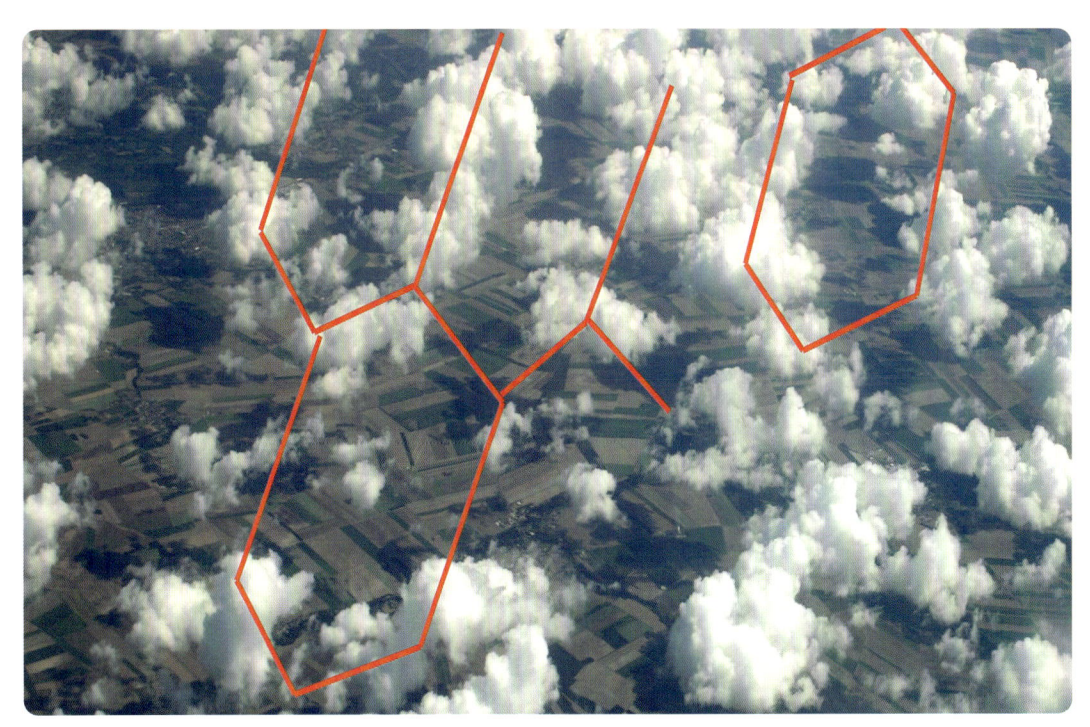

11.9 Hexagon clouds with wind. *With wind, one side of the hexagon gets longer and becomes a cloud street. This has some important conclusions for the XC pilot. First, it means that cloud streets do not go on for ever. Instead, they will have a limited length, which in light winds will be 6km, and will be longer as the wind speed increases. It also gives an important clue as to what to do when you come to the end of a cloud street. The end of a cloud street is simply the end of one side of a hexagon, so you should look to fly at 60 degrees to the line of the cloud street to the left or right. After 6km on this course you should expect the beginning of the next cloud street. I took these photos from 10,000m one day when taking a scheduled airline. They explain better than words how the hexagon theory works in practice. The hexagon theory is not so much a rule but a way of interpreting the clouds in the sky. As soon as there are strong thermal sources on the ground the hexagon pattern breaks down, but if there are only weak thermal sources then the pattern can hold quite well. The pattern can also explain why some thermal sources work and others do not. It is the thermal sources that coincide with the hexagon pattern that are going to work the best. Photo: Bruce Goldsmith*

11.10 *Below: Bruce Goldsmith on the way to becoming world champion in Australia. Photo: Martin Scheel / azoom.ch*

When is a lee side not really a lee side?

When you fly in the flatlands you should never fly over the back of a ridge with a 20km/h wind blowing. You will get rotored immediately. However, in the Alps every valley is in the lee side of some mountain and yet people fly when the wind is stronger than 20km/h. Why? When is it safe to fly in the lee and when is it unsafe?

These are difficult questions and there is no simple answer. I can offer some advice from my own experience of flying different mountain sites all over the world.

In paragliding school every pilot learns that he or she should not fly in the lee. Flying in the lee is obviously dangerous because of leeside turbulence and rotors. These rotors can be violent leading to collapses and accidents. On the lee side even a reserve parachute may not work if the air is too turbulent.

However, a meteorologist once told me that all thermals start on the lee side! If you fly in major competitions you will see top pilots flying on the lee side on a regular basis! What about protected flying sites, such as Gréolières in France where you often fly on the lee side? How can it be safe to fly in the lee sometimes and unsafe at other times? How can you tell when it is safe or not? What is conical hill convergence?

None of these are easy questions to answer, but I hope these words of advice will help to give pilots some of the answers to these questions.

Every thermal starts as a rotor

Thermals start when the sun heats the air unevenly. If the wind is constantly blowing in a smooth fashion over the ground, then the ground will therefore heat the air in a similarly smooth and constant fashion which is not ideal for thermal formation.

However, for thermals to form what we need is differences in air temperature. As soon as you introduce an obstruction into the airflow such as a house, a fence or a hill, you get an area of turbulence behind the obstruction.

Sometimes the obstruction will cause the air to remain calm for a time, protected from the wind, which gives the air a chance to warm up. Then the turbulence may separate the bubble of warm air from the ground releasing it into the wind above as a thermal.

The same thing can happen on a small or large scale, so you may get thermals being kicked off behind a fence, a house

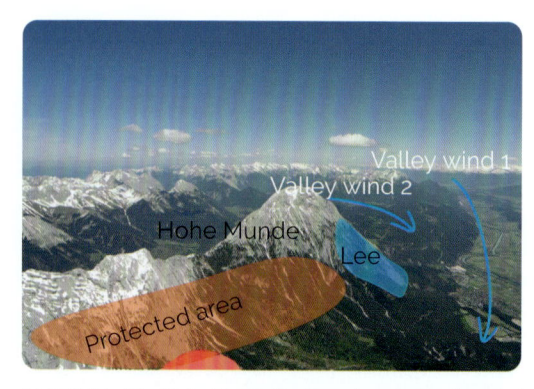

11.11 Leeward rotor made visible.

11.12 Behind the Hohe Munde the Bavarian wind (valley wind 2) blows into the Inn valley (valley wind 1). The blue area is a known turbulent lee region. The red zone is protected from the Bavarian wind, as the ridge above it is high enough to block the wind.

or a hill. You can even get wind shadows or a rotor behind a thermal which can act as an obstruction itself.

So the lesson to be learnt is that a rotor is just as much a friend to the thermal pilot as a hazard.

Size matters

It is difficult to say when it is safe to fly in the lee of an obstruction. The simple rule is if in doubt, don't! That is of course the cover-your-butt / limited liability answer that you can get from any paragliding school or textbook. However this does not really solve your problem, it's just the safe answer.

My own experience says that the single most important factor is the size of the hill. The bigger the hill or mountain the more protection it will offer. For example, you can almost never fly in the lee in England where the hills rarely reach more than 500m. On the other hand, in Tenerife nearly all the flying is done on the lee side of Mount Teide which towers to 3,000m. You can fly in the lee in Tenerife even when the prevailing wind is as much as 50km/h; however, you can expect strong leeside thermals and strong winds if you stray outside the protected area.

Wind strength

The lighter the wind, the less dangerous it is likely to be flying in the lee. Wind strength is extremely important to the safety of flying in the lee. Flying in the lee when the wind is only 5km/h should pose very little problem but if the wind is greater than 20km/h leeside flying is likely to be extremely dangerous.

Solar heating

Thermal heating of the lee side helps a lot. This means that even if the air is turbulent on the lee side it is being heated by the sun and so the air will generally have an upward motion. This is also the case in Tenerife where the site of Taucho faces southwest into the afternoon sun. Other sites such as Gréolières and Monaco offer a similar thermal-powered protection.

Sea breeze

If the heating is combined with a sea breeze or a valley wind system the protection from the prevailing wind is even greater. The presence of the sea tends to lead to a larger scale air movement than simple rotor, helping to make the air less turbulent.

11.13 Flying on the protected lee side of Teide, Canary Islands

11.14 Rio de Janeiro, Brazil

Conical hill convergence

When air flows around an isolated hill or mountain, the air divides on the upwind side of the hill and then flows together again on the downwind side of the hill. The area in front of the hill is therefore an area of divergence and the area behind the hill is an area of convergence.

Therefore, where the air is converging it can produce lift especially if there is some thermal activity as well that helps to produce some upward movement in the air when the air converges. If the air is not going up due to thermal activity it may be falling just as strongly as it could be lifting.

The photos below show how classical conical hill convergence works. You can get an area of lift downwind of a hill rather than an area of rotor, which is normally what you would expect, as is shown in the photo on the right of the two. There are many different factors that can mean that you will get lift behind a hill rather than a rotor. Factors that will help you get lift are:

1. **The size of the hill**, the bigger the better.
2. **Heating from the sun** on the downwind side of the hill.
3. **The stability of the air**. If the air is unstable it may flow over the top of the hill instead of around the side, meaning that the air will come crashing down in an area of descent behind the hill. So a layer of stable air to stop the air displacing vertically in front of the hill can help.
4. **The exact shape** of the hill.

Leeside flying in summary

The main factors to consider in flying in a lee are:
1. Wind strength
2. Size of the obstruction
3. Solar heating on the lee side
4. Air stability
5. Shape of the hill
6. See breeze or valley wind considerations

There can be no hard and fast rules as to whether it is safe for flying in the lee. Everyone must make their own decision based on their own skill level and their ability to be able to cope with any turbulence likely to be encountered.

One last consideration is that it is often the edge of the lee side that is the most dangerous area. If you are completely in the lee, you may be fully protected, but if you are at the edge of the protected area, then you may well encounter the maximum amount of turbulence.

If you intend to fly in a protected area you need to go all the way into the lee. It is often more dangerous to test the waters by feeling around the edge of the protected area than flying all the way into it.

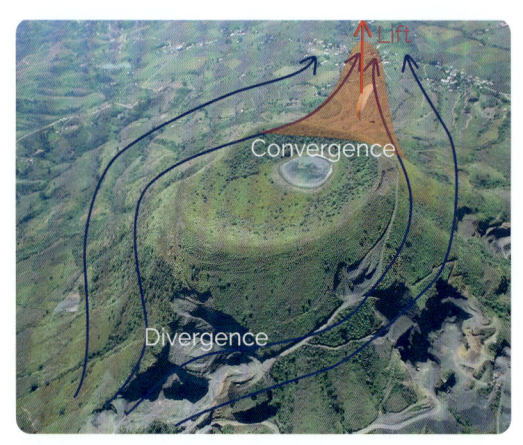

11.15 *Behind the conical hill could be lift or a rotor!*

11.16 *Valle de Bravo, Mexico. Photo: Mads Syndergaard.*

One final word. Leeside flying is only for the experienced pilot, or for pilots under the instruction of a very experienced pilot flying in controlled conditions. Please take all possible precautions when considering flying in the lee.

The importance of observation

To a large extent flying is a guessing game. In order to fly safely or to simply fly down from launch to landing pilots need to know all kinds of information about the air and the way it is moving.

- What is the wind direction?
- Where is that thermal?
- What size and shape is it?
- Where is the core?
- What is the turbulence like behind that hill?

But what makes flying so fascinating is that the air is invisible so you cannot see it directly. Pilots can only deduce what the air is doing by its effect on visible objects. These things include most obviously the clouds, the ground and of course other flying objects, both other pilots and birds. So it is not surprising that observation is the key to understanding what the air is doing, and hence the key to becoming a good pilot.

This sounds simple and logical enough but in reality it is not so easy. Pilots who do not fly so often need most of their concentration to control the glider. They simply don't have the spare capacity to be concentrating too hard on looking around and observing the world.

However, as the act of flying becomes more automatic pilots can free up their minds to pay more attention to their surroundings, and to a large extent this is what makes more experienced pilots so much better at flying. It is precisely because the act of flying their wing has become automatic that they have more time to be able to look around and observe more details in the surroundings.

There are literally hundreds of useful things to observe, so the more you observe the better your understanding of the way the air is moving, and therefore the better decisions you can make. This applies to nearly every situation a pilot can find himself in from launch, to landing, thermalling, ridge soaring, gliding, and of course competition flying.

Thermalling

When thermalling you should pay great attention to any other pilots in your thermal or within easy gliding distance. If any pilot starts climbing faster than you, you should leave the lift you are in to join the stronger lift. There is no excuse for being out-climbed by someone close to you.

You should always join him before he goes past you. The same goes for birds or even a floating bag getting sucked up in a thermal. Thermalling should always be a quest to climb the fastest.

When thermalling watch the relative climb rates of all the pilots around you. If you think someone is climbing faster than you, try to estimate his height relative to you, each time you go round a 360.

For instance one pilot may be 50m lower, and the next time he comes into sight this height difference could have dropped to 30m, so gently readjust your centre of turn to join into his circuit in the thermal.

11.17 Castejon de Sos, Spain. Photo: Bruce Goldsmith

On glide

The same goes when on glide. I always look closely at all the pilots close to me to see if they are entering lift. If they start to climb I normally start gliding towards them before they have even started to turn. In competition seconds count and the earlier you can react the better.

I find that it is quite easy to see when someone you are gliding with starts to enter lift, you can see their glider start pitching around as they begin to enter the turbulence around the thermal, you can also see their height relative to your own and relative to the pilots nearby.

If you are behind a group of pilots you will actually be able to judge better where the best lift is, easier than the pilots themselves because you can see how all of them move relative to each other.

This type of observation is exceedingly important. Placing yourself in a group so you can see more easily where the best lift is, is another tactic worth considering.

11.18 Manilla, Australia during the Worlds, Photo: B.Goldsmith

Ridge soaring

Such strategies are not only limited to competition flying. It is equally important for pilots ridge soaring on a hill. If you are trying to catch thermals, you should not only be thinking about what you are doing but you should be carefully looking at every pilot on the hill.

If someone gets up, you should know where he got that lift from. You should be looking at every move each pilot makes and see if their strategy worked. This can save you making the same mistake, or if the option was a good one, it will tell you the way out.

Competition

In competition flying this is even more important. You should know exactly what everyone in your field of view is up to, why they are doing it, and whether it works.

Sometimes I see a pilot turn 90-degrees to the course and fly off for no apparent reason in that direction. I immediately look for the reason of this decision. Have they seen a bird that I have not seen or another pilot climbing in the distance? So then I start to try to see the same thing. Is there a bird, is there another glider climbing over there? Sometimes I might decide to follow the pilot even before I have spotted what he is after, this just depends on the reason he was flying in the other direction in the first place.

When you see someone making a decision you should keep watching them to see if that decision worked.

Do not let someone out of your sight for more than a few seconds, especially if you are on glide with him and hunting for thermals. I often have to really stretch my neck and try to look above and behind me to be able to see everyone I am with.

When flying on a hill with a load of gliders if you are trying to get high to go XC, you should be trying different ideas to get up. Also, watch everyone else's ideas of how they are trying to get up.

If someone succeeds you should know exactly how he did it. Where he found that lift or how he flew to get up. You should also link your observations with the weather, eg "The last time the sun came out over there the guys in that little bowl on the end of the ridge got high."

Ridge soaring example

Today I had an interesting example of this same kind of thing. I was watching a group of pilots who were struggling about 300m below me a little further down the ridge. We were also not doing very well, but had been only just maintaining our height for about 15 minutes.

Because these pilots were not doing very well the pilots with me were ignoring them. But I always try to keep an eye on everyone, so I was glancing over at them every 30 seconds or so. They had been climbing 100m or so from time to time, but all the lift had been weak.

But then a couple of them hooked into a thermal that looked a bit better than any of the previous little bumps of lift they'd been climbing in. I made my move over to them immediately, arriving well above them and before they had climbed up to my altitude, and I was very happy to find some good lift. The rest of my group then came over to join us just 30 seconds later as the lower group had just climbed up to our level, but none of them could catch me as I quickly climbed away.

Making my decision earlier basing it on their relative climb rate rather than waiting for the group to get high enabled me to make the decision earlier and get in on top of the thermal, rather than in the back end of it.

Landing

Judging the wind speed and direction on landing is important for all pilots. There are the obvious things to look at like the windsock in the landing field and we should all know to watch the way the trees and bushes are moving.

I have a few other things that I like to keep an eye on before landing. I look at any pilots who landed before me and watch carefully to see if they made a good landing. If they pile in tailwind you can normally see it from way up.

Another one of my favourite hints is to look at the direction in which birds land or even the way they stand. Yes, the way they stand. Birds always like to stand facing into the wind. This is very obvious when brids are standing on wires. Birds get the feathers ruffled the wrong way if they stand facing downwind, and they just don't like that, so a bird standing is as good as a windsock.

Hints
- Look around all the time.
- Don't let people out of your sight. If you lose sight of someone it is very likely that they are doing something that you had not considered.
- Peripheral vision is important, do not wear a helmet or glasses that restrict your side vision.
- Get used to your glider and equipment so that you can spend more time observing your surroundings.
- Do not spend much time looking at your instruments, looking around is much more important.

11.19 Cuzco, Peru. Photo: Bruce Goldsmith

How close to the ridge should you fly?

If you are flying on a ridge with a thermal breeze flowing up it is difficult to decide exactly how close to the ridge you should fly. Should you try to stick your wingtip in the rocks to climb fast or should you be hunting thermals out front?

In the first chapter of this book there is an interesting study by meteorologists who investigate the upslope thermal wind in the Inn Valley in the Austrian Alps. This study helps, giving some information on how to decide the best distance to fly from a ridge to find the best lift. Often people just think that the closer to the ridge the better, but this study says otherwise.

The thermal updraught is caused by the sun heating the sun-facing slope causing convection up the slope. Close to the slope the friction between the slope and the air causes the updraught to rise slower. These two opposing effects produce an updraught profile which is shown in the attached graph. Their study showed that the best distance on average was between 20m and 30m from the ridge.

On an average day in the summer in the Inn Valley I am sure this is correct. However the real beauty of flying is that every flying site on every day is different and even if you fly the same ridge every day what can be true one day can be completely false the next day because the weather is always changing. This is true for the distance you should fly from a slope. Some days you climb best by clinging as close to a ridge as you can and on other days the best thermals can be found 100-200m out in front. It just depends on the weather and the site.

Here are the main factors to consider.

The smoothness of the slope. The smoother the slope the less the updraught will be slowed down by any roughness. Therefore if a ridge is tree covered then the lift will be better further out. If the ridge is smooth grass from top to bottom skimming along close to the grass could well be the best way to fly.

The features below. If there is a small break in the slope or even a hedge line or a line of trees then this line of trees can kick off the thermals before they arrive at the part of the ridge where you are flying. Many ridges are double ridges and the smaller lower ridge can often produce better thermals than the upper bigger ridge, so you can climb better by flying far from the main ridge so you need to imagine that you are thermalling over the peak of the lower ridge rather than soaring on the upper ridge (see photo 11.23).

Small cliffs. When a ridge has a small vertical section in it, the lift is always

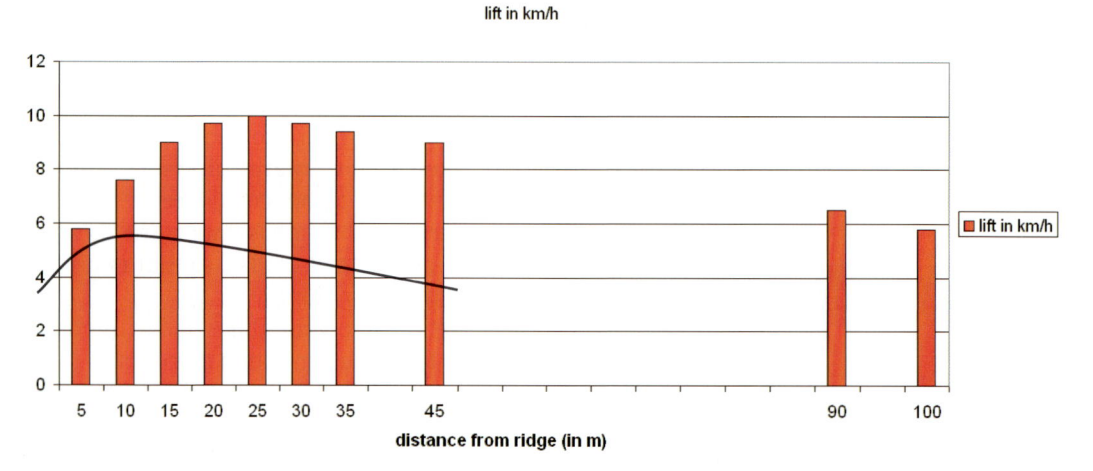

11.20 The upslope thermal wind in the Inn Valley in the Austrian Alps as measured by meteorologists

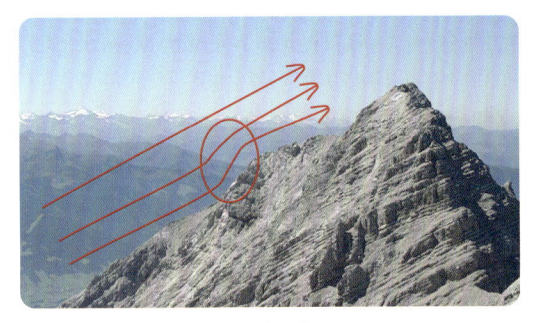

11.21 Extra strong lift at top of cliff.

much better precisely at this vertical part of the ridge. Typically this would be a cliff or rock outcrop. Often you can stay up where the ridge is vertical but you go down where the ridge is just very steep. I think part of this is that you can get your canopy close to the area of best lift without the pilot being too close to the ridge. Personally I reckon that little cliffs are so important because they produce a kind of mini Venturi as well in front of the top of the cliff, accelerating the lift in this area much more than you would expect from the small size of the cliff.

The level of turbulence. Safety is always the prime consideration when flying and how close you dare go to the ridge must be primarily a safety decision. If the air is turbulent then you cannot fly as close to the ridge as if the air is smooth. This decision also depends on your skill level and the kind of glider you have. You may feel happier to fly closer to the ground on a glider you feel more confident with.

When I fly in England in smooth ridge lift I feel quite safe and confident to fly close to the ridge. As the thermals start popping in, I tend to start to fly further from the ridge and start hunting for thermals further out.

The picture below demonstrates nicely two of these points. On the left side of the picture you can see a lower ridge which is minor compared to the higher ridge to the right, but on several days during the competition the thermals were better on the lower ridge than the upper one, and the best way to climb on the upper ridge was to fly 500m in front of the main ridge.

The second point is the mini cliff halfway up the main ridge on the right. This is a typical example of a small vertical part of the slope that will produce much better lift than the slope below or above it. This small cliff may also act as a thermal trigger – thermals are then found directly above this cliff and not close to the slope.

In some sites, like Àger in Spain, conditions during the day are strong and turbulent and it is just not safe to fly close to the ridge due to the high level of turbulence and rocky terrain.

Lower ridge may produce better lift than the higher ridge.

11.22 Extra strong lift at top of cliff. Photo: Bruce Goldsmith

11.23 This small vertical cliff produces much better lift than the slopes below or above

Seeing turbulence

After a career flying paragliders and hang gliders spanning decades, I would like to share some of my thoughts and experiences about flying in turbulence, and at the same time dispel some common misconceptions.

It's a naughty pleasure to climb to cloudbase and play in the misty swirls around the bottom and sides of a cumulus cloud. I have often done this and been intimidated by huge towers of thick cloud that swirl and tumble around the edge of the cloud as it surges up though the air around it with impressive power and grace. The surprising thing is that even though these huge eddies of air look large, powerful and turbulent, when you actually fly through them, the air feels practically smooth.

The first time this happened to me I thought that somehow I had missed the turbulence, and that it would be just around the corner, waiting to catch me out the next time. But I have now done this dozens of times and I have never been hit by the turbulence: it's just not there!

What we can learn from this is that the gliders we fly actually cope well with what looks like a really serious piece of turbulence.

The other side of the coin is to ask what does turbulence look like when it is so strong that it would cause a paraglider to collapse? I have never had the chance to actually see turbulence that is so strong it collapses a paraglider.

Can you fly in dust devils, or are they not so evil after all?

You expect to get your ass kicked when you go into a dust devil, but time and time again I have done it and found that it's just another thermal.

The only difference between a dust devil and a thermal is the dust! You can actually see the air in a dust devil, so it looks worse than it really is, simply because we are not used to seeing how turbulent the air we fly in is.

Not all dust devils are violent, but some of course can be. The problem is that dust devils are visible only when they are close to the ground; and when you are close to the ground you do not want to be taking chances with potentially violent air, so I cannot advise pilots to fly in dust devils.

Also, if a dust devil is visible and it is not close to the ground, then beware. It must be very strong to be able to keep the dust airborne far from the ground.

However, I would just like to reconfirm my own experience that dust devils normally look worse than they actually are. As a footnote, I would also add here that if you do enter a dust devil then you should fly in the opposite direction to that in which it is turning. That is because if you enter a thermal in the same direction as the thermal is turning it will feel rougher and more difficult to centre and you won't climb as well.

Every thermal has some rotation, some clockwise, some anti-clockwise. If you turn in the same direction as the rotation then you will end up rotating faster in the thermal because in effect you are flying downwind. If you fly against the rotation you fly more slowly and make fewer rotations per minute. This is more efficient and a smoother way to fly.

In the northern hemisphere you should generally turn left, and in the southern right, but this not a hard-and-fast rule. It is only 70% of thermals that follow that rule. If in doubt, follow a bird!

Wake turbulence behind other aircraft

The tip vortex of a wing produces wake turbulence behind the aircraft. There are two main factors that make the turbulence stronger. These are:

The weight of the aircraft: the heavier the aircraft, the stronger the turbulence.

The speed: the slower the aircraft, the greater the turbulence. Yes, that's right. I said slower. This is quite surprising, but it means that you can expect more turbulence from a slow plane like a Cessna, than from a high-speed military jet.

The reason for this is quite simple. The turbulence left behind by a wing relates to the amount of lift that piece of air has produced.

The Cessna and the jet may have a similar weight, but the jet will be flying at 500km/h and the Cessna only 100km/h. This means that in the same time, the jet covers five times more distance. So the weight of the jet is supported by five times more air, and you could expect the wake turbulence to be five times less.

You can therefore expect the biggest wake turbulence from big and heavy slow-flying aircraft, like a Hercules transporter rather than a high-speed jet.

It is for this reason that the wake turbulence behind aircraft is worse when landing than at other times, and so aircraft need to pay special attention to this at airports.

What about wind turbines?

Years ago I was involved in a Facebook discussion about a photo where you saw wind turbines and rotating clouds behind them. Comments such as: "Don't try landing or flying behind those babies!" were posted on the thread, and all the pilots seemed to be very scared of wake turbulence from wind turbines.

I have actually flown behind wind turbines in Llandinam in Wales, and I found the air surprisingly smooth.

The first thing to say is that the speed that the wind turbines are going around is not important at all in relation to the amount of turbulence they would produce. This must be similar to an aircraft wing. It is not the speed of the wing that is important, rather it is how much energy the blades are producing. Of course, this is not at all visible to the outside observer.

Perhaps the blades I flew behind in Llandinam were not producing much energy at the time, but yet again I find that this is an example of how smooth the air is when I expected it to be turbulent.

11.24 Horns Rev wind turbine field in the North Sea, Denmark. Photo: Vattenfall

A final word

The objective of this chapter is to try to give an idea to the pilot how flying does not follow strict rules. It is useful to know the rules but often there are two or more different concepts that can apply to any situation, and so understanding which rules to apply when, can only be decided upon by the clues in the sky. Being open to interpret these clues quickly with the ability to change the mental model is what makes a great pilot.

"If what you're doing is not working then do something else" is the oft-used phrase. The opposite also applies: "If you are winning, then don't change what you're doing."

This saying was going though my head constantly during the last task of the Paragliding World Championships when I won back in 2007. It set my strategy for the whole day.

One of my favourite stories is an example of how this saying was applied to soaring what appeared to be a simple slope on the side of a valley. Our pilot was one day flying down a windward-facing ridge, and even though he was on the windward side of the valley he was in bad sink. He could not understand why he was having such a bad time and was going down fast.

Our pilot thought to himself, "If it's not working doing what you're doing then do something else." So he crossed the valley and flew into the lee side of the mountain. To his amazement he found nice smooth lift and the day was saved.

The explanation is that the airflow in his valley was basically a huge vortex that caused the flow to reverse on the valley floor. He needed to change his mental model to understand what was going on. Conventional thinking was wrong. Clues that may have helped him to change his mental model were the descent he was in and signs of the wind direction at the bottom of the valley.

If you have a very good level of flying

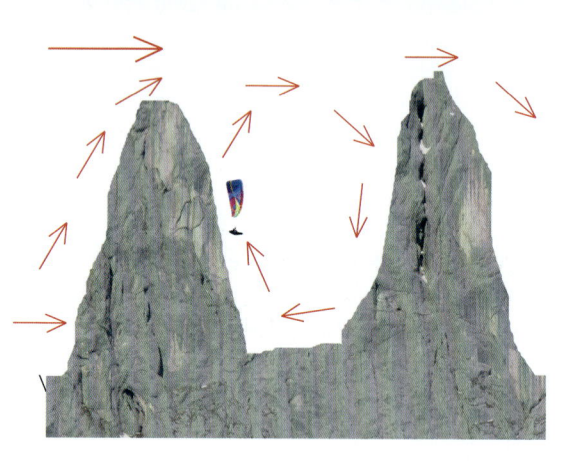

11.25 *"If what you're doing isn't working, then change what you're doing."*

and you feel that you can get yourself out of most problems then I often find that you can try the 'suck it and see' method of flying. You can test out your mental models by trying different things by going to fly somewhere to see what happens. If you get bad turbulence or sink then turn around and go and try something else.

It is suprising how many of our mental models of flying are wrong and do not follow conventional lines of thought. This is the beauty of flying. I always say that my best flights are when I manage to do a flight that I thought was physically impossible.

I hope this chapter helps pilots to 'expect the unexpected' in flight as well as in your earthbound lives.

Enjoy your flying! Gourdon, France. Photo: Martin Lifka / BGD

Thermalling on a hang glider

By Peter Achmüller

On our planet there is no travelling without using energy. All the systems we know of which use energy have one thing in common – the energy needs to be replenished to keep them working.

Depending on the form of travel we use a variety of places to refill: petrol stations on the motorway, huts along mountain bike routes through the mountains, or alternatively and much more difficult to recognise and find, the next thermal on a glide towards our flying goal.

One other point regarding travelling: if you don't fill up before the last drop in your tank, take enough muesli bars or find another thermal to regain some height, you'll end up stranded along the way.

Therefore, the question of how to replenish energy while underway is of utmost importance, and the more efficient we are at refilling, the faster we can travel – see Formula 1 racing.

This is where the challenge begins – how to find the next energy station. Where no road signs exist, it's easy to sail straight past one, and then park our glider on the next field, demonstrating once again one of the world's most unreliable transportation systems.

Recognising thermals

Not every flight has to end this way. There are several hidden signs we should look for when approaching the next thermal. We just need to develop the necessary sensitivity to recognise them.

An important sign is to observe how thermals suck up the air around you. When you approach a thermal with a hang glider, you will tend to be pulled towards its centre, even if you try and maintain a straight course. Follow the signs, turn in the direction you are being sucked, because the thermal is going up somewhere there.

Another indication is turbulent air or strong sink at the edge of a thermal where air currents are mixing. Together with the wind drift, you should be able to begin to visualise the centre of the thermal, and head towards it.

11.27 *Above the haze in the valley on a spectacular blue day in the Ennstal Alps, southern Austria. Photo: Sasha Serebrennikova*

11.28 *Gerolf Heinrichs in Meduno, Italy in February. Photo: Sasha Serebrennikova*

Coring well

How do we turn our best guess at where the thermal's core is into height gain? In other words, how do we start filling the tank as quickly as possible even though we can't see the petrol pump? Begin to turn, and move the centre of your turn towards the area of increased lift. During this you begin to see how big the thermal is. Once you're in a thermal, the first job is to stay in it, and then to use it as efficiently as possible. This means we have to position our turns and adjust the turn radius and speed to match the thermal we're in.

The most important safety factor is the speed at which we are flying. In turbulent air we need to fly faster. Thermal turbulence is normally proportional to the climb rate, and inversely proportional to the thermal's diameter. This gives us this rule of thumb: *the faster and tighter a thermal is, the faster you need to fly.*

Personally, I use the VG to set the speed I want to fly at. This minimises resistance and reduces the amount of force needed to fly a turn, but it does also reduce the responsiveness of the glider with every metre of rope you pull through the cleat.

One method, which you might like to try, depending on your own personal constitution and preferences. The strong tight thermals typical for the Alps are great for training; there is always room for improvement even after years of flying.

One special technique for optimising climb rates should also be mentioned: high siding to quickly centre laminar thermals with large diameters. Normally you push out the bar on a hang glider to reduce speed. If you are flying a turn, then doing this automatically reduces the turn radius, which is not necessarily our goal in a large diameter thermal.

Through doing the following (which requires a bit of force) you can push out the bar without reducing your turn radius: when you push out, move your bodyweight to the outside of the turn. This helps to keep your turns flat, while reducing your speed and sink rates. This method is one of the best ways of getting the most out of the weakest thermals when half-on VG doesn't help any more.

Hanging in there

Thermals ascending in the lee of steep rock faces often tend to spit you out, rather than keep you in them. These are raw energy sources, which often cost the pilot more than what they pay back. Here are a couple of tips: you can generally recognise a lee thermal immediately on entry. If you get sudden strong climb rates after a turbulent entry, then I recommend making a steep and fast turn into the thermal. Once you've manoeuvred your glider into the core, then you can start working on optimising your speed and turn radius. The first seconds in a lee thermal are critical – here you really need to concentrate. Once you get up higher things get smoother, wider and more laminar.

Weak climbs can also have a few surprises in store, especially in mountainous regions. The weaker climb rates are, the greater the roles of wind shears and inversions. Pilots who merely keep the same turn radius throughout the climb find themselves automatically on the edge after a time.

You can often observe this on the launch thermal of a site on a day with one or more inversions. Gaggles build at the top of the first inversion, and only a few pilots make it through to the blue skies or cloudbase above. These pilots are the ones who have managed to follow the wind drift through the inversion.

Here you need to carefully observe how the wind shears at the inversion, and re-centre your turns accordingly, sometimes this might take you several hundred metres sideways before you make it through.

Moving on

Once you're back up at cloudbase, your tank is full again and you can glide on. My last tip: always try to choose a route which will take you over regions with updraughts. For example, in Pinzgau, Austria, you can often just follow the other thermalling pilots in front of you. If you're up high enough, then you can miss out on a box stop, just fly at minimum sink through rising air, and return to MacCready speed in between: dolphin style can often take you 30-50km along east-west ridges without a single turn.

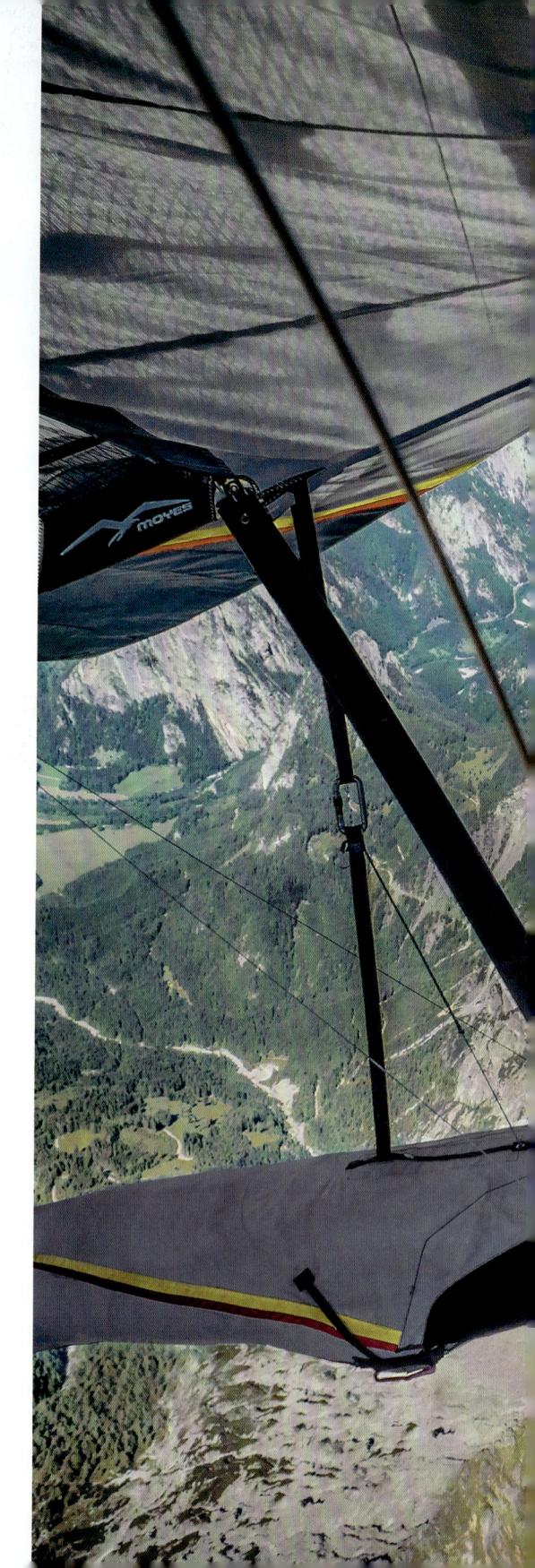

11.29 Super high above Tolminski Kuk (2,085m) in Slovenia. Photo: Sasha Serebrennikova

11.30 Now the journey really begins. Photo: Skywalk

Thank you for reading

You have reached the end of this book, but of course it is not the end of your adventure in paragliding or hang gliding – it should be only the beginning. Learning to fly a paraglider or hang glider well is a lifelong journey, you genuinely never stop learning in this sport.

Hopefully Thermal Flying will find its way onto your bookshelf, as it has with thousands of pilots around the world already, and you will return to it regularly. There is no substitute for real-world experience, which means flying as much as you can. But there are shortcuts to learning the knowledge that you need to do the basics well, and I hope I have explained some of this knowledge in an understandable way that has kept you interested as well as informed.

Free flight is an incredible adventure and opens doors to people, places and destinations all around the world. I encourage you to make the most of it, to fly as far as you can, to learn the art of cross country flying, to take part in competitions and to fly everything, from single-skin wings to tandem paragliders. The boundaries of our sports keep expanding, and that is amazing to see.

If I have one small piece of advice it is to take your time and to enjoy the learning process. Don't be in too much of a rush to skip through the basics and the easy stuff – these are what build the foundations of your flying career.

Spend time learning to groundhandle well, take SIV courses, read, watch and listen to everything about your sport so you stay up to date. And focus on really honing the art of thermal flying. Learn to thermal to the left and to the right equally well; work on climbing without using a vario; experiment with wide circles and then see what happens when you tighten up; explore the bountiful lift under the clouds before you head off on XC.

None of this time will be wasted, every second spent developing your foundation thermalling skills will make you a better pilot, whatever you fly and however far you progress in the sport.

Paragliding has given me a lifetime of excitement, adventure and pleasure. I hope you find as much joy out of learning the art of thermal flying as I do.

Many happy landings,
fly high and go far!

Burki Martens

Cross Country

In the core, since 1988

STAY CONNECTED

More journal than magazine, Cross Country has kept pilots stoked with inspiration and information since 1988. Learn to fly better with technique, weather and safety articles, read the latest glider and gear reviews, and be inspired with adventure and flying stories in every one of the ten issues you'll receive throughout the year. Respected as independent and authoritative, Cross Country is a reader-supported publication read in over 100 countries.

- Ten issues per year delivered in high quality print, Zinio digital - or both

- Includes a free 100+ page Travel Guide or Gear Guide

- Beautiful photography, simple design and the highest production values from our passionate editors - we've all been flying for 20+ years!

- Subscriber Prize Draws: twice a year, a lucky subscriber wins a new paraglider of their choice

Every issue is packed with insight, inspiration and education

Advice to help you fly better

Glider, harness and instrument reviews

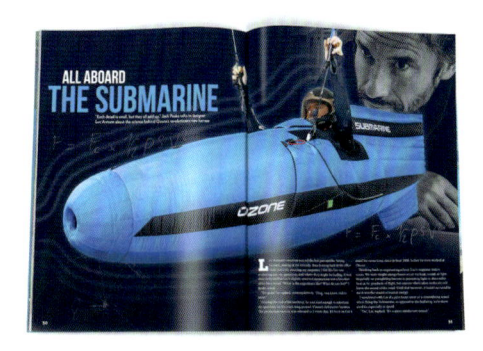

Insightful features

Inspirational photography

Travel, new destinations and sites

New equipment and gear news

"I just subscribed, the first copy arrived yesterday and I immediately fell in love with it."
Massimo Gulli, new paraglider pilot, Italy

Subscribe today at *xcmag.com*. Find us on social media #xcmag